CELT AND SAXON

Peter Berresford Ellis

CELT AND SAXON

The Struggle for Britain
AD 410–937

CONSTABLE · LONDON

First published in Great Britain 1993
by Constable and Company Limited
3 The Lanchesters, 162 Fulham Palace Road
London W6 9ER
Copyright © Peter Berresford Ellis 1993
Reprinted 1993
Paperback edition 1994
Reprinted 1995, 1996
ISBN 0 09 473260 4
The right of Peter Berresford Ellis to be
identified as the author of this work
has been asserted by him in accordance
with the Copyright, Designs and Patents Act 1988
Set in Linotron Sabon 11pt by
Rowland Phototypesetting Limited
Bury St Edmunds, Suffolk
Printed in Great Britain by
St Edmundsbury Press Limited
Bury St Edmunds, Suffolk

A CIP catalogue record for this book
is available from the British Library

To the memory of my Celt and Saxon forebears: to the first Helias; the original 'Dweller by the Barley Ford'; to 'Wolf Shield', Du Lac and the Ó hEodhusa; with the hope that Saxon may finally learn to understand Celt and both may come to live alongside each other in mutual respect and amicability.

Contents

List of Illustrations

between pages 96 and 97

between pages 192 and 193

Iona, I-Shona, the Holy Island of Colmcille
The Book of Durrow
Glamis Manse (Angus) Pictish stone dated to the 8th Century
The Monymusk Reliquary
Statue of Nominoë, king of Brittany
The Norrie's Law hoard of Pictish silver
The Cross of Cong, made in Co. Mayo, 1123–1136 AD

Introduction

The world has become a place of bondage,
frequent are the acts of oppression;
where Briton once was, now there is Saxon . . .

Iolo Goch (c.1320–c.1380)

APOLEON BONAPARTE once remarked with cynicism:
'What is history but a myth agreed upon?' So far as the
period covered by this study is concerned, popularly known
as 'Dark Age Britain', hardly any two authorities can be found to
agree the 'myth'. The period is replete with cause for scholastic
debate. There is even a dispute as to whether the Anglo-Saxons
invaded Britain at all! Nicholas Higham, an archaeologist and historian, heads a new school which has resurrected an old theory that
England was created by comparatively small groups of Anglo-Saxons
who staged a series of *coups d'état* in the British Celtic kingdoms
and then intermarried with native women, imposing their language
and social structures on subsequent generations without any ensuing
conflict. Dr Martin Welch, a fellow archaeologist and Anglo-Saxon
expert, points out that the argument simply ignores the contemporary
and near contemporary evidence of annalists and chroniclers. 'It
argues that we know much better than both contemporary and
slightly later commentators who wrote about events in Britain.' So
there is even a difference on the first fundamental – how the Anglo-
Saxons arrived in Britain.

In *Celtic Inheritance* (1985), in which I made an attempt to present
an outline of the phenomenon known as 'The Celtic Church' for the
general reader, I called attention to some of the pitfalls of dealing
with the history of the period: the cut and thrust of discussion,
sometimes couched in rather unacademic language, ranging over
various theories and hypotheses. I pointed out: 'Even the simple

assertion of dating provides grounds for lively scholastic debate. The accuracy of the majority of dates during the entire period can be opened up to question. Many scholars of the period seem to fix their own chronology and defend it with verbal violence against all comers.'

The chronology that I have put forward in this volume is that now generally accepted by the consensus of modern students of the period. I have found myself revising some of the dates that I have previously adhered to, having, in some cases, been swayed by new evidence in the course of ongoing studies.

The Early Middle Age period is the one period where historians have to admit that there is no such thing as 'academic objectivity'. There has recently been a tendency for some groups of historians, particularly those recently engaged in Irish studies, to maintain that they can write an 'objective' history, and can view historical events in the manner of a judge sitting in splendid isolation (or at least according to the popular notion of the role of a judge, who is supposed to view the events and people paraded before him dispassionately). But the truth of the matter is that the historian is just as caught up, just as involved and biased as any of the historical characters who pass before him or her for scrutiny. Consciously or subconsciously, historians will contribute to both historical characters and events something of themselves, giving their own values, judgements and reactions.

A history book will tell you more about the historian than about historical facts. Historical narratives are full of the personal judgements of the historian. Beware of the historian who tries to tell you that this is not so and that he or she is possessed of some will-o'-the-wisp secret of 'academic objectivity'. Mark Twain put it very succinctly in *Following the Equator* (1897): 'The very ink with which all history is written is merely fluid prejudice.'

But, some may ask, what of *facts*? Facts can't be changed . . . or can they? The very form in which the historian selects and relates the facts conveys judgement and prejudice. Let me make a statement of 'fact'. The bottle is half-empty. It is a quantifiable fact which surely cannot be argued. Yet if the same fact were put another way – the bottle is half-full – it provides us with an entirely different perception or interpretation of that very same fact. We see the same fact from an entirely different angle or perspective. History then is not simply about the enumeration of facts. It is about individual selection and interpretation as well as individual moral judgement of facts.

Instead of pretending that I am seeking to write an 'academically objective' view of the struggle which took place between AD 410 and AD 937, as Celt and Saxon fought for the mastery of the island of Britain, I admit to starting from a thesis propounded by the sociologist and historian Francis Ambrose Ridley (b. 1897). I was stimulated by meeting Frank Ridley in the 1960s when he was finishing what he considered was going to be his *magnum opus* entitled *The Rise and Fall of the English Empire*, of which, regretfully, only the first section was published (by the Medusa Press, London, in 1976). This was a limited printing and copies are extremely rare. The manuscript remains in the possession of Ridley's literary executor, the author and London Labour politician, Ellis S. Hillman.

Ridley's reputation as a polemic social historian has been considerable. He has not only analysed history but sets out the logical lessons of that history. In 1936 he pointed to the inevitability of a European war in *Next Year's War*, arising as an historical consequence of the conflict of 1914–1918. As early as 1944 he had discussed the inexorable arrival, and the dangers, of *The United States of Europe*, a theme to which he returned in 1947 with a study entitled *Unite or Perish*.

The main thesis of his new work was one that he had argued over many years in several publications. Ridley maintained that there was no such thing as a British Empire but that, in reality, it was an English Empire. Firstly, the Anglo-Saxons had to invade the island of Britain and conquer the indigenous inhabitants – the British Celts – or such a major proportion of them as to render Saxon settlement of the island permanent and dominant. The Anglo-Saxons created 'England' in part of the island but were not able, at that time, to entirely eradicate or control the Celts confined to certain areas of the island. Therefore, independent Celtic kingdoms remained in Britain until modern historical times. But the Anglo-Saxons never lost the imperial dynamic, reinforced by a Norse (both Danish and Norman) intermix, which eventually proceeded to the conquest of the remaining Celtic areas, as well as pushing on to the conquest and annexation of their Celtic neighbours in Ireland. Once a base was finally secured, first by Oliver Cromwell and then by William of Orange, and England attempted to create the concept of a homogeneous 'Britishness' –

what Winston S. Churchill saw as 'The Island Race' – then the English thalassocracy could expand on a more universal scale. The dynamic of the empire was therefore English and England's Celtic neighbours were only incorporated in the empire in the subordinate role of colonial conquests. The Celtic peoples were no more at the centre of empire than the Hausa or Hindustanis. Ridley's contention was that it would be a logical nemesis in the realm of historical dialectic that the English empire should end where it began with the re-emergence of the Celts as self-governing communities.

A parallel example to this thesis was, ironically, seen in the break-up of the Soviet Union. The former Tsarist Russian Empire had, in 1917, changed its political structures from monarchical autocracy and imperialism to what was popularly believed to be Communism based on the social theories of Marx, Engels and Lenin. In both cases, Tsarism and 'Communism', Russia was still the dominant imperial power, controlling, with centralized bureaucracy, the many nations within the empire. The empire remained intact until 1991. The creators of the new Soviet Russian Empire had ignored a fundamental principle of the founding theoreticians of Scientific Socialism which was, perhaps, best summed up by V.I. Lenin himself when he wrote in 1917:

> The principal condition of a democratic peace is the renunciation of claims of annexation. This must not be wrongly understood in the sense that all powers should recover what they have lost, but according to the only true meaning, which is that *every nationality without exception in Europe and in the colonies should obtain freedom* . . . [my italics].

A few years later, Lenin was dead and Stalin and the founders of the Soviet system, while claiming Lenin as a philosophical totem, ignored his teachings on 'the equality of nations' and their right to self-determination put forward so succinctly in *The Socialist Revolution and the Right of Nations to Self-Determination*. When the western world claimed that 'Socialism had failed' in 1991, it would have been more precise to argue that politicians had failed Socialism: the system, in maintaining the centralist structures of the Tsarist empire in new guise, had, to use Lenin's own words, 'committed treachery to Socialism'. Soviet Russia had ignored Lenin's fundamental commitment to the basic right of national communities to self-government and the right of secession from multinational states and federations. It was historically inevitable that the peripheral nations of the Russian Empire would eventually rise up and, given the opportunity, demand to be allowed to go their own way.

The fundamental point is that, whatever system of imperial government is used, benign or malign, the domination of one nation over another releases an inexorable historical process which can only result in the complete destruction of the dominated national community or its re-emergence in an attempt to regain its cultural and political integrity. Whether the process is peaceful or bloody usually depends on the dominating power, not on the dominated. And, in whatever form the destruction or the emergence of the subdued national communities evolves, it is simply a process of logical historical nemesis.

The lack of understanding of the dynamic for national self-determination has caused many historians to make comments which, if seriously analysed, must bring a smile even to those who seek justification for empire. John Mitchell Kemble, writing in *The Saxons in England* (London, 1876), could make an asinine justification for the harsh treatment of the British Celts by the Anglo-Saxons: 'We learn that at first the condition of the British under the Saxon rule was fair and easy, and only rendered harsher in punishment of the unsuccessful attempts at rebellion.' His argument, therefore, is that if the Celts had not resisted Saxon conquest they would have received better treatment at the hands of their conquerors.

Taking the first part of Ridley's thesis as the theme of this work, I have attempted to examine those first important years during which Celt and Saxon struggled for the control of this island of Britain. What follows is my interpretation of those events and from it, in my concluding chapter, I am drawn into a consideration of whether the latter part of Ridley's thesis can be sustained by asking, 'Do "The British" Really Exist?' In other words, before we are able to identify a 'British Empire', can we actually define a 'British Nation'?

This is my position, the starting point for this study.

The documentary evidence remains the same. We must still rely on the work of Gildas, Nennius, Bede, the *Anglo-Saxon Chronicles*, *Annales Cambriae*, as well as the works of many other annalists, both Celt and Saxon, and observers from other lands. It is not the evidence that is new but only the interpretation. In writing a history for the general reader, I have attempted to sketch the most recent interpretations on the period as well as propounding my own. Modern thinking, of whatever school of interpretation, is coming to view the so-called 'Dark Ages' as a misnomer. Indeed, Lloyd and Jennifer Laing, in their recent study *Celtic Britain and Ireland* (Dublin, 1990), argue that, for the Celts, this period was 'an historical dawn' when, freed from the constraints of druidism, which had forbidden them to commit their vast store of scholarship to written form, as a religious prohibition, they began to write extensively in their own languages as well as Greek and Latin. Moreover, in their enthusiasm to impart their knowledge to others, Irish missionaries were primarily involved in the groundwork of Christianizing the pagan Saxons and bringing them literacy and learning. According to the Laings: 'The most difficult battle of the Dark Ages must be fought nowadays: against previous scholarly attitudes and approaches. There can be no doubt that the Dark Ages attract their followers partly due to their own view of themselves. Like those of Greece, the British and Irish "Dark Age" was an "Heroic Age".'

This volume is my contribution to the Laings' battle: an attempt to throw some light on the realities of the Dark Ages and, in doing so, to seek an understanding of the seemingly ages-old racial antagonism which still exists, in varying degrees, between Celt and Saxon.

In writing for the general reader, I have attempted to follow the style and purpose of *The Celtic Empire* by making this area of history available in all its complexity for the non-specialist while presenting a 'Select Bibliography', covering a representative range of reading, for those who wish to research further into the period. While I have tried to follow a chronological form, the very nature of the study causes some areas to be treated in a thematic form. To help readers follow the course of events, I have presented a 'Chronology' at the end of the work.

[1]

The End of Empire?

The Roman empire is beheaded ... all things born are
doomed to die ... but who would have believed that Rome
would crumble?

Eusebius Hieronymus (St Jerome)
(c. AD 342–420)

S OME time during the year AD 446 the wealthy Romanized
families of southern Britain wrote an appeal to the Supreme
Commander of the Army of the Western Empire of Rome, the
Consul Flavius Aetius, seeking military help against the increasing
attacks by Saxon raiders. According to the British Celt, Gildas, writing in his *De Excidio et Conquestu Britanniae* (On the Ruin and
Conquest of Britain) around AD 560, Britain was suffering constant
attack. Aetius was told: 'The barbarians drive us to the sea and the
sea drives us back to the barbarians; death comes by one means or
the other; we are either slain or drowned.'

Aetius, however, was preoccupied with more pressing matters than
giving military aid to an island which had left the empire thirty-six
years before and now had its own king and army. Attila and his
Huns had been pressing the Eastern Empire along the Danube valley.
About this time Attila had inflicted a devastating defeat on that
Eastern Empire and would shortly be attempting to smash his way
into Gaul to challenge Aetius and the Western Empire. Meanwhile,
Aetius was trying to stabilize the Rhine frontier against the aggressive
attacks of the Germanic tribes. The Franks, one of the leading Ger-
manic groups, were already poised to spread south and to change
Gaul into Frankia (France). Military aid to protect the former Roman
colony of Britain was not an option for the hard-pressed commander.
However, within the year following the sending of the appeal, two
Gallo-Roman bishops arrived in Britain. For Germanus of Auxerre

(b. *c*.AD 378, d. 448), who had once practised as an advocate in Rome, it was his second visit to Britain. During the previous visit, just over fifteen years before, Germanus had actually taken command of a British militia and led them to victory against raiding bands of Saxons in a battle which had become known as the 'Alleluia Victory'. Germanus had led his Britons into battle encouraging them to shout 'Alleluia!' Accompanying Germanus on this second trip to Britain was Severus, bishop of Trier, once capital of the Treverii Celts. Eusebius Hieronymous, St Jerome, had lived in the city only a generation before and compared the local Celtic spoken there with the Celtic spoken in Galatia.

Both bishops had close links with Aetius. Germanus was well respected in Roman diplomatic circles. It has therefore been argued, and seems entirely likely, that Aetius, unable to spare any part of his armies, decided to send a 'fact-finding mission', consisting of Germanus and Severus, to see the extent of the problem in Britain and, perhaps, advise on how best the Britons could organize their own defences against the Saxon menace. The Saxons had been making raids on the coast of Gaul as well as Britain, particularly along the coastline of the Armorican peninsula, in conjunction with attacks of the Franks in northern Gaul. Perhaps Aetius saw the problem in terms of overall strategy.

Gaul, too, was a changing land. Julius Caesar had conquered it for Rome, destroying what was regarded as the very heartland of the Celtic world. Yet Gaul had not meekly settled to the *pax Romana*. While the Celts of Gaul had never again risen as a united people, as they had during the years 54–51 BC, there had nevertheless been uprisings in 44 BC, 33 BC, 30 BC and between 25 and 7 BC. As late as the fifth century we have Gaius Sollius Apollinaris Sidonius (*c*.AD 430–480), who became bishop of the Arverni, saying that it was only in his day that the *leading families* of Gaul were trying to throw off 'the scurf' of Celtic speech. Therefore, the Celtic language was still widespread as a *lingua materna*, with Latin as the *lingua franca*, when the Germanic tribes began to push into the country and settle.

We can see from this state of affairs that Germanus and his companion Severus, journeying to Britain in AD 446, were not entering a country which was alien to them. Their Gaulish Celtic would have been understood by British Celts, while in addition Latin was a *lingua franca*. But Germanus found a rapidly changing situation in Britain.

For 350 years, Britain, or rather the southern part of the island, south of Hadrian's Wall, had lived, often restlessly, under the *pax Romana*. The Brigantes, a tribal confederation whose territory spread over what is now northern England, 'from sea to sea' (as Ptolemy states), north of the Mersey and the Don and south of the Eden and the Tyne, were particularly prone to insurrection throughout the entire Roman occupation. Towards the end of the fourth century, the Roman Empire was weakening, beset by its own internal contradictions and power struggles as well as by the increasing threat of the Germanic tribes, raiding and pushing forward along the northern borders of the empire.

The situation in Britain was often confused. It was far from being the stable, peaceful Roman province so many writers like to imagine. The indigenous Celtic population, the Britons, had not entirely given up hope that one day they would be able to throw off the yoke of Rome. Additionally, the Roman colonists were agitating against restrictive control from Rome. In AD 286, M. Aurelius Carausius, the commander of the Roman fleet in British waters, declared Britain the centre of an independent empire. Carausius was murdered in AD 293 by his finance minister, Allectus, who took over control of the government. In AD 296 the emperor Constantius arrived in Britain with an army, defeated and slew Allectus. Constantius attempted to subdue the Britons north of Hadrian's Wall but was so exhausted by the fruitless task that he died at York where his son, Constantine the Great, was declared emperor.

As early as AD 296, a panegyric addressed to Constantius Chlorus spoke of the Irish (Hibernii and Scotii) apparently making common cause with the Picts of northern Britain and raiding the Roman province.

During the fourth century, southern Britain came under increasing attacks from the Irish and the Picts of northern Britain. The Romans generally used the term Scotii, or raiders, for the Irish while the British Celts, among whom some of the Irish settled in large groups, called them the Gwyddel. Scholars argue that this name was then transported back to Ireland in the form of Góidel and thus we have the modern terms Gael and Gaelic. It is also argued that the name Gwynedd, which emerges as the major kingdom of north Wales, has a similar derivation and was named after Irish settlers who were later driven out by Cunedda and his sons who led their own settlement of the area from the land of the Votadini (the Gododdin) in south-east Scotland.

What seems to have concerned the imperial administration more, in the dying century of the empire, was the increasing number of raids emanating from the expanding Germanic tribes on the European continent. Raids on the eastern coast by the Saxons caused the Roman authorities in Britain to devote their military energies to driving out invading armies on more than one occasion. During the third century the Romans, to counter these attacks, had built a series of coastal fortresses known as the 'Saxon shore' under the command of a special officer known as *comes litoris Saxonici*. Even before southern Britain left the Roman Empire, the *ferocissimi Saxones* had become a fact of life to the Britons of the east and southern coasts.

The regular Roman garrison in Britain grew even more political during the later part of the fourth century and resented what appeared to them to be an indifferent attitude from Rome. They decided once more to set up their own rulers and claimants to the imperial throne.

In AD 383 the Roman legions in Britain declared their commander, Magnus Maximus, to be emperor. He was a Roman from Spain who became remembered in Celtic folklore as Macsen Wledig (*gwledig* meaning ruler). He had married a native Briton, Elen Lwddog, daughter of a chieftain named Eudaf, from whom later Celtic rulers would claim descent to legitimize their claims. Maximus took the Roman garrison troops from Britain and marched on Rome to seize the throne. He was finally defeated, captured and put to death on 28 July AD 388. Ammianus Marcellinus, the Greek-born Roman historian, reports that Maximus's battle standard was a dragon on a purple background which Welsh historians claim as the origin of the red dragon flag of Wales.

Maximus's widow, Elen, who had accompanied her husband as far as Gaul, now returned to Britain with her family, many of whom were to become leading members of the British Christian movement, as did Elen herself. Many place-names are tributes to the influence of Elen and her children in Christianizing the country. Others of her family are regarded as founding Celtic dynasties in Britain while a daughter, Severa, is said to have married the ruler Vortigern, whom we shall discuss later.

The victorious Roman emperor, Theodosius, sent troops to Britain to replace those defeated legions which had been commanded by Maximus. Flavius Stilicho was given the task of pacifying Britain. While Stilicho was engaged in this work, Theodosius died and left the empire divided between his sons Arcadius and Honorius. This is accepted as the point at which the division between the Western and Eastern Roman Empires became final with Honorius (AD 395–423) ruling the Western Empire from Rome. By the time Honorius died, however, the Western Empire had disintegrated into several warring states. Against this background, the poet Claudian was singing Stilicho's praise for subduing Britain and driving back the Picts. Stilicho was also praised for defeating the Irish who were not only raiding Britain but establishing settlements there. This was the period when the Irish settled the Isle of Man, changing it from a British Celtic-speaking island to Irish Celtic-speaking. They also settled 'the seaboard of the Gael' (Airer Ghàidheal, Argyll) and formed a new kingdom of Dàl Riada in northern Britain. Settlements were also made in what were to become Dyfed and Gwynedd, in Wales, as well as in Cornwall. Indeed, during this period it was recorded that the Irish High King, Niall Noigiallach (of the Nine Hostages), died during a raid on Britain on shipboard off the Isle of Wight. It has been generally accepted that this event occurred in AD 405. However, Professor J. F. Byrne has argued that the date is in error and that all the people with whom Niall was associated lived a generation later. Professor Byrne argues that Niall, in fact, died c.AD 452. But it is certain that Stilicho did check Irish territorial ambitions. Of the two Irish settlements in Britain which survived any length of time, Dàl Riada grew and prospered while that of the Dési in Dyfed was eventually absorbed into a British Celtic ethos.

But during the summer of AD 401 Stilicho was being forced to withdraw his troops from Britain to meet another threat to the Western Empire, this time that of the Visigoths, led by Alaric, who had crossed into Italy and were threatening Rome itself. By AD 405 the remaining Roman garrisons in Britain were trying to set up their own emperors once again. Marcus, Gratian and Constantine were named as emperors by the enthusiastic troops and asked to organize a defence of their British interests. All the claimants met with fairly swift deaths.

Yet again Rome was being torn by internal disputes. At one point, Alaric, leader of the Visigoths, formed an alliance with the Roman senate against their emperor Honorius. In AD 410 Alaric managed to enter and sack Rome.

In this same year of AD 410, Zosimus, the late fifth-century Greek historian, states that the 'Britons', by which he undoubtedly means the Roman colonists in Britain and the leading Romanized Britons, had sent an appeal for aid to Honorius and that Honorius had issued a 'rescript', which was a way of issuing instructions and reinforcing the law. Honorius's 'rescript' is supposed to have told the Britons to organize their own defences. Historians, liking certainty, accept this date as 'the end of Roman Britain'. Of course, it was not so clear-cut as this, not as specific as when twentieth-century Britain set dates to pull out of its former colonies and when those colonies attained their freedom. Professor Peter Salway is dubious whether this appeal was ever made; and if Honorius did, indeed, issue a 'rescript' he was in no way announcing his intention of abandoning Britain for ever. If the date of AD 410 marked the end of Roman Britain it only did so with hindsight.

What is certain is that when Germanus, the bishop of Auxerre, made his first visit to Britain in AD 429, and organized the Britons to turn back an attack of the Saxons, there was no Roman garrison in the country. The Roman system was slowly disintegrating and Britain no longer gave any allegiance, politically or economically, to Rome. The soldiers had gone and the ruling class looked to local leaders. Zosimus reports that the native British had now actually expelled the Roman colonial administrators and established their own government.

Celtic Britain, held in check for 350 years, began to re-emerge. Latin was still the language for a great many Romanized southern British and the colonial families who had settled in Britain from other parts of the empire as soldiers, administrators and entrepreneurs. If we accept Zosimus's report, how many of these colonials remained in Britain after the re-emergence of a native government? We can reflect on the answer, which cannot be given specifically, by remembering how many families of the 'British Raj' remained in India after independence in 1948: not all that many. And in the Britain of post-Roman times, all the Roman colonial families had to be bilingual in Latin and the native language. British (P-Celtic) was spoken everywhere on the island of Britain, although there were also pockets of Irish (Q-Celtic). Therefore, the language of independent

Britain which emerged in this period was not a language whose structures had been changed by Latin (as among the Iberians): it was British Celtic, the ancestor tongue of Welsh, Breton and Cornish.

Christianity was now the major religion in southern Britain. It had been introduced very early on. Gildas claimed it had been introduced some six years after Christ's crucifixion. The Church was in a very strong position and would become the backbone of resistance against the pagan Saxons. Elen, the widow of Maximus, had taken a prominent role in asserting the position of the Church in Britain during the decades before the Roman withdrawal. Indeed, as we shall subsequently see in Chapter Eight, the British Celts were prominent in the early Christian movement and provided several leading theologians who were respected throughout Europe.

Just back from Rome at this time was Ninian, son of a British chieftain from Carlisle. He had been ordained by the Pope. He was greatly impressed by the teachings of Martin of Tours (d. AD 397). Martin is now looked upon as the 'Father of Celtic Monasticism'. He was not a Celt, being born in Pannonia, but settled in Gaul where he introduced the asceticism of eastern monasticism. It was this concept of the religious life that Ninian brought back to Britain, to his home territory around the Solway Firth. He established his monastery at what is now Whithorn in Wigton, Galloway. He called it Candida Casa, the pure or white house, after the establishment of Martin of Tours, his mentor. The Gaulish Celts had called Martin's monastery 'the place of the big family', *mor-munntir*, which survives as Marmoutier. Candida Casa was translated by the Anglo-Saxons into *hwit aern* – Whithorn. Whithorn became the first influential monastic centre in Britain and by the time Ninian died, about AD 432, he had acquired a reputation throughout both Britain and Ireland, as his dedications show. The next abbot of Candida Casa was Caranoc who, according to a tradition recorded in the *Book of Ballymote*, compiled in 1390, first took Christian teaching to Ireland and there baptized a British hostage named Patrick.

The most influential British Christian of the period was undoubtedly Pelagius, born c.AD 354. He went to Rome in AD 380 and was there when his fellow Briton, Ninian, was visiting. Pelagius was distressed by the laxity of moral standards he found among Christians in Rome. He blamed this squarely on the doctrine expounded in the writings of Augustine of Hippo which maintained that everything was preordained. Pelagius believed that men and women could take the initial and fundamental steps towards their salvation, using their own efforts and not accepting things as pre-ordained. He argued that Augustine's theories imperilled the entire moral law. If man were not responsible for his good and evil deeds there was nothing to restrain him from an indulgence in sin with the excuse that it was preordained.

Pelagius's argument was condemned by Augustine's supporters as an attempt to re-establish druidism, the pre-Christian religion of the Celts. This might not be too far from the truth, for the druidic philosophy was an intensely moral one and Christianity had found it easy to coalesce with the ancient religion.

Pelagius was undoubtedly a man of his culture.

He managed to avoid Alaric's sack of Rome by leaving the city beforehand in the company of a friend, an Irishman named Celestius, and they travelled to Africa and the Middle East. But Augustine, stung by Pelagius's criticism of his philosophies, published several denunciatory letters and his friend, Orosius Paulus of Spain, began to orchestrate an attempt to accuse Pelagius of heresy. Criticism was first made of Celestius and, when a church council condemned him, the attack was opened directly on Pelagius. Pelagius was able to clear himself before two church councils in Jerusalem and Diospolis (Lydda), and he finally wrote a treatise, *De Libero Arbitrio* (On Free Will), to explain his views. Augustine pressed remorselessly on with his campaign to discredit Pelagius, finally convincing the African bishops at Carthage and Milevius in AD 416 who condemned him as 'anti-Christian'. They persuaded Pope Innocent I to excommunicate him. But Innocent's successor, Zosimus, immediately pronounced Pelagius innocent of heresy having studied his works, especially *Libellus Fidei* (Statement of Faith). Augustine was outraged, and he and his supporters renewed their campaign. The emperor Honorius (AD 395–423) now denounced Pelagius, which left the Pope with little choice but to revoke his finding and condemn the British Celtic theologian. Pelagius remains a 'heretic' in Rome to this day.

Ammianus Marcellinus, regarded as the last great Roman historian who wrote in Latin, although he was a Greek born in Antioch (c.AD 330–395), was a man without religious prejudice. As such he could observe: 'No wild beasts are so cruel as the Christians in their dealings with each other.' Certainly, he was proved right within a few years judging from the way Augustine and his followers hounded Pelagius and drove him from the Roman Church.

The teachings of Pelagius were to cause concern to the orthodoxy of Rome during the next century in Britain and a Pelagist 'movement' was condemned at the second Council of Orange in AD 592. Prosper of Aquitaine wrote a verse repeated by Bede which contained more than a touch of racialism against the British Celts.

> Against the great Augustine see him crawl,
> This wretched scribbler with his pen of gall!
> In what black cavern was the serpent bred,
> That from the dirt presumed to rear its head?
> Either the coast of Britain saw his birth,
> Or else his heart pours its own venom forth.

The important point here is that Pelagius had not evolved a new philosophy but was a representative of British Celtic culture with its philosophy of free will and its social concepts. With regard to the latter, we find that Pelagians were condemned as being 'proto-socialist' by nineteenth-century writers. A fifth-century Pelagian, known as the 'Sicilian Briton', a British Celt writing in Sicily whom Dr Haslehurst believes to be identifiable as the British bishop Fastidius, wrote a *Tractatus de Divitiis* – a tract on wealth – in which he saw mankind divided between wealth, poverty and sufficiency. He argues: 'Overthrow the rich man and you will not find a poor man . . . for the few rich are the cause of the many poor.' Heady revolutionary stuff, but perfectly acceptable to the egalitarian social order of the Celts with their lack of absolute private property, their electoral methods of kingship and officialdom, and their lack of the concept of primogeniture. What Rome saw as the teachings of Pelagius winning converts in Britain was no more than the British Celts abiding by their own social order.

In spite of this, several British Celtic early Christian theologians were well respected by Rome. Fastidius himself, according to Grennadius of Marseilles, 'a bishop of the Britons', wrote several works which were 'sound in doctrine and worthy of God'. In about AD 411, in a tract entitled *De Vita Christiana*, Fastidius apparently confirms the Greek historian Zosimus's view of an administrative metamorphosis in Britain in AD 410 by speaking of the political changes in Britain which, according to Dr John Morris's interpretation, represented a violent overthrow of government. Indeed, this would support the report of Zosimus that the Britons had expelled the Roman administrators and set up their native government. Fastidius writes:

> We see before us many instances of wicked men, the sum of their sins complete, who are being judged at this present moment, and denied this present life no less than the life to come. This is not hard to understand, for in changing times we expect the deaths of magistrates who have lived criminally; for the greater their power, the bolder their sins . . .

This, indeed, could be taken as evidence that the change from Roman imperial administration to native government was not achieved without violence; that the native Britons sought to punish profligate colonial administrators and collaborators.

Fastidius is clear what the Celtic Christian attitude should be in these troubled times. He asks:

> Do you think yourself Christian if you oppress the poor? . . . If you enrich yourself by making many others poor? If you wring your food from others' tears? A Christian is a man who . . . never allows a poor man to be oppressed when he is by, . . . whose doors are open to all, whose table every poor man knows, whose food is offered to all.

Another British Celt, Faustus, about this time, became a leading churchman in Gaul and abbot of Lérins. His writings were extremely popular during his lifetime but condemned after his death for Pelagian attitudes.

There were few areas in Britain where the Christian religion had not been preached at the time of the coming of the pagan Saxons. Christianity was the major religion and there was an identifiable British Church, based on British Celtic social concepts. Each tribe had its own bishop and priests, both under the control of the local abbot. The diocese was merely the district and towns occupied by the various tribes. The tribal assemblies allotted land to their clergy for their support, the land usually being looked after for the clergy under the supervision of a layman. The Celtic attitude to land owner-ship, not recognizing the right of absolute ownership, was a constant source of dispute with Rome where property ownership had become an important concept. The Pope and Roman clergy were developing as temporal princes and eventually emerged as feudal barons. The creation of the Papal States in AD 756 ensured the Pope's place as a secular ruler as well as a spiritual one. The Celtic clergy usually lived in communities in which male and female *religieux* lived and worked together; they were often married with children. The clash between the differing religious concepts was another factor which under-scored the animosity between the Celts and Saxons.

Christianity was also spreading in Ireland during this period. The British Celt, Patrick, was not, as is popularly supposed, the first missionary to take Christian teaching into Ireland. He was un-doubtedly the most successful missionary but, as already pointed out, we find Caranoc, mentioned by the *Book of Ballymote*, as the first recorded Christian in Ireland. According to Prosper of Aquitaine it was Pope Celestine I (AD 422–432) who sent a missionary called Palladius to be 'the first bishop to the Irish believing in Christ', thereby implying that there were already Christian communities in Ireland at that date. Palladius was a Gaulish Celt who had been deacon at Germanus's monastery of Auxerre. According to some scholars, Palladius is supposed to have died in Britain about AD 431 and been replaced by Patrick. Professor James Carney, however, maintains that Palladius worked in Ireland for many years with three other missionaries from Rome, Secondinus, Auxilius and Iserninus. Professor Thomas O'Rahilly argues that Palladius did not reach Ireland but died in Britain.

Professor Carney argues that it was Secondinus who founded the religious centre of Armagh, which is now the seat of the Irish primacy, in AD 444.

We can argue that Secondinus's companion, Iserninus, was cer-tainly in Ireland long before Patrick, having been imprisoned by the petty king of Leinster, Ende Censelach, and released only after Patrick's arrival and the conversion of Censelach's grandsons.

Patrick was a British Celt. According to early traditions, he was born at Bannarem Taberniae, which has been identified as Alcluyd (Dumbarton) and was originally named Sucat. His father was a

Christian deacon using the Latin name Calpurnicus. Patrick was taken as a hostage, when aged sixteen years, during an Irish raid by a chieftain named Milchú. He was forced to work in the area of Slemish, Ballymena, Co. Antrim. He eventually escaped to Gaul and joined a Christian settlement there, taking the name Patricius. Traditionally, this foundation was said to be Lérins where the British Celt, Faustus, was abbot. Patricius went on to Auxerre when Germanus was bishop there. The date of Patrick's mission to Ireland is disputed. It is agreed that he replaced Palladius as 'bishop to the Irish believing in Christ', but Carney argues that this was in AD 456 while O'Rahilly suggests AD 461. The formerly accepted date of AD 432 is no longer considered tenable.

He is reported as landing in Strangford Lough with a follower named Seginis. We are told that, on hearing of his arrival, Milchú, the chieftain who had taken him hostage in Britain, burnt himself to death. If this is true, one wonders what manner of man would instil such fear as to cause self-immolation. Mochaoi, Milchú's grandson, became one of Patrick's followers. There survive copies of Patrick's *Confessio* recounting his life, and a letter addressed to a British Celtic ruler named Coroticus, whom we can identify as Coirthech, or Ceretic (Caradoc), king of Patrick's original homeland, the Strathclyde kingdom, around AD 450–480. His name appears in the Harleian genealogies as the first historical king of Strathclyde, grandson of Cinhil, whose capital was at Alcluyd, where Patrick was reputedly born. Patrick addresses Ceretic as a fellow Christian, and ruler of a Christian kingdom, but accuses him of leading raiding parties on Ireland and carrying off his newly converted Irish flock and selling them into slavery to pagan kingdoms. It would seem from this that the raids by the Irish and Picts on the Christian British Celts were not a one-way venture.

If we are to accept Dr Morris's interpretation, based on the writings of the bishop Fastidius and Zosimus, the natives had risen up and overthrown the last Roman imperial administrators in Britain in AD 410. In the years following, the native British Celtic chieftains or princes had re-emerged with strong powers. Many of these native local rulers had been tolerated by Rome during the occupation, more or less as the Indian princes were tolerated by the 'British Raj' in India. Native Indian princes ruled half the land mass of India and one quarter of the population during the days of the empire. Indeed, there were 600 ruling princes in India who accepted imperial suzerainty. So what emerged in Britain in AD 410 was a number of self-governing Romanized *civitates*, or city 'states' (Gildas says that Britain was adorned with twenty-eight chief cities) and numerous rural areas occupied by tribes still ruled by local chieftains in the traditional Celtic way. The High Kingship system seems to have been quickly adopted, or rather readopted, with the rural chieftains and city magnates electing a central monarch, based in London, who ruled with the aid of a council or assembly of 300 representatives. The total number of members of this assembly may well have some cultural significance as it corresponds exactly to the number of members of the assembly of Celtic Galatia, the first Celtic state of whose political administration we have evidence.

The Celtic tribal system seems to have survived fairly intact in those areas outside the *civitates*.

Southern Britain had emerged from Roman imperial dominance not only as a Christian state with a sound political structure but also as a prosperous country. There was no decline in the material comfort and welfare of the state, as J. N. L. Myres has demonstrated. British rulers continued to strike their own coinage. Gildas asserts that there was a long period of high prosperity after the break with Rome. There is certainly evidence of wealthy houses still being built in the years following Roman departure. Indeed, neither the provincial ruling classes nor the great mass of pastoral and agricultural workers were adversely affected. But there does seem evidence of damage to the mercantile classes, those merchants cut off from European markets by the Germanic advances on the Continent. There is also evidence of the destruction of centres of pottery and glass manufacture as a result of Saxon raids. The British weaving industry, the export of metals and metal work were also restricted. All this was due not to a change of government but simply to the concurrent increased raiding of the Saxon 'pirates' whose ships plundered the seas surrounding Britain.

For over a century the British had become used to encounters with the Saxons and Franks, who were reaching across the sea and conducting savage raids on the coastal populations. It would be an obvious measure for the new government of Britain to maintain the 'Saxon shore' defence system of the Romans and man these forts along the coast.

Until the mid-fifth century, the British Celts had been dealing simply with raiding parties. It was at this stage that the Saxons decided to do more than raid Britain; they decided to occupy areas of land and form permanent settlements.

[2]

Mutiny of the Mercenaries

The priests and the people, without any respect of persons, were destroyed with fire and sword, nor was there any left to bury those who had been cruelly slaughtered.

Bede (c. AD 673–735),
Historia Ecclesiastica Gentis Anglorum

WHEN Germanus of Auxerre arrived in Britain in AD 446 with his companion, Severus of Trier, they found the southern half of the island ruled by one man. Gildas, writing about a hundred years after the event, does not name him but calls him a 'great tyrant'. He undoubtedly meant the term in the original Greek sense of an 'absolute ruler'. It was not until some centuries later that Nennius put a name to the man and called him Vortigern. But Vortigern is not a proper name. *Vawr-tighern* simply means 'overlord': it is a description of his position. Dr John Morris has argued that his name was probably Vitalinus and that the original text of the genealogies, which gives us this information, listed 'Vortigern, that is Vitalis' (or Vitalinus) which was then misinterpreted as 'Vortigern, son of Vitalinus'. Interestingly, Welsh tradition lists him as 'Gwrtheyrn Gwrthenau'; the name Gwrtheyrn also means 'supreme leader'. But we will continue to call him Vortigern for it is by that name that this ruler is popularly known. And, as Vortigern, he has become the arch-traitor in Celtic tradition. He is accused of betraying Britain to the Saxons. Many hostile accounts circulated among the Celts, especially of Wales, until Nennius recorded their traditions.

Vortigern became High King of southern Britain in about AD 425. That he was able to do so and retain power for nearly thirty years is indicative of some initial popularity among the people. Tradition has him among the wealthy landowning classes and therefore either of a prominent Latinized family or even of Roman colonist ancestry. The latter suggestion seems unlikely, if we accept Zosimus's view of the ousting of Roman colonial administrators. Geoffrey of Monmouth repeats several popular traditions of the time, even making him a descendant of the famous British king Cunobelinos (Shakespeare's Cymbeline) who ruled southern Britain before the Roman conquest in AD 43. It is certainly more than likely that he was the descendant of one of the native ruling families. Tradition also has him as marrying Severa, the daughter of Magnus Maximus and Elen, perhaps to reinforce his kingship claims. Later medieval Latinists were anxious to claim Roman ancestry for leading Celtic figures of the time and such claims should be taken with a great degree of scepticism.

In spite of the hostility towards Vortigern, the kings of Gwrtheyrnion (Radnor) claimed descent from him to reinforce their claims. So did the ninth-century king of Powys, Cyngen ap Cadell. Two of Vortigern's three sons bore native Celtic names, Vortimer and Categirn. The main traditions about Vortigern were set down by Nennius and expanded by Geoffrey of Monmouth in his *History of the Kings of Britain*, written *c.* 1136, but this cannot be trusted as an authentic history.

When Germanus of Auxerre paid his second visit to Britain, Vortigern was still 'overlord' or High King of southern Britain. But he was now a king under pressure from raids and settlements by the Irish on the western seaboard, from raids by the Picts of northern Britain and from attacks by the Saxons along the eastern seaboard. We can suppose that there were already small settlements of Saxons along the eastern seaboard of the country by this time.

To recapitulate: the Celts had sent their appeal to Aetius and it seems likely that, in answer to this, Germanus and Severus arrived on their fact-finding tour. According to Germanus's biographer, Constantius of Lugdunum (Lyons), the bishop was more concerned with finding and condemning Pelagian 'heretics' than considering the local political and military situation. (Constantius's *Life* is one of the few sources for what was happening in Britain at this time.) According to Constantius, Germanus arrived in the Selsey or Southampton area and was given hospitality by Elafius, probably the chieftain of the Belgae, whose chief city was Venta Belgarum (Winchester). Constantius says that adherents of Pelagius's teachings were found, handed over to Germanus and Severus and officially expelled from Britain. Nennius later reports that Germanus, 'with all the clergy of Britain', condemned Vortigern. He has Germanus hounding Vortigern to his death at Caer Guorthigern on the Teifi for his Pelagian heresy. While this is plainly unbelievable, it might be an instance of tradition simply underscoring the fact that there was enmity between Vortigern and Germanus.

Germanus and Severus departed from Britain without apparently achieving much by way of practical steps to aid the Britons in their military plight.

Vortigern now decided, unwisely as it turned out, to fight fire with fire and, like many another ruler before and subsequently, he decided to employ a band of mercenaries. The mercenaries he chose have been identified as a group of Jutes led by two brothers called Hengist and Horsa. It is Bede who identifies them as Jutes. The Jutes, according to Bede, came from northern Jutland and were a band of Germanic warriors. However, Sir Frank Stenton has argued that available evidence shows the Kentish Jutes to have closer connections with the Franks of the Rhineland; he therefore believes them to have come from that area rather than Jutland. It seems acceptable, from his evidence, that the three shiploads of mercenary warriors, with their women and children, who came to Britain in the employ of Vortigern sailed, not from the fjords of Jutland, but from the mouth of the Rhine and were Franks. This is to some extent confirmed by a letter of Pope Gregory I (AD 509–604) to Theuderic and Theudeberht, the Frankish kings, in which he refers to the Germanic settlers of Kent (the Kentings) as 'your subjects'. Indeed, in AD 551 Theudeberht sent an embassy to Constantinople asserting his claim over the Germanic kingdoms in Britain by right of the migration of his people there.

The mercenaries were, of course, culturally related to the Saxons, speaking a slightly divergent dialect but basically the same Germanic language and sharing the same culture and religious philosophies, which we will consider later. According to Dr Mario Pei, it is generally supposed that Jutish and Saxon were the progenitors of Kentish and southern English dialects, while Anglian gave birth to the Midland and northern dialects, and that all three (Jutish, Anglian and Saxon) formed the basis of standard English, linguistically recognizable in Old English for which Anglo-Saxon is an alternative but imprecise term.

The early chroniclers have it that Vortigern gave the mercenaries, by way of payment, the Isle of Thanet in Kent as a place of settlement. In spite of this early settlement Thanet has retained its Celtic name, 'the bright island', cognate with the British *tan* for bright or fire.

But the mercenaries of Hengist and Horsa were not the first Germanic settlers in Britain: there is archaeological evidence that there were already settlements of Angles and Saxons in the coastal areas of Yorkshire and Lincolnshire, and even inland at Dunstable and Abingdon where archaeological remains indicate small communities of merchants, though why these places were chosen as commercial centres is unclear. Angles were also already arriving and settling in what was to be East Anglia.

The Jutes (we shall continue to call them by the name Bede ascribed to them) soon set to work for Vortigern. But when did they actually arrive? The chronicles are confusing. Bede places the date of their arrival in AD 449, three years after Germanus's visit. The anonymous *Gallic* or *Gaulish Chronicle* claims that it was in AD 442 that Britain 'passed into the control of the Saxons'. Now this, of course, is far too early for any significant political rise to have occurred among the Germanic settlers in Britain, let alone for them to have started to carve out their own kingdoms in the country. AD 449 seems a reasonable date for the arrival of the Jutish mercenaries.

For a while it seems that the Jutish mercenaries served the British ruler without any problems, checking the marauding attacks on the east coast by their own Germanic kinfolk, meeting the enthusiastic raids of the Celts of Caledonia, the Picts. There is even evidence that they were used in attempts to stop the raids and settlements of the Irish in the west of the country.

The 'honeymoon' period was soon over. Hengist and Horsa began to voice their discontent at their pay and conditions, the complaint of most mercenaries from time immemorial. The Jutes claimed legality for their subsequent mutiny by stating that the Celtic king was paying them neither adequately nor regularly. Hengist informed Vortigern that if matters did not improve then they would consider that their agreement with him was at an end and lay waste his entire kingdom.

What had happened was that the numbers of the Jutes had grown considerably during the preceding year. The *Anglo-Saxon Chronicle* says 'the Saxons multiplied their numbers, and the British could not feed them'. Obviously, Vortigern could not raise sufficient taxes to maintain his mercenary army. Indeed, it may well have been because of the imposition of taxes that Vortigern's popularity was declining. Earlier, in the late AD 430s, Vortigern had found himself with a civil war on his hands as well as pressures from outside. Resistance centred around a man known in Welsh tradition as Emrys, who bore the Latin name Ambrosius Aurelianus. Dr John Morris argues that there were two men named Ambrosius Aurelianus, father and son. Ambrosius the elder was the one who fought Vortigern in the 430s, while the younger Ambrosius led subsequent British resistance to the Saxons. Nennius reports a battle at Guoloph in AD 437 between Vitalinus and Ambrosius. If we accept Dr Morris's contention that Vitalinus was actually Vortigern, then the clash makes sense. According to Gildas, Ambrosius Aurelianus's parents had 'worn the purple', which implies that he was descended from one of the Romano-British imperial claimants such as Marcus, Gratian or Constantine.

At the time of the Jutish mutiny, Vortigern seemed to be relying heavily on his mercenaries to keep him in power. He was encouraging even more mercenaries to arrive in Britain. According to Nennius, repeating the view that Hengist was a shrewd and experienced leader, there then occurred an incident which gave the Jutes a legal claim over the kingdom. Hengist is said to have had a beautiful daughter. He held a feast for Vortigern, contrived to get the Celtic king drunk, and then arranged for his daughter to flirt with him. Vortigern was so taken with the girl that, through his interpreter, Ceretic, he offered the girl half of his kingdom, if she would marry him. Now this is a common romantic morality tale which we should take with more than a few grains of salt. However, Nennius gives it as the reason why the Jutes then claimed all of Kent, for he has Hengist telling his daughter to demand Kent from the High King.

> So the girl was married to Vortigern ... So Hengist gradually brought over more and more ships, till the islands whence they came were left uninhabited, and his people grew in strength and numbers, [and were] established in Canterbury.

Canterbury, which translates as the *burg* of the Cantware, or people of Kent, now changed its name from the original British form of Durovernon (the fort by the swamp) to the Germanic name. It is the place where the earliest Saxon pottery has been found. This reinforces the idea that the Saxons, or Jutes, were in occupation of the town at a very early date.

Now the mercenary warriors of Hengist and Horsa were ready to strike. The year is recorded as AD 449. But if we accept the year as AD 450 it would make more sense, allowing the Jutes to have served Vortigern for one summer campaign before they rose up against the British king. It is very unlikely that the mutiny would have occurred in the same year that Hengist and Horsa arrived to serve the British king. Vortigern had, apparently, been oblivious to the build-up of the Jutish threat. Hengist's assault on the British did not rely merely on the mercenary troops; he apparently issued a call to the Angles and Saxons settled throughout Britain. Gildas speaks eloquently of the consuming fire of their attack: 'Once lit, it did not die down. When it had wasted town and country in that area, it burnt up almost the whole surface of the island, until its red and savage tongue licked the western ocean . . .'

Hengist and Horsa's men could not have been in a position to devastate Britain from the east coast to the west by themselves, although Gildas talks of the great towns of Britain falling to the Jutes. There is archaeological evidence of the rising among the Angles' settlements in East Anglia, but elsewhere any rising appears to have been contained at a local level or, as with the case of the settlements at Dunstable and Abingdon, the Anglo-Saxon settlers appeared too weak to cause trouble.

Gildas laments the fate of the British towns.

All their inhabitants, bishops, priests and people were mown down together, while swords flashed and flames crackled. Horrible it was to see the foundation stones of towers and high walls thrown down bottom upwards in the squares, mixing with holy altars and fragments of human bodies, as though they were covered with a purple crust of clotted blood, as in some fantastic wine-press. There was no burial save in the ruins of the houses, or in the bellies of the beasts and birds.

Allowing for the embellishment of Gildas's purple prose, the rebellion of the Jutish mercenaries must have been devastating for the British. Excavations have tended to prove that certain towns did, indeed, fall to the Jutes. At Caistor by Norwich, for example, thirty-six charred bodies from the period were found in the remains of a burnt building. There are signs that many inhabitants of the towns had fled before the Jutes attacked; hordes of coins have been found, having been hastily buried by the departing Celts never to be reclaimed.

Vortigern probably awoke from his idyll and tried to organize resistance. In spite of the claims of Gildas, the British Celts did not even have to evacuate Kent, the main centre of the Jutish uprising, for another thirty years according to the *Anglo-Saxon Chronicle*. If this is so, then Celtic resistance, after the initial shock, was successful. How much of this success can be ascribed to Vortigern is questionable. Bearing in mind the increasing criticism of the policies of Vortigern, during the Jutish mutiny, many of the local leaders of southern Britain had now ceased to acknowledge Vortigern's supreme authority. They were legally entitled to do this according Celtic law. While Roman law had held general sway during the occupation, it is obvious that Celtic law was reasserting itself in Britain. The earliest surviving codifications of native law show that it was little influenced by Roman concepts. The basis of kingship was that a king or chieftain was elected to office, usually from the same families who were used to office, but elected nonetheless. The Roman law of primogeniture, the eldest surviving son inheriting, was not part of Celtic law. Moreover, if the ruler did not pursue the commonwealth of the community then he could be deposed by the assembly who elected him. Only if he refused to promote the commonwealth or abide by the wishes of the tribal assemblies could there be bloodshed.

This was a concept which has been a recurrent problem for the Celtic peoples. Celtic rulers thus removed from office, and knowing about the laws of primogeniture current among their neighbours, often went to seek military aid to regain their thrones and were supported on the basis that a ruler has an inherited right to be and remain ruler. Thus did Madubratius (whose name in Celtic ironically means 'black traitor') persuade Julius Caesar that, as son of Imanuentius, ruler of the British Trinovantes, he should be helped to regain his throne after his people had thrown him out; thus did Maol Callum a' chinn mhoir (Malcolm Canmore) of Scotland persuade Edward of England to give him military aid to overthrow MacBeth (1040–57), on the basis that Maol Callum's father had been king; and thus did Dermot Mac Murrough, the king of Leinster, persuade Richard, Earl of Pembroke, to send an army of Norman knights to Ireland in 1169, to reinstate him as king of Leinster when he was chased out of his kingdom by his indignant people.

Quite frequently a Celtic ruler would resign office and retire to other things – often, in the early Middle Ages, to a life of monastic study or to go to Rome. In many respects, Celtic kingship was more like the presidency of a republic than the divine right of kingship which developed among the Anglo-Saxons. Celtic kingship is not unique among world cultures, but it did conflict with the Anglo-Saxon perception of the position. It should be pointed out that D. A. Binchy, in his *Celtic and Anglo-Saxon Kingship*, argues that the British Celts eventually came to recast their traditional kingship patterns after the Anglo-Saxon model whereas the Irish held to their original concepts for a lengthier period.

At the time of the mutiny of Vortigern's mercenaries, it would seem that there was a great deal of dissatisfaction with the way the High King was dealing with events. Nevertheless, Hengist and Horsa had failed to achieve their prime targets. They had not captured Vortigern's capital at London nor even secured themselves in Kent. Vortigern's son, Vortimer, had organized an army and counter-attacked the Jutish strongholds in Kent. Vortimer is said, by Nennius, to have driven the Jutes back to the Isle of Thanet but to have been killed in the process. Hengist had to send envoys to his compatriots in the homelands on the Continent, asking them to send more warriors and ships as reinforcements. The campaign to push the Jutes back into Thanet lasted for over ten years, according to the *Anglo-Saxon Chronicle*.

The Celtic sources maintain that Vortimer fought one battle on the River Darent (the British name means 'river by the oaks'). Another battle was fought at a ford called Rithergabail, where Hengist's brother, Horsa, was killed and Vortimer's brother, Categirn, also died. Vortimer then went on to win a decisive victory at Ritupis (the port of Richborough) where, Nennius says, 'the barbarians were beaten and put to flight, drowned as they clambered aboard their ships like women'.

The *Anglo-Saxon Chronicle* lists the same battles but gives them different names and reverses the order of the first two; however, the fact that the two disparate sources should agree on the three battles seems to confirm their authenticity. It is said that Horsa was killed at the first battle at Aylesford. The second battle was listed as Crayford, two miles from the junction of the Cray (meaning, in Celtic, 'fresh or clean') and the Darent. The Saxons claim this as a victory in which they slew 4000 Britons whereby the 'British forsook Kent and fled to London'. This is obviously a boast, or the evacuation was a brief one, for British Celts were soon back in Kent and fighting the Jutes in a third major engagement. The third battle was called Wippedsfleot, the estuary or inlet of 'Wipped'. The Saxons record the death of a thane called Wipped here, after whom they presumably named the stretch of water which is clearly Wantsum channel at Richborough, between Thanet and the mainland. The *Anglo-Saxon Chronicle* also claims that twelve Celtic chieftains were slain here but significantly it does not claim the battle as a victory. Nennius, on the other hand, does so claim it. And it was here that Vortimer was slain at the hour of his triumph.

It is Nennius who records that, during his last victory, Vortimer was mortally wounded. Before his death he told his men to bury him, presumably in Richborough, prophesying that if they did so then the Jutes would never be able to capture or settle in Britain. This is a common Celtic legendary motif, whereby the tomb of a dead leader gives a mystic protection to the land in which he is buried. We find the same motif in the *Mabinogi*, where the head of Bran the Blessed was taken to London and buried on Tower Hill. So long as it remained undisturbed, it would protect Britain from foreign invasion. In Ireland there also occurs a tradition of kings and chieftains being buried in a standing posture, arrayed in full battle dress, with the face turned towards the territories of their enemies. It was a Celtic belief that while the body of the king remained in this position, it exercised a malign influence on his enemies who were thereby always defeated in battle. There are many examples, such as that of Eoin Bel in a *Life of Cellach*. The king, mortally wounded, instructed his followers to bury him in the standing position facing his enemies to protect his lands from them. But Vortimer's men did not obey him and he was buried elsewhere, thus giving the chronicler a quasi-religious reason for the subsequent devastation of Britain.

Both British and Saxon sources agree that the Jutes were confined in Thanet for five years and then, reinforced, they managed to break out. If the mutiny occurred in AD 449/450 then the Celtic victory at Richborough would have occurred in AD 460 and therefore we would have to take AD 465 as the date of the Jutish break-out from Thanet. And this does accord with the *Anglo-Saxon Chronicle*'s claim that Crayford was fought in AD 456. There now began a warfare with shifting frontiers, covering a large battle front.

Vortigern, faced with the break-out of the Jutes from Thanet, decided to make a treaty with Hengist. Nennius says that Hengist's daughter played a large part in bringing this about. Hengist invited Vortigern and the 300 members of the British council to a meeting to agree a treaty which would, in effect, partition Vortigern's kingdom, creating a Jutish kingdom in Kent. Knowing that the members of the council were not as easy to persuade as Vortigern, Hengist ordered his men to go into the meeting with their arms concealed and, at a given moment, kill the Celts, sparing only Vortigern who was then obliged to cede his lands for fear of his life. Again, this story is similar in incident to others in Celtic history. It is reminiscent of Mithridates V (the Great) of Pontus, who invited the sixty Celtic chieftains of Galatia to a banquet in 88 BC, knowing the Celts would not enter a feasting hall armed, because of social and religious taboos, and then taking advantage of this fact to slaughter them all.

It seems that following this débâcle a new British Celtic leader emerged. Gildas specifically mentions Ambrosius Aurelianus, known in Welsh tradition as Emrys, as the leader of a successful British counter-offensive against the invaders, while Nennius has Ambrosius making a prophecy that the red dragon (the British Celts) would eventually overcome the white dragon (the Anglo-Saxons). The site of this prophecy was at Dinas Emrys, the fort of Emrys or Ambrosius, at Bedgelert. It is a small hill-fort, still viewable, whose main defences seem to belong to this period and containing a pool and artificial cistern constructed in the fifth or sixth century.

Tradition has it that Ambrosius overthrew the weak Vortigern and rallied Britain. Only one early source speaks of Vortigern's fate: the suspect version of Nennius has Germanus hounding him to death. A fourteenth-century chronicle claims that Ambrosius attacked and burnt down Vortigern's fortress and the former High King perished in the flames. The same source also claims that Ambrosius killed Hengist in battle. But there is no evidence closer to the period to support these claims.

That Emrys, or Ambrosius, was able to check the Jutes is best seen from the fact that the *Anglo-Saxon Chronicle* is significantly silent for the next few years. No further victories over the Celts are recorded until AD 473.

Gildas has nothing but praise for the 'modest, strong and faithful' Ambrosius. 'Though brave afoot, he was braver still on horseback', implying that Ambrosius was a good cavalry tactician. 'The Britons fled to him like swarms of bees who fear a coming storm. They fought the war with Ambrosius as their leader.'

By AD 473 Hengist's son Aesc emerges as his father's right-hand man. In that year, the *Chronicle* records that Hengist and Aesc fought the British Celts again in Kent and caused them to flee while the Jutes took 'uncountable spoils'.

The *Chronicle* records that in AD 488 Aesc became king of Jutish Kent, succeeding his father Hengist, who we may suppose died in that year. Aesc remained king for twenty-four years. Ambrosius Aurelianus disappears as abruptly as he had appeared. Was he slain in battle or did he, having held the Saxons to their beachheads, die of respectable old age? Some eager Arthurians have attempted to merge Ambrosius with Arthur to create a single hero.

By the time Aesc became king of Kent in AD 488 it can safely be said that the indigenous Celtic population, the descendants of the Cantii who gave their name to the area and were the first to face the landings not only of Julius Caesar but of Aulus Plautius one hundred years later, had either been massacred by the new settlers or driven westward out of the area; perhaps a few had been retained as slaves by the Jutes to be absorbed eventually in their German culture.

According to Bede, Aethelberht of Kent (*c*.AD 580/93–*c*. 616/18), accepted as the first 'historical king of Kent', was descended from Aesc, and the kings of Kent became known at that time as the Oiscingas after Aesc, or Oisc as it was originally spelt. The people were called the Kentings, thus the Celtic tribal name, the Cantii, survived in the language of the new settlers.

Kent had become the main beachhead of the Anglo-Saxon invasion and conquest of Britain.

[3]

The Coming of the Saxons

They sought help from Saxonland, and continually and considerably increased, and they brought over kings to rule over them in Britain.

Nennius, Historia Brittonum
(c. AD 830)

THE people who now began to settle extensively in southern Britain were the Saxons. Linguistically and culturally, they were little different from the other Germanic peoples who had settled in Kent (the 'Jutes') or from the Angles to the north-east. So it was, in Celtic perception, that the term 'Saxon' became the descriptive word for all the Germanic conquerors coming into the island of Britain. Even after the 'Jutes', Angles and Saxons coalesced with the Danes and the Norman French (themselves 'Norse-men'), and adopted the name English (Aenglisc) from the Angles, the Celts, linguistically, lumped them all together as Saxons. In the modern Celtic languages the word for the English remains the same: Sais (Welsh), Saoz (Breton), Saws (Cornish), Sasanach (Irish), Sasunnach (Scottish Gaelic) and Sostynagh (Manx). In much the same way, the Saxon invaders arrogantly dismissed all the native Britons as 'foreigners' – Weilsc or Wealhas, or in modern English, Welsh.

The news of the rich pickings to be had in Britain was taken to the tribes of the Angles and Saxons on the Continent. Stories of the success of Hengist in carving out a kingdom in Kent were attractive to the leaders of the other Germanic tribes. Among them was Aelle, a warrior chieftain of a Saxon tribe in south Jutland. Within a few years of Hengist's final battle with the British, which established his kingdom in Kent, Aelle decided to attempt a settlement of his own. In AD 477, with his three sons, Cymen, Wlencing and Cissa, he landed his followers from three ships on the south coast of Britain.

The place of his landing was later called after his son Cymen, Cymenesora (Cymen's shore), a spot near Selsey Bill, Sussex, which the sea has now claimed having extensively encroached along this coastline. Some scholars think it is probably Owers Bank, found a little off the coast on Admiralty charts.

The Saxon warriors were met on the coast by the British. But the Saxons were successful in driving the Celts back into a great wood which covered the major part of this area of south-eastern Britain, stretching from Sussex into Kent, and which was to become Andredsweald. The Saxons added their name for woodland, *weald*, on to the name of the nearby town of Anderida (Pevensey). The Celtic name of the town meant 'the place of the great fords'. The battle allowed Aelle and his Saxons to gain a beachhead. But it was not for another eight years that a second battle was recorded by the *Anglo-Saxon Chronicle*: 'Aelle fought against the Welisc near the bank of *Mearc raedes burna*.' Attempts to identify this river site have been unsuccessful, though some scholars favour the River Arun.

It was not until AD 491, fourteen years after first landing at Selsey, that Aelle, who had slowly fought his way eastward, successfully attacked the town of Anderida and had all its British inhabitants massacred. The *Anglo-Saxon Chronicle* boasts: 'Aelle and Cissa besieged the city of Anderida and slew all that were therein; nor was one Briton left there afterwards.' The chronicler points out that the Saxons did not rebuild the city, but later they seem to have formed a new settlement nearby and renamed the place Pefen's river (Pevensey).

Although the idea of a policy of annihilation of the native British Celtic population by the Saxons is viewed with discomfort by later generations of English historians, who would prefer to think that invader and native intermarried with little conflict, the massacre at Anderida was to foreshadow the Saxon method of clearing the native inhabitants from the lands which would eventually become England.

In terms of the settlement of Sussex, the eminent Sussex archaeologist Dr E. Cecil Curwen has said: '. . . for Sussex the evidence of place-names and of agricultural economy supports the view that the Britons, worn down by two centuries of raiding, were virtually exterminated.' The linguist, Dr Mario Pei, adds his support to the 'extermination theory', which we will examine in depth later. Dr Pei states:

One might imagine that the Celtic of the original Britons would have supplied a fertile field for loan-words to the Anglo-Saxon. Such is emphatically not the case . . . The reason for this seems to lie in the scantiness of social relations between the two races, the English considering the Celts as inferior and their own race and tongue as superior.

Robert McCrum, William Cran and Robert MacNeil, in their book *The Story of English* (London, 1986), agreed entirely.

The extent to which the Anglo-Saxons overwhelmed the native Britons is illustrated in their vocabulary. We might expect that two languages – and especially a borrowing language like English – living alongside each other for several centuries would borrow freely from each other. In fact, Old English (the name scholars give to the English of the Anglo-Saxons) contains barely a dozen Celtic words.

Archaeology also shows us what was happening during this time. Many of the old pre-Roman Celtic hill-forts, like Cissbury near Worthing, were being refortified by the Celts as a defence against the new enemy. When Cissbury was captured the Saxons seem to have renamed it after Aelle's son, Cissa – Cissa's burgh, or fort. The towns, such as Noviomagus Reginorum (New Place of the Regni – Chichester), were also attacked and destroyed along with the populated hill-forts, villages and undefended farmsteads. Most of the hill-forts which the Celts sought to reoccupy had not been in use by them since the Romans invaded. One hill-fort, at Highdown near Ferry, once cleared of its Celtic defenders, was used by the victorious Saxons as a place to bury their dead. The indigenous populations were slowly driven out of the area and, according to Bede, 7000 Saxon families now settled in their stead. In Sussex, particularly, very few of the original Celtic place-names survive, showing a fairly immediate and complete change of population.

The Saxons made an instant change from the native Celtic agricultural system in the area. They created an open field system, well suited to the valley claylands of the area. As a consequence the old hill-forts, villages and upland Celtic field systems were left derelict and the Downs were left to become pastureland. Saxon settlements were set up and the Saxon chieftains appear to have made no effort to take over the rich villas or townships of the dispossessed. According to Dr Curwen: 'No remnant of the defeated Britons remained to till their ancestral hills ... thenceforth the Downs were left to solitude and the tinkling sheep bell – a paradise for the lover of nature and for the archaeologist.' Since Dr Curwen wrote this in 1939 large areas of the Downs have been cleared with bulldozers, constituting a threat to archaeologists in search of pre-Saxon evidence.

After the destruction of Anderida in AD 491, nothing more was heard of Aelle, the founder of the kingdom of the South Saxons (Sussex), although Bede refers to him as the first Bretwalda, overlord, of the southern Saxons. The fact that Aelle was thus regarded would indicate that he led a powerful confederation of Saxons against the Celts. It is significant, in my opinion, therefore, that after AD 491, Aelle disappears from any mention in the chronicles and not even the names of his successors are known. The date coincides with the period in which the shadowy figure of the Celtic leader, Arthur, emerges as checking the Saxon incursions in Britain. I believe that this indicates that the supremacy of the Bretwaldship of Aelle collapsed at this time.

The Saxon title Bretenanwealda, usually contracted to Bretwalda, meant 'lord of Britain'. The *Anglo-Saxon Chronicle* applies the title retrospectively to Aelle in Sussex, Ceawlin of Wessex, Aethelberht of Kent and Raedwald of East Anglia. It signified the dominance of a Saxon king over his fellow kings and the title was given as the political and military fortunes of the kings waxed and waned. Northumbrian kings claimed the title, then Mercian kings and finally Wessex kings. Adomnán claimed that Oswald had been 'ordained' by Aidan as 'emperor of all Britain'. The title was usually a grandiose boast for it was never recognized by all the kings whether Celt or Saxon. Athelstan in the tenth century claimed the title Bretwalda with more cause than most of his predecessors, declaring himself '*rex totis Britanniae*'.

Aelle's sons did leave their names in the new place-names of Chichester (Cissa's *ceastar*) and Lancing (Wlencing's place). But we know nothing of them or their descendants during the next hundred years.

What is clear, however, is that Aelle's kingdom of the South Saxons was established by the end of the fifth century. At this time, it was merely a coastal strip from Selsey to Pevensey and, during the next century, the Saxons gradually extended their territory inland.

Four years after the Saxons destroyed Anderida, according to the *Anglo-Saxon Chronicle*, in AD 495, another Saxon chieftain named Cerdic, with his grandson Cynric, landed at Cerdicesora, placed as Totton near Southampton, and began to conquer and settle what was to be the most famous of the Saxon kingdoms – that of the West Saxons (Wessex). Some Wessex genealogists give Cynric as the grandson of Cerdic, the son of his son Creoda. If so, it would make the time-scale of Cynric's activity plausible. Most sources, however, maintain the tradition that Cynric was Cerdic's son. The *Anglo-Saxon Chronicle* says Cerdic landed with five ships and that the British met him and fought a major battle, disputing his landing. The British Celts were beaten back and the Saxons established a foothold in what is now Hampshire.

Who was Cerdic and why does this Saxon chieftain actually bear a Celtic name (the British Ceretic or Caradoc) as, indeed, do his successors to the Wessex throne – Ceawlin and Caedwalla? Had this Saxon family a Continental Celtic ancestor? This could be more likely than the belief of some scholars that he had a British Celtic ancestry. Dr D. J. V. Fisher states that 'The name Cerdic, regarded as derived from the Celtic Ceretic, is too unusual to have been invented.' The Wessex royal line became known as the Cerdicingas.

Bede uses Gewissae as an alternative name for the West Saxons. According to J. N. L. Myres, the name serves merely as a distinction between the royal family and their people. Gewis appears as a royal ancestor and the phrase *rex Gewissorum* is applied to the royal family and their dependants. Some have claimed the name to mean 'confederates' but, according to Myres, this means a rejection of Gewis, claimed as an ancestor of the family. He believes that the uniform 'C' of the names of the early kings of Wessex denotes a common ancestor, namely Gewis – the 'g' mutating from a 'kw' sound.

Dr Fisher argues that the importance of Cerdic's invasion and settlement was boosted by later annalists to glorify the West Saxon royal dynasty and that Cerdic was, in reality, the leader of a small but significant wandering war band which made contact with other Saxon settlers in the Upper Thames valley, in Abingdon for example, and that it was from this area that Wessex really began to spread.

This is a fine argument and we shall simply follow the historicity of the *Anglo-Saxon Chronicle*.

That Cerdic's conquest was not easy is demonstrated by the silence of the *Anglo-Saxon Chronicle* for a further six years before it records, in AD 501, someone called Port, with his two sons Bieda and Maegla, arriving at a place called *Portes mutha*, and defeating a young Celtic chieftain and his men. This entry has been dismissed as a plausible myth to explain the place-name Portsmouth. But Port was a personal Saxon name, and the fact that *mutha* can be combined with such a name is demonstrated by 'Eadgylses mutha', occurring in a charter relating to the Isle of Wight.

It is not for another seven years, in AD 508, that Cerdic and Cynric are recorded as being victorious in another major battle against the British Celts when they defeated a local chieftain named Natan-leod, killing him and 5000 Celtic warriors. The *Anglo-Saxon Chronicle* says the area they conquered was afterwards known as *Natan-leaga* as far as Cerdicesford or Charford. The site has been identified as Netley Marsh. There has been some scepticism as to whether Natan-leod existed or if the name derived from the Saxon *naet-leah*, wet marsh. In AD 514 Cerdic was reinforced by two other Saxon chieftains, his nephews Stuf and Wihtgar, who landed in three ships at Cerdicesora and won a victory over the British Celts. The *Anglo-Saxon Chronicle* makes the curious comment that in AD 519, about the same time as Arthur's great victory over the Saxons at Mount Badon, Cerdic and Cynric 'took the kingdom' and in the same year they fought with the Britons. The wording seems to imply that it was only after they had been fighting for a quarter of a century that their settlement around Southampton was assured.

Of course, the British Celts in this area appear to have been exceptionally tenacious. Although the Saxons had killed Natan-leod and 5000 Celtic warriors around Charford in AD 508, we find them still having to fight a fierce battle at the same place in AD 519, eleven years later. And then in AD 527 Cerdic and Cynric were still fighting the British Celts in *Cerdices leaga*, which they had first attempted to capture twenty years before.

By this time, several settlements of Saxons, Angles and 'Jutes' were emerging along the eastern seaboard of Britain and becoming powerful military centres, subduing and driving the native Celts westward. Tribes of Angles began arriving from their homelands in Schleswig during the latter half of the fifth century AD, settling the areas which were to become East Anglia, Mercia and the lands north of the river Humber which would become one of the most powerful kingdoms of the English – Northumbria.

The Fenlands in which the Angles moved seemed to have a curious fascination for them. The tribal area of the famous Iceni, who, under Boudicca, had almost succeeded in turning back the Roman conquest, was seen as a place of material and spiritual terrors by the invaders. St Guthlac (c.AD 673–714), a Mercian, became a hermit on the Welland in the Fens. When Felix wrote a *Life* of the hermit (*Vita Guthlaci*) he talks about the saint's struggle with spirits and demons in the haunt of lost souls and masterless mortals. Then he adds a fascinating piece of information by stating that Guthlac was also disturbed by the activities of Celtic-speaking Britons, 'those bitter enemies of the Saxon people'. Could isolated groups of Celtic-speakers have survived to this later period (the late seventh, early eighth centuries) so far east? The terrain could make it possible but such survival could not have been on a large scale and Felix indicates their isolation from their Anglian neighbours.

The Angle settlement of East Anglia and Middle Anglia, the area to the west of the Wash, must have taken a considerable time. Archaeological evidence has shown, however, that there is no other region of England where there is such a significant concentration of Germanic grave goods dating from the end of the fifth century. Here, also, it seems that the Angles settled in what were already Celtic sites, driving out the native inhabitants, especially around Cambridge; these indigenous inhabitants either took refuge in the neighbouring Fens or moved westward. This is not to say every site was taken over. Prosperous villas and major pottery centres were also totally abandoned by the Celts at this time and remained abandoned. Soon these Anglian settlements were defined as between the 'North folk' (Norfolk) and the 'South folk' (Suffolk).

J. N. L. Myres suggests a 'not inconsiderable British survival' in the Brandon area of west Suffolk for a century or so after the initial settlements. The Celtic influence was so strong that Nennius points out that the East Anglian kings found it advisable to claim a descent from Roman Britons as well as from Woden.

The kingdom of Mercia grew from the westward and northward expansion of the East and Middle Angles as the invaders pushed out of the Fenlands by way of the Welland, Wreak and Soar towards the Trent. For a while, into the sixth century, the Trent became the boundary between the Celts on its northern bank, forming the British kingdom of Elmet, and the Angles on its southern bank. The meaning of Elmet is obscure but it is obviously cognate with Elfet, a cantred in Wales, mentioned in the *Red Book of Hergest*, and with the personal name, Elmetiacos, mentioned in an ancient Caernarfon inscription. The Angles remained by the Trent long enough to accept the use of the Celtic river name which meant 'trespasser river'; that is, a river liable to flood. Then they pushed north-east, forming, for a while, a kingdom of Lindsey, whose northern border was the Humber but which soon became part of Mercia. The name of one of its earliest kings was Caedbaed, which seems to be a Celtic name with Cad, meaning 'battle', as its first element.

There is no early Anglo-Saxon literary evidence for the settlement in East Anglia as there is with Kent, Sussex and Wessex. Nennius says that the first major ruler in this area was Wuffa, the son of Wehha, who founded the East Anglian ruling family known as the Wuffingas, and that his grandson, Raedwald, ruled the kingdom just before the death of Aethelberht of Kent in AD 616. Raedwald, according to Bede, briefly exerted his authority over the Middle Angles and Mercians.

To the south of the East Anglians, another Saxon kingdom was developing: that of the East Saxons or Essex. The *Anglo-Saxon Chronicle*, however, is silent about the early kings of Essex, as is Bede. The only point of difference between them and their fellow settlers elsewhere is that, instead of claiming descent from the god Woden, they claimed descent from Seaxneat, a god still worshipped by the Continental Saxons in the eighth century. However, little is known of his function except that he was regarded as a major god. The *Merseburg Charm* lists 'Thunor, Woden and Seaxneat' as the three major gods. It is also interesting that the Essex kings invariably carried names beginning with the letter 'S'.

Another kingdom was also emerging in the Thames valley: the land of the Middle Saxons, Middlesex, which included Surrey. Of its origins nothing is really known and there are no traces of a separate series of kings. As early as AD 568, Ceawlin of Wessex and Aethelberht of Kent were disputing claims to the land of the Middle Saxons. The kingdom did not develop until after the middle of the sixth century, when London had finally fallen to the Saxons. The Saxons were making early settlements around London; this is supported by archaeological evidence with Saxon burial grounds at Croydon, Beddington and Mitcham and the emergence of many early Saxon place-names south of the Thames. But, during the late fifth century, the area was dominated by Celtic London, the city still, at this period, being firmly in British hands.

London, strategically, separated the East Anglians and East Saxons from their brethren in Kent, Sussex and Wessex. Therefore, it had been constantly under threat since the time of Hengist who had realized its strategic value. If London fell, the invaders could join from the Trent to the south coast and begin to push the British even further westward. London, in the fifth century, had come a long way from the original Celtic settlement called *londo* (the wild place). The Roman conquerors had built their major administrative and trading centre on the spot and the British Celts were continuing to use it as such. In the last decades before Roman withdrawal, the city's defences had been rebuilt with new walls along the banks of the Thames. The city was still a distributing centre for Continental trade.

It is likely, from what evidence we have, that London, though under British control, had within its walls, by the end of the fifth century, a sizeable community of Anglo-Saxons and also Frisians, the most adventurous of the early Germanic traders. Many Frisian coins (*sceattas*) have been found, although these do tend to date from after the Saxons captured the city. When did London fall to Saxon control? Certainly sometime in the sixth century, perhaps in the wake of the disastrous battle of Camlann in which Arthur was killed. What can be said for certain is that Aethelberht of Kent, ruling in the late sixth century, exerted his authority over the city and, having been converted to Christianity by Augustine in AD 597, had the first Saxon church built there.

To the north of the River Humber, more Germanic settlers were establishing themselves. By the end of the sixth century there had emerged two distinct Anglian settlements. At the mouth of the River Tweed, whose Celtic name means 'powerful river', tribes of Angles had made a settlement which they called Bernicia. Archaeological evidence shows that they were hard pressed to survive on the coast during the next fifty years, meeting strong opposition from the native

Celts. But gradually their settlements spread southwards and soon they had a strong centre at Bamburgh, originally a Celtic fortress called Dinas Guoroy. According to the *Anglo-Saxon Chronicle*, the Anglian king Ida built the settlement in AD 547, and Bede says it was named after a queen called Bebba. But Bebba seems to have been the wife of Aethelfrith who ruled much later in AD 593–617. Like their fellow Germanic settlers in Wessex, the Bernicians traced the ancestry of their royal house to Baeldaeg son of Woden. The first recorded king was another Aelle who died in AD 588.

The second northern settlement of Angles was on the coastline of modern Yorkshire and called Deira. Sir Frank Stenton claims that it was the British who called the invaders 'the Dere', or 'the water dwellers' because they formed their settlements along the rivers which converged on the Humber. The word is still found in the modern Brythonic Celtic languages – *dofr* (Welsh), *dovr* (Cornish), and *dour* (Breton). Dover is one 'English' place-name that retains the clear original Celtic form – the meeting of the waters. The evidence is that the settlements of Deira were constrained by the British and that it was not until the third decade of the seventh century that the Angles reached the valleys of the Aire or the Wharfe. The Deiran royal pedigree contains a line to Woden through names which are not mentioned in other genealogies.

At this stage we should examine who these invaders were – the Angles, Saxons and 'Jutes' who collectively are seen in Celtic perception as 'Saxons'. They were a branch of the Germanic peoples, speaking dialects of a common language. The modern Frisians, who still live in the marshy islands and coastal areas of Holland, speak a language which is the closest form to Old English and give us an indication of how the ancestors of the English spoke. Words for boat (*boat*), bread (*brod*), butter (*butter*), cow (*ko*), dream (*dream*), dung (*dong*), goose (*goes*), lamb (*lam*), and ox (*okse*) are easily comprehensible to the English speaker of today as well as to the Frisian. Indeed, most Frisian words are closer to English than to Dutch. With some thought we can also understand a little rhyme:

> Brod, butter en grene chiese
> En wat dat net sayse ken
> Is kin uprjuchte Friese.

Bread, butter and green cheese,
And who cannot say that
Is no upright Frisian.

Christianity was unknown to these Germanic newcomers and we will examine, in Chapter Ten, their pagan religious attitudes and practices. The Anglo-Saxon scholar, Dr Ray Page, points out that the first thing about their society that strikes us is the violence of its way of life. He has stated: 'The settlement of England was violent . . . Even after the settlement had established the pattern of Anglo-Saxon occupation, strife did not cease, for the small early Anglo-Saxon kingdoms were constantly clashing with one another and with the remaining Celtic peoples.' Whether fighting the Celts or fighting with each other, the Saxons were constantly at war. A state of perpetual disorder seemed to exist. Blood feuds were common and the mortality rate was high. The average person, surviving to adulthood, did not live much beyond his or her thirties and the average life of a king was no more than forty years. There were exceptions, especially after the conversion to Christianity and among the clerics.

We have some fascinating very early examples of ritual killings from the homeland of the Angles; these people were slain some centuries before the Angles arrived in Britain but their bodies were preserved in peat-water. One man was strangled and another had his throat cut. They are known as the 'Bog People' or Moorleichen. (P. V. Glob, *The Bog People*, London, 1969). These leathery corpses were ancestors of the Angles who landed on the eastern seaboard of England.

They were generally a pragmatic people concerned with practical affairs, with mercenary gain in the world of reality. Once they learnt the art of literacy from their Celtic neighbours, their poetry and sagas showed a depressing melancholy strain, regretting the passing of life and lamenting the decay of temporal power and goods and the loss of their kin by death. This was in total contrast to the exuberant Celtic philosophy which had no regrets for life nor fear of death: death was simply a passing of place, and life continued in the Otherworld, which, when the Celts accepted Christianity, was reinforced in the concept of a Christian 'Land of Eternal Youth'. The brooding Anglo-Saxon was unconvinced by the Christian claims of life after death and rather sought out the material comfort of life in this world. Thus Celt and Saxon contrasted strongly in their spiritual philosophies.

Saxon society was hierarchical with everyone knowing their place: the king, his *ealdormen*, his thanes, churls and slaves. The kings traced their descent back to their gods. Most kings claimed descent from Woden, god of battles, with only the East Anglians claiming descent from a little-known god named Seaxnat. Thus Saxon kingship had become mystical and formal, as opposed to the Celtic concept whereby rulers could claim descent from heroes but to claim divine descent was an alien idea. After the Saxons converted to Christianity, the Saxon Church introduced the ceremony of consecration – the first recorded consecration of a king was in AD 787 with Ecgfrith son of Offa. The 'divinity' was thus reinforced with the Saxon Church formally recognizing the king as 'Christ's deputy'. Herein was the basis of the 'divine right of kings' which eventually cost Charles I his life at the hands of his Parliament.

In pagan Saxon society, the kings were war leaders. Tacitus tells us (in *Germania*) that on the field of battle it was a disgrace for the king to be surpassed in valour by his companions and for the companions not to come up to the valour of their king. It was a sign of lifelong infamy and shame, if any left the field of battle alive after the king had fallen. The society was a strictly military one, holding little pity or concern for the fate of those it fought.

In such a society, women do not appear to have been allowed any prominent role. They are shown as passive, suffering hardship and discrimination but doing little about it. An Anglo-Saxon gnomic verse states that 'A woman's place is at her embroidery', which is reminiscent of the nineteenth-century English saying, 'A woman's place is in the home'. Women, at all levels of society, could be bought by men. They appear at the aristocratic level as decorative and their duties confined to being the congenial hostess. The Saxon queen appears mostly as a ceremonial object in a male-dominated world. The influence of the Celtic missionaries, converting the Saxons to Christianity, persuaded women to take an equal part in Church affairs and so we have the rise of women like the famous abbess Hild. One notable exception to the general secular trend was Aethelflaed (d. AD 918), the eldest daughter of Alfred, who became the ruler of Mercia for seven years after her husband's death and achieved a reputation as a strong leader. Another exception was Aethelburgh, wife of Ine of Wessex, who personally led an attack on the fortress of Taunton and then persuaded her husband to retire to Rome. But, generally, the lot of the average Saxon woman was not a happy one. Archaeologists have made several sinister finds of early Saxon graves in which female bodies have been unceremoniously thrown on top of a carefully placed male body. And at Sewerly, Yorkshire, we have a grave dated to the sixth or seventh century of a woman, of some position, carefully laid in a coffin with some earth scattered over it, and then another woman, her body contorted as if by a violent death, thrown carelessly on top. Did the pagan Anglo-Saxons sacrifice female slaves to accompany their master or mistress into the world of the dead? It would seem so.

The woman's place in Saxon society was in total contrast with the happier position of her Celtic sisters. But Celtic woman seems to have enjoyed a unique position. She could be elected as chief, lead her clan into battle in defence of the territory and, in law, she remained mistress of all she had brought into a marital partnership. She could divorce or hold any office a man could hold. She was carefully protected by law and if she died a violent death attributed to malice or the neglect of a man, various penalties were imposed. Offences against a woman's honour and person were severely punished. If the woman committed an offence against the law such as a premeditated murder, execution was strictly forbidden. By contrast, the Saxon punishments against wrongdoers were harsh, with summary execution in numerous cases but more frequently a long and varied list of maimings, from the putting out of eyes and removal of tongues to the chopping off of limbs.

The class system of Saxon society was based on property and wealth. A man's social position was defined by his *wergild*, his financial value in law; the fine payable if he were killed. The Saxon imperative was to gain property and wealth. The Irish-educated Northumbrian, Alcuin (AD 796–804), wrote sadly to Aethelred, king of Northumbria:

Some labour under an enormity of clothes, others perish with the cold. Some are inundated with delicacies and feast like Dives clothed in purple, and Lazarus dies of hunger at the gate. Where is brotherly love? Where the pity which we are admonished to have for the wretched? The satiety of the rich is the hunger of the poor . . . Be the ruler of the people, not the robber; the shepherd, not the plunderer.

At the bottom of the social pile were the slaves, who had few rights. Celts taken prisoner were usually equated with slaves. The chief way to gain freedom was by escaping, although a slave could buy his freedom if he could get the money, or he could gain freedom through the goodwill of his master. The Saxon Church generally accepted this inequality of society, though some, like Alcuin, spoke out, while the Celtic missionaries encouraged the freeing of slaves and the suppression of the export trade in them which the Saxons conducted.

There is a tradition that the churls (*ceorls*), the backbone of the Saxon society, consisting of the vast mass of society – the working class, if you like – were fiercely independent and, in the pastoral and agricultural society, worked their own land and defended their own homesteads. But as soon as the Saxon kingdoms were formed, because of the drive for land and wealth, their position was immediately encroached upon by the stronger *ealdormen* and thanes. These began to amass large estates by their military strength where the churls simply worked at their bidding, and the movement to the feudal pattern became inexorable.

Dr Page points out that between war, blood-feuds and constant training for warfare, which was such a marked aspect of Anglo-Saxon society, feasting was 'the pleasure of the rich and the solace for the poor'. The accounts by the Saxons of their own feasts describe great quarrel-ridden drinking contests which left many a man dead. Anglo-Saxon literature is full of descriptions of arguments and death caused under the influence of drink. How much saner the Celtic law and custom which forbade anyone going into a feasting hall to take their weapons with them. The harp, interestingly, appears as the most frequently mentioned instrument among the Saxons. They appeared to like music, and enjoyed horse-racing, swimming, running, archery and contests of martial arts.

These, then, were the people who were having such a devastating effect on the life of the native British.

The threat to the southern British Celts did not, however, all emanate from the invasions of the Anglo-Saxons. During the time that the Anglo-Saxons were establishing themselves on the eastern and southern seaboards of Britain, there were threats on the western seaboard and from the north of the country which we also have to take into account.

I have already mentioned the panegyric addressed to the emperor Constantius Chlorus in AD 296 which gives the first mention of marauding Irish bands which the Latin writers call the Hibernii and, more popularly, the Scotii. The Irish seemed to make common cause with the northern British, the Picts, as early as AD 360. Ammianus Marcellinus writes of even later expeditions by the Irish to northern Britain. Julius Honorius, at this time, notes that the Irish had taken possession of the Isle of Man. Indeed, it has been shown that the language on the island was originally Brythonic Celtic and that this was displaced through its rapid assimilation into Goidelic Celtic at the time Honorius speaks of.

The Irish were not slow to seize the opportunity provided by the withdrawal of Rome and the advent of the Saxon invasions. Gildas talks of 'devastations' by their raiding parties and we find in the lives of many fifth- and sixth-century saints that British hostages were numerous in Ireland. Among them, of course, was the famous Patrick, to become Ireland's patron saint.

But the Irish invasions were not confined to raids in search of wealth and hostages. Gildas noted that many bands of Irish came as settlers. We have the example of an ancient Irish story, *Inndarba inna nDési*, 'The Expulsion of the Dési' which, Professor Kuno Meyer claims, dates back stylistically to the third century AD. The name of their ancient clan lands still survives in Co. Meath. They were expelled from their homeland by the High King, Cormac Mac Art (*c*.AD 254–277) and, under the leadership of Eochaid Mac Artchorp, sailed to modern Dyfed in Wales. Here they settled and their king became known as Eochaid Allmuir (Eochaid beyond the Sea).

The Irish kingdom of Demetia (Dyfed) prospered and was accepted by the British Celts. Eventually it became absorbed into a British Celtic cultural ethos. Teudor Mac Regin reigned there in the eighth century as a direct descendant of Eochaid, and an eleventh-century Welsh pedigree showed that Elen, wife to Hywel Dda ap Cadell (d. 950), traced her descent from the Dési rulers. What is astonishing is the corroboration between the Welsh and Irish sources of the genealogy. The settlement of the Dési, according to Cecile O'Rahilly, 'must be regarded as a well-established historical fact'.

As Rome was in control at this period it is arguable that the settlement was made with the consent of the Roman authorities and under condition of some military service. It has been argued that the Atecotti, who are placed as allies of the Scotii and Picti, were in fact Irish and were, moreover, Irish soldiers recruited in Britain for service in the Roman legions.

The concurrent traditions of Welsh and Irish sources indicate that the Dyfed settlement was not the only one and that a series of settlements, some of a temporary character, were taking place in the west of Britain at this time. Settlements were formed on the Lleyn peninsula and on Anglesey (Mona). Here, we have evidence that Cunedda, mentioned by Nennius, came to north Wales from Manaw of the Gododdin, whose capital was in Edinburgh, and established his kingdom, driving the Irish out. Cunedda became the founding figure of the first dynasty of the kingdom of Gwynedd. Cunedda is believed to be contemporary with Magnus Maximus (d.c.AD 388).

Another Irish kingdom being established in Britain at the time was to take on a more permanent aspect. This was on the peninsula of Kintyre, 'the head of the land' on the 'seaboard of the Gaels' – Airer Ghàidheal, modern Argyll. It was called Dál Riada. According to Irish sources, Cairbre Riada founded a kingdom in Ulster, in Co. Antrim, having been driven there by a famine in his native Munster. This kingdom, too, was called Dál Riada – 'of Riada's part'. Nine generations later, his descendant, called Fergus mac Erc, began another migration across the strait separating Ireland and northern Britain, and formed the second kingdom of Dál Riada. The kingdom of Dál Riada and the Pictish kingdoms of the Cruithne-tuatha were eventually to form the kingdom of Alba with its capital at Sgàin (Scone).

We will return to the fortunes and influence of the Irish settlements in Britain later.

The situation of the southern British Celts at the end of the fifth century AD is clear. They were surrounded by invaders on all sides. Along the eastern side of the island, fierce, rapacious Germanic tribes were settling and driving them westward. From the north the Picts, who were their brothers, speaking the same Brythonic form of Celtic, were in league with the Irish (Scotii) and raiding them, while, to the west, the Irish were raiding and, where they could, forming settlements. But it was in the east that they faced their greatest peril for the Germanic settlers were conducting a war of systematic extermination.

It is at this point, in the closing years of the fifth century, that the besieged southern British Celts needed a saviour: a military commander who would halt the inexorable onslaught of the Saxons and unite the Celts in an attempt to turn back the conquest and settlement of Britain. The shadowy figure of Emrys, Aurelius Ambrosius, after his initial successes, seems to have disappeared. It is in this age that the even more shadowy figure of the legendary Arthur emerges.

[4]

Arthur: Fact or Fiction?

A wild boar's fury was Bleiddig ab Eli ...
But he was not Arthur, and he fed
Black ravens on Catraeth's walls.

Aneirin, Y Gododdin
(c. sixth century)

O F the historical Arthur we know hardly anything. The first reference to him occurs in a poem by Aneirin, written in the late sixth century, entitled *Y Gododdin*. It tells of how 300 picked warriors of the Gododdin, whose capital was at Dineiddyn (Edinburgh) and who were known to the Romans as the Votadini, were led by their chieftain, Mynyddawn Mwynfawr, in an attempt to recapture Catraeth (Catterick) from the Angles. Names of several of the warriors are mentioned including Bleiddig ab Eli whose fury is compared to that of a wild boar, but, we are told, he was not Arthur and so he fed the black ravens on the walls of the enemy's fort. All the Gododdin but one, three in another account, went to their slaughter.

The worth of this throwaway remark ('but he was not Arthur') is that Arthur had a reputation as a warrior and general by the late sixth century. Gildas does not mention Arthur by name but indicates that a British Celtic victory over the Saxons, at Mount Badon, occurred in the year in which he was born. Further, he states that this victory stemmed the Saxon advance for a generation. It is Nennius, the Celtic chronicler writing in the early ninth century, who not only records this battle but names Arthur as the victorious commander. Nennius gives a total of twelve victories by Arthur, of which Badon is the last and most outstanding. More significantly, he refers to Arthur as a 'leader of battles', a 'warlord' (*dux bellorum*) rather than a king. 'Arthur fought against the Saxons alongside the

59

kings of the Britons but he himself was the leader in the battles.'
Nothing could be more clear as to Arthur's exact role as a general
and not a king.

It is the *Annales Cambriae*, compiled *c.*AD 955 and thought to be
based on earlier chronicles, which record the date of Badon as being
AD 516/518. The same source places the death of Arthur at a battle
called Camluan, or Camlann, in about AD 537/539 and records that
Medraut, the Mordred of later legend, was slain in this same battle.

Who was Arthur?

That he was a British Celtic chieftain who achieved a widespread
military reputation among his fellow British Celts for halting, if only
for a few years, the Saxon conquest, is unquestionable. He became
the major British Celtic hero of the age and as with all heroes, following his death in battle, the Celtic bards and poets began to embellish
his story with old mythological themes which bear a more than
passing resemblance to the earlier tales of the Irish warrior Fionn
Mac Cumhail, as we shall see. By the time Geoffrey of Monmouth
(*c.* 1100–1155) produced his *Historia Regnum Britanniae* (History
of the Kings of Britain) on which all later Arthurian saga is based,
the character of Arthur had developed out of all proportion to the
historical character. Arthur was finally given permanent form in
popular legend in Malory's *Morte d'Arthur*. From a Celtic chieftain
fighting against the Saxons he had been turned, ironically, into an
English king cloaked in romantic medieval chivalry.

What can be rescued of the real Arthur? The answer is precious
little in spite of the countless Arthurian studies which, since the
nineteenth century, have become a veritable industry. Everyone has
their own pet theories and interpretations.

The name Arthur has been claimed as a Roman one, Artorius, and
some have eagerly pointed out that there was a Roman officer named
Artorius Justus, who served in Britain in the third century, and
Arthur could have been his descendant. But what is overlooked is
that Art, Artur, etc. are also Celtic names. And Arthur would not be
an unusual Celtic name of this time. Artur, son of Nemed, in Irish
mythology, leads his people in battle against the Fomorii at Cramh
Ros. Art Aenfer (Art the Solitary, son of Conn Cedcathach) became
High King of Ireland, in AD 220–250, according to the genealogies.
J. D. Bruce believes the name has its origins in the Celtic deity Artos
Viros (bear man), corresponding to the Welsh Arth Gwyr. In Gaul

Artio, protector of bears, was often invoked, usually in female form as a fertility goddess. A bronze group from Muri near Berne shows Artio offering fruit to a large bear. In other words, there are no grounds for supposing that Arthur bore a name other than one showing his Celtic identity.

Geoffrey, who gives the date of Arthur's death as AD 542, some ten years after the date given by the *Annales Cambriae*, also gives him a family tree which makes his father Uther a brother of Ambrosius and both sons of the claimant to the throne of the Western Empire, Constantine. This must be treated as legend but the tradition which Geoffrey records could merely serve to underscore the wish to make Arthur a prominent figure in society and not simply 'an unknown'.

We may conjecture that a Celtic warrior, Arthur, had made himself acceptable as a military leader to the desperate British Celtic chieftains sometime in the late AD 490s or early 500s. Most Arthurian scholars claim Arthur for Cornwall because of the preponderance of place-names associated with Arthur in that area. Place-name evidence is tenuous. Could it be argued, a thousand years from now, that Nelson Mandela must have had close links with Glasgow, in Scotland, because streets have been named after him in the city? Because Arthur's early victories are clearly placed in Lincolnshire, with the British fighting the encroaching East Anglians, would it not be more probable to suggest that he was a war leader of Elmet, the British kingdom to the west of the Trent, and that his victories caused the other British kings to give him supreme command of their armies in the struggle? This is only a suggestion, for with the story of Arthur we can do little more than speculate.

What we know is that Arthur won his first major engagement, as commander of the British, at the mouth of the 'River Glein'. Now there are two River Glens; one is in Northumbria while the other is in Lincolnshire. The name is a British Celtic one meaning 'clean, holy and beautiful'. It would make sense if Arthur's battle was at the mouth of the Glen in Lincolnshire because the subsequent battles in the sequence are clearly identified as being in Lincolnshire.

The Angles were moving westward towards the Trent. They were building a strong settlement at Peterborough, so what better move for the British to make than to threaten them in this area where the River Glen runs? Here, Arthur gave the Angles the first major check.

Nennius says, 'The next four [battles] were on the banks of another river called Dubglas which is in the region of Linnius.' Professor Jackson has pointed out that Linnius is the Lindsey district which is bordered on the north by the Humber. Lindsey comes from the Celtic name for an island and, indeed, the district was practically an island before the fens on the Witham were drained. The Witham must then be our River Dubglas, for its Celtic name is not certain before the Angles named it after 'Witta's ham'. In spite of Ekwall's contention that Ptolemy was referring to the Witham when he mentioned a river called the Eidoumanios, which Ekwall thinks could be altered into Widumanios and that made to be identical with the Welsh *gwydd*, thus 'river in the forest', there are too many 'ifs' to find the etymology. Apart from these 'ifs', it is unclear that Ptolemy was even referring to the Witham. It seems a much better bet that the Celtic name for Witham was the 'black-blue coloured river' – Dubglas. No other river in the Lindsey area provides a suitable alternative.

If we accept this, we can also identify the sites of another four battles which Arthur fought against the Angles, in the same area as his first conflict at the mouth of the River Glen.

Nennius gives a sixth battle as being fought on the banks of the River Bassas whose location has not been identified. An Anglo-Saxon named Basa certainly gave his name to some sites, including Basa's ford across a river in Nottingham, not far from the locations of the other battles. Could this sixth victory of Arthur be sited near here?

Having checked the incursions of the Angles, the warlord then marched his army northwards to face another enemy, the marauding Picts and Irish (Scotii). We are told his seventh victory was in the wood of Celidon, that is Cat Coit Celidon, which the Latin reference calls Silva Calledoniae, the wood of Scotland. The wood of Celidon emerges in Welsh Arthurian literature.

The next victory was secured at a fortress called Guinnion which has a tantalizing Celtic sound to it but, sadly, is unidentifiable, although it could well be in southern Scotland. Nennius tells us that in this battle Arthur carried an image of the Virgin Mary on his shoulder 'and there was a great slaughter of them [the enemy] through the strength of Our Lord Jesus Christ and of the Holy Mary his maiden mother'. Even this could be evidence that Arthur, a southern Christianized Briton, was fighting the Picts, for the evidence is that at this time the Picts were generally non-Christians, although there had been some proselytizing among them. The Christian symbolism could underscore the difference in religious culture.

The next battle site is clearly identifiable. Nennius says, 'The ninth [battle] was in the City of the Legion.' Now Castra Legionum is Chester. This fact has thrown Arthurian scholars into a quandary for Chester is in the west of Britain, away from the advances of the Saxons. Geoffrey Ashe, in explaining the site of the battles, confesses, 'The City of the Legion is frankly awkward.' Not so. Arthur came south from his campaign against the Picts and Scotii (Irish) because the Irish had landed in the Mersey and attacked Chester. One should notice that the statement says the fighting was *in* the city not outside it. Arthur had to drive the Irish marauders out of the city.

Then he was drawn back northwards to Caledonia again where his tenth victory was gained at a river called Tribuit. This is placed in southern Scotland and is a battle described in a Welsh poem which mentions a Celtic warrior named Bedwyr (the original for Bedevere) as fighting for Arthur.

Having checked the Picts and Scotii, Arthur returned south because the Angles had begun to move forward again. He won another victory over them on a hill called Agned. Professor Jackson has suggested that Rochester is the site. This was his eleventh victory and, if we accept Professor Jackson's argument, it was won over the Angles of Deira.

Nennius records: 'The twelfth was on Mount Badon, in which – on that one day – there fell in one onslaught of Arthur's, nine hundred and sixty men; and none slew them but he alone, and in all his battles he remained the victor.'

Badon is a major battle between Celt and Saxon, whose first recorded mention is by Gildas, born in the year it was fought. But where is its site? A favourite candidate is the oval hill-fort called Liddington Castle, which dates to the sixth century. This is near Swindon and has a village at the foot of the hill named Badbury – Baddan-byrig. But other sites have been suggested. Geoffrey regarded it as identical with Bath. Others have suggested Bradbury Rings in Dorset. One Arthurian enthusiast even suggests Greenan, in Ayr. But it is fairly clear that it was a battle in which the defeat of the West Saxons was encompassed. One of the most likely sites, one which fits in with what Gildas says, has been put forward by John Morris. This is Solsbury Hill, near Batheaston, in Somerset.

Only one Anglo-Saxon king is directly stated to have fought at Badon and that was Aesc of Kent. Here we can make a conjecture. Aelle, of the South Saxons, disappears before or about this time, and he was regarded by the chroniclers as being Bretwalda, or overlord of the Saxons. The South Saxon kingdom being so small, and with little military power compared to the other Saxon kingdoms, it is an obvious speculation that his leadership would not have been enforced by conquest. More likely Aelle was simply recognized by his fellow Saxon rulers as being a good strategist. We can make another specu- lation here: did Aelle, overlord of the Saxon kingdoms, fall at Badon? And did Aesc fall with him? Such a catastrophe would certainly have halted Saxon designs for a while.

In the *Annales Cambriae*, which record the battle, it is stated under AD 516/518: 'The battle of Badon in which Arthur carried the cross of Our Lord Jesus Christ, for three days and three nights, on his shoulders and the Britons were victorious.' This, of course, means, that Arthur was using the cross as a symbol on his banners. Badon is referred to as a siege by Gildas, Nennius and Geoffrey. Who was besieged, and by whom, are not explained. John Morris argues that the Celts liked mobility and moved with cavalry, while the Saxons were mainly infantry. He suggests that the Celts, led by Arthur, were besieged on Solsbury Hill, by Saxon infantry, and fought for three days and nights until they were able to sweep down on the Saxon lines, destroying them. The victory was absolute and, arising from it, tales of the hero Arthur started to become popular through the Celtic world.

The *Anglo-Saxon Chronicle*, which generally omits mention of Saxon defeats, is also sadly silent about Badon.

For the next twenty-one years, the Saxons were checked. Skir- mishes followed but there were no major attempts to expand the territories they had already secured on the eastern seaboard of Britain. I would argue that many of their most powerful chieftains had been slaughtered at Badon and so they had to rebuild their structures and societies. The fascinating question, at this point, is why the British Celts did not appear to follow up their major victory and move against the Saxon settlements. Once more we are in the realm of speculation.

While the Germanic tribes in Britain had suffered defeat, elsewhere in Europe their star was in the ascendant. Rome itself had been swept by the Germanic tribes. In AD 486 Clovis, king of the Franks, had killed the Roman Syagius and taken his kingdom, overrunning the Alammanu of south-west Germany, occupying Bohemia, acquiring the Visigoth kingdom in Aquitaine and forcing the Burgundian kingdom to acknowledge his suzerainty. The Germanic Franks totally dominated central Europe. The Ostrogoths now controlled the Italian peninsula, setting Theodoric on the throne in AD 489.

Everywhere, the Germanic tribes were powerful.

The only place they had been given a check was in Britain, where their attempts to absorb the entire island had been defeated by Arthur and his British Celtic army at Badon. The kingdoms of the Angles and Saxons began to consolidate and rebuild themselves as individual statelets, each suspicious and envious of the others.

And for the Celts, a new Britain was emerging. While the Celts still recognized themselves as British, they were beginning to divide into smaller kingdoms with no central authority or High King of southern Britain. While Arthur had been general of an apparent confederation of British kingdoms, there had been no overall king during this time and would not be again. And twenty-one years after Arthur's victory at Badon, he was no more.

The *Annales Cambriae* record under AD 537/539: 'The battle of Camluan in which Arthur and Medraut were slain: and there was death in Britain and Ireland.' The date of this battle has caused some debate. Geoffrey claims it was in AD 542 while the *Annals of Tigernach* place it in AD 541; the *Anales Toledanos* (Toledo, as a centre of British Celtic clergy, had a direct link to British traditions, as we shall discuss in Chapter Seven) record it in AD 580. This late date is unacceptable and the *Annales Cambriae* would appear to give the most accurate date. There have also been several suggested sites, including Camboglanna (a fort on Hadrian's Wall at Birdoswald, Cumberland), the River Cam in Somerset and the Camel in Cornwall. But Cam, meaning 'crooked', is a very popular Celtic place-name and there is little hope of pinning down the place.

Camluan is not claimed as a victory by the *Anglo-Saxon Chronicle*. If the Saxons had had a hand in the death of the Celtic leader who had encompassed their earlier defeat it would be inconceivable that the *Chronicle* would not boast of it. Therefore, it would seem that it was not a Saxon victory but an internal squabble or a fight against the Picts or Scotii. We certainly have a history of internal conflict, and there is the fascinating tradition of Medraut (Mordred), the arch-traitor in Arthurian legend, who kills Arthur and is himself slain, and who is actually mentioned in the *Annales Cambriae*. Or it could have been a battle fought against the Picts and Scots, which makes Camboglanna seem a likely site for it.

Tradition has it that there were seven survivors of this battle. A number of survivors are mentioned in the story of Culhwch in the *Mabinogi*. Among those who were claimed to have been there and survived was the abbot Petroc who became one of the most important British saints in the sixth century. His dedications and place-names predominate in Devon and Cornwall as well as in south Wales. *Lives* and traditions would indicate that he came from south Wales to the Camel estuary and established his monastic centre in Padstow (Petroc's Stow) before withdrawing to a hermitage on Bodmin moor. Another *religieux* named Derfel was also said to have survived the battle. But of who fought, apart from Arthur and Medraut, and why they fought, there is no record.

Before we leave the shadowy Arthur, who was nevertheless one of the greatest opponents of Saxon settlement and expansion, perhaps we should give some consideration as to how he ceased to be a Celtic war chieftain and achieved a world-wide place as a romantic hero. Arthur's death must have been an enormous blow to the Celts and, as was their cultural tradition, they soon fell to telling tales about him. The Celtic story-tellers began to embellish their tales of Arthur with elements from traditional Celtic myths and legends. They began to use older themes associated with the Irish hero, Fionn Mac Cumhail. He was given a special circle of élite warriors, similar to Fionn's Fianna, and these grew into the 'Knights of the Round Table'. He was also given a magic sword, for every Celtic hero had one, and this was named after the sword of Fergus Mac Roth – Caladcholg (hard dinter), which, by means of a Latin corruption of the name, became Excalibur. Another essential Celtic ingredient was added: the magic cauldron of plenty, which developed into the search for the Christian Holy Grail.

Around the British Celtic firesides, during the decades following Arthur's death, the war leader who had decisively defeated the

Saxons, the Picts and the Scotii began to grow into a mythological hero, a symbol of British Celtic resistance.

Arthur was too excellent a hero, and the stories were too fascinating, to be ignored by other cultures. The tales were soon being written. As we have seen, the first surviving reference to Arthur comes in a late sixth-century poem by Aneirin. But the earliest known fully fledged Arthurian tale is that of 'Culhwch and Olwen', which only survives from eleventh-century texts. This, with three later Arthurian tales, appears in the *Mabinogi*. Arthur also makes a cameo appearance in a tenth-century poem tale, 'The Spoils of Annwn'. From British Celtic, or Welsh as we must call it now, the tales transferred easily to Ireland. There are at least twenty-five identifiable Arthurian tales in Irish surviving from the medieval period. However, popular though these tales must undoubtedly have been, they did not overtake in popularity the tales of Fionn Mac Cumhail in Ireland during the period.

Arthur began to make the leap into world literature through Geoffrey of Monmouth (c. 1100–1155) and his Latin *Historia Regnum Britanniae* (History of the Kings of Britain), in which the character of Arthur was developed into its popularly accepted form. Geoffrey, of Breton origins, whose family had followed the Normans to settle in Wales, claimed he was doing no more than translating 'a very ancient book in the British language'. His superior, Walter, the archdeacon at Oxford, had given it to him. But from the nineteenth century, scholars have accused Geoffrey of fabricating the book because they were unable to find a Welsh model for it. Yet a manuscript does survive in the Vatican Library, dated 8 October 1474, which is a Latin translation of a work called 'The Prophecy of Merlin', written by John of Cornwall in the tenth century. This early date is confirmed by glosses in the original Cornish.

From Geoffrey of Monmouth's work in Latin, whether it is a translation of an original Celtic book or simply a recording of Celtic traditions, Arthur began to head off into European literature. The Norman poet Wace wrote his *Roman de Brut* based on Geoffrey's work, in which Arthur is depicted as a medieval knight and the 'Round Table' makes its first appearance. Chrétien de Troyes (fl. 1160–1190) of France added the idea of courtly love and adapted the earliest version of the 'Holy Grail' legend. Then Layamon (fl. 1198–1207) added more Celtic folk traditions. In the thirteenth century, Gottfried von Strassburg and Wolfram von Eschenbach, in Germany, both embellished the saga.

In England, two more innovations were made with *The Alliterative Morte d'Arthur* (c. 1360) and *Sir Gawain and the Green Knight* (c. 1370). The latter is regarded as the greatest single Arthurian work in Middle English, introducing two major motifs – the 'Beheading Game' and the 'Temptation to Adultery'. However, neither is original and both are borrowed from Celtic sources appearing in the 'Red Branch Cycle' of Irish mythology.

In the fifteenth century, Sir Thomas Malory's *Le Morte d'Arthur* gave the ultimate shape to the saga that William Caxton chose for printing in 1485. From then on there is hardly a European culture which has not celebrated the Arthurian legends in some form or another.

It seems ironic that the deeds of a remote Celtic war chieftain, fighting to hold back the invaders of his country in the early sixth century, particularly the Saxons, should have inspired so many stories in the literatures of the world for ten centuries. The greatest irony is that Arthur's very enemies, the descendants of the people he was fighting, now claim him as their own. Arthur is acclaimed as a king of England! But then, irony – by which I mean the condition whereby one is mocked by fate – seems a constant companion in Celtic history.

However, the reality for Britain was that by the mid-sixth century Arthur was dead and the Saxons were once again encroaching on Celtic territory.

[5]

The British Celtic Kingdoms

The Saxon is conquered, the seas tranquil – Britain is safe.

Claudius Claudianus, In Eutropium (c. AD 400)

B Y the mid-sixth century, in the years following the death of Arthur, the Celts of Britain were once more facing an aggressive, land-hungry people. But now the British were reorganized into eleven separate kingdoms, the most northerly of which, the kingdom of the Picts, had yet to feel the Saxon threat. Of the south-western kingdoms we obtain a glimpse of their rulers through the rather harsh eyes of the cleric Gildas, who had little good to say about the contemporary rulers of the British kingdoms. Gildas chose to launch a savage attack on the Celtic rulers of his time, whom he blamed for some of the suffering of the people. The implication is that they were too busy feathering their own nests to organize proper defensive policies against the Saxons. Gildas is speaking about those rulers in power about twenty-five years after the death of Arthur.

Gildas names five rulers. The first he attacks is Constantine, king of Dumnonia, a kingdom which had emerged covering originally part of Hampshire, Dorset, Somerset and Devon, in which the name still survives. It is my contention that Dumnonia did not incorporate Cornwall as is popularly thought. Cornwall, it is generally accepted, did not emerge as a separate kingdom until after the fall of Dumnonia in the eighth century. I believe the evidence shows that Cornwall was already a separate kingdom in the time of Gildas. It is also arguable that Cornwall was ruled by its native chieftains even during the Roman occupation, in the manner of the autonomous Indian principalities during the 'British Raj'. We will return to the issue of Cornwall later. Dumnonia's eastern borders fluctuated before the West Saxon advance; at the time Gildas wrote, the boundary was around the

69

Hampshire-Dorset border. In the name 'Dorset' we can still see the Celtic tribal name of the Durotriges ('kings of strength') who occupied the area, a rich trading people whose lands stretched into Wiltshire and Somerset. We have evidence that some of the old pre-Roman Celtic hill-forts in Dorset had been refortified at this period: South Cadbury, for example, was still occupied by the Celts at the start of the seventh century.

Gildas dismissed Constantine of Dumnonia as a 'whelp' of the lioness of Dumnonia and accuses him of immorality, perjury and sacrilege. Further, says Gildas, this ruler, disguised as an abbot, entered a church and slew two 'royal princes', undoubtedly rivals for power.

The next king he attacks is Aurelius Caninus, which latter name is probably the Latin guise for the Celtic name Conan. To support this Gildas makes a pun on his name, calling him a 'puppy' (Conan means 'hound-like'). This king is described as a man grown old in iniquity, the last survivor of a noble race, who had started a civil war and who was a murderer and immoral. Gildas does not name his kingdom but since he places the king in a list between Dumnonia and Dyfed it is likely that this Conan ruled in the lower Severn in Gwent, the old Silurian territory. And could the 'civil war' he started have something to do with the conflict which brought Arthur and Mordred to their deaths at Camluan?

The third king was Vortepor whom he calls 'tyrant of the Demetians'. Demetia was the Latinization of Dyfed and this Vortepor (Gwrthefr) does appear in the genealogies of the kings of Dyfed as son of Aircol, a descendant of Eochaidh Allmuir, who had led the Irish Dési to settle in the area. A memorial stone from the period, which originally stood in the churchyard at Castell Dwyran, Dyfed, until 1895, bore the inscription 'Memoria Vorteporigis Protictoris'. Gildas accuses 'Vortepor the Protector' of incest and murder.

The ruler of Powys, to the north, covering central Wales and Shropshire, was the fourth king. This was the former territory of the Cornovii and was now ruled by Cuneglas (Cynlas). The name means 'tawny hound' and Gildas puns his name as 'tawny butcher'. A Cynlas, son of Owain, son of Einion, son of the legendary Cunedda, appears in the genealogies of the kings of Gwynedd, which would make Cuneglas the cousin of the fifth king attacked by Gildas. Gildas condemns Cuneglas for immorality and the violence of his life. Gildas places Cuneglas's fortress, 'the bear's fortress', Dineirth, east of Conway in Rhos.

The fifth king is undoubtedly the most powerful in southern Britain at the time – Maglocunus or Maelgwyn, a great-grandson of Cunedda who is recorded as dying of a plague in AD 547/549. Gildas was writing about a decade later. Indeed, there is confirmation from other sources of a great plague sweeping Britain at this time. Maelgwyn was ruler of the kingdom of Gwynedd, north of Powys. Gildas condemns him for having murdered his uncle to become ruler when he was a youth and then murdering his first wife and his nephew. Maelgwyn had gone into a monastery to repent but then returned to seize power 'like a dog to his vomit'. Gildas sneers at him for employing bards to compose panegyrics to praise his ego. He places his capital at Degannwy on the shore of the Conway.

Gildas does not speak of the other British kingdoms to the north. This is not because he knew nothing about them although, at about this time, he was either living at St Illtyd's monastery at Llanilltyd Fawr (Llantwit Major in Glamorgan), or had migrated to Brittany. The tradition is that Gildas was born in the kingdom of Strathclyde at Alcluyd. Alcluyd was later named by the Scotii Dùn Breatann, fortress of the Britons – today Dumbarton. Arthur Wade Evans contends, based on a *Life*, that he was the son of Caw, a Pict, who became a Christian during a raid on Alcluyd. If this is so, then Gildas would have had extensive knowledge of these other British kingdoms, but he was being selective about those rulers he was criticizing: it was not meant as a blanket criticism of all the British Celtic rulers as has been implied by some. Whether Gildas was justified in his fierce denunciations we can only speculate. There is no other evidence and no reason to doubt his word. What is amusing is the attitude of pro-Saxon historians who will accept Gildas most readily while he speaks about the laxity of morals of the Celtic rulers but reject him out of hand when he talks of the massacres and migrations caused by the Saxons.

We can fill in the gaps left by Gildas as to the British kingdoms. However, before we come to the northern kingdoms, let us return to the issue of Cornwall. Was Cornwall a separate kingdom from Dumnonia? Kernow, which the Saxons later called Kern-wealhas, the land of the foreign Kerns – Cornwall – is often confused in medieval texts with Kernev (Cornouaille in Brittany). The evidence is that Cornwall was the tribal area of the Cornovii, according to the *Ravenna Cosmography*, who are not to be confused with the Shropshire or Scottish Cornovii. Celtic tribes often shared a name while being geographically separated; for example, the Tectosages of southern Gaul and the Tectosages of Galatia. The Cornovii were scarcely touched by Roman military influence during the occupation, though there is evidence of a good trade with the rest of Roman Britain. During the fifth and sixth centuries Christian missionaries, not only from other British Celtic areas but also from Ireland, visited and Christianized the area. There is some evidence that the Irish settled a small community in north Cornwall. Six Ogham inscriptions, the earliest form of written Irish, are to be found in Cornwall, five in the Camel estuary, perhaps indicating the Irish point of entry.

There is a host of traditions involving these sixth-century early Celtic missionaries or 'saints', and several *Lives* which mention local kings, like the pagan Tewdrig, or Tudor, of Hayle who persecuted the missionaries with torture and death. But Cornwall, generally, quickly accepted Christianity and Chi Ro monograms are found dating from the early and middle fifth century. In St Just-in-Penwith, a memorial to one Selus dates from the first half of the fifth century, while another early fifth-century monument, found at Carnsew, commemorates Cunaide, aged thirty-three. There are several such memorials.

But no memorial of this period, religious or secular, is more poignant than the stone standing near Fowey by Castle Dore, the ancient pre-Roman hill-fort still in use until the seventh century AD. Castle Dore features in the legends of Tristan and Iseult and King Mark of Cornwall as the 'palace' of Mark. The stone reads, '*Drustanus hic iacit Cunomori*', 'Here lies Drustanus, son of Cunomorus'. It is dated to the mid-sixth century. Drustanus is philologically identified as Tristan. King Mark in ancient sources is called Marcus Quonomorus or Mark Cunomoros. Wrmonoc of Landévennec, writing his *Life of Pol de Léon* in AD 884, speaks of 'Marc whose other name is Quonomorus'. The names are purely Celtic. Mark comes from *marc'h* (horse) and Cunomoros means 'hound of the sea'. In one early version of the legend we are told by Beroul that Mark has 'ears like a horse'. So we can identify historically two of the great mythological figures of the time and we find that Tristan is the son of Mark, not his nephew. The legend of Iseult becomes that much

more poignant when we realize that Tristan elopes with his step-
mother.

We find that Cunomoros also ruled in Kernev (Cornouaille, Brittany) from Carhaix. Cunomoros is supposed to have supported
Chramm, a rebel son of the Frankish ruler, Clothair. About AD 560,
both Cunomoros and Clothair were killed in that war, according to
the interpretation of Dr Morris, while Dillon and Chadwick think it
more likely that Cunomoros was killed when his own people rebelled
against him. The traditions about him show him in a bad light.
Wrmonoc of Landévennec says that Cunomoros had been warned
by a prophet that one of his own sons would kill him and so he
murdered his wives when they became pregnant. His fifth wife,
Trephina, daughter of Wroc'h of the Venetii, managed to give birth
to a son, Tremeur. Gildas himself is reported as giving protection to
her and her son. The boy was brought up by the monks at Gildas's
foundation at Rhuys. Eventually Cunomoros found the boy and
killed him and the monks later dedicated a church to his memory
at Carhaix. St Trémeur's church still stands, though dating from the
sixteenth century now. Legend has it that Gildas carried the boy's
head to Cunomoros's fortress where, at the sight, the battlements
fell and killed him, which provides a good symbolic Celtic ending.
Certainly, as well as in Cornwall and in the tragic tale of Tristan
and Iseult, Mark Cunomoros lives on in Breton tradition: Penmarc'h,
Mark's Head, a brooding headland of southern Cornouaille, is
named after him and from it, so locals tell you, on a dark and stormy
day, you may see Cunomoros riding out to sea on his winged horse
(*mormarc'h*).

In Cornwall, we find another sixth-century memorial at the Men
Scryfa (written stone) in West Penwith, this time to Rialobran son
of Cunoval – 'royal raven' son of 'the hound of Bel'. Traditions of
separate kings, such as Padernus, also emerge at this time. In other
words, Cornwall was not simply the western part of Dumnonia. It
was already an independent and influential kingdom in the sixth
century, buffered by Dumnonia. It would not face a serious Saxon
threat for another two centuries.

Immediately to the north, covering central Britain, was the kingdom
of Elmet, stretching from what is now the Shropshire border eastward to the mouth of the Humber. As previously explained, the
etymology of the Celtic name is uncertain although it is preserved in

local names found at Sherburn and Barwick. Dr Ekwall maintains it is identical with Elfed, which occurs in Wales. The name could derive from the same root as *elfydd*, a region or country. We have no records of Elmet except that Nennius refers to Gwallawg of Elmet as one of the British chieftains engaged in attacking the Angles of Bernicia and besieging them on Lindisfarne. The sixth-century poet, Taliesin, celebrates Gwallawg's martial qualities. Elmet remained independent until the seventh century. Its last Celtic ruler was Ceredig (Caradoc) who was driven from the kingdom by Edwin of Northumbria in AD 625. The territory was conquered, incorporated into Northumbria, and its Celtic population annihilated or driven westward.

To the north-west of Elmet, covering Lancashire and Cumberland and straddling Solway Firth into Galloway, was the kingdom of Rheged, whose chief city was at Caerliwelyd (Carlisle). The earlier name was Lugovalus (wall of the god Lugos), which then had the Celtic word for fortress, *caer*, placed before it. In the late sixth century it was ruled by Urien who, according to Nennius, was a powerful leader. So powerful does he appear that some Arthurians have tried to identify him as Arthur. Urien was the subject of poems attributed to Taliesin. One of them celebrates the 'Battle of Argoed Llwyfain' in which Urien and his son Owain are the leaders of a victory over the Angles. 'King of the Golden North, I will praise your deeds,' Taliesin sings. Another of Taliesin's poems laments the death of Urien's son Owain, 'a vivid man above his many-coloured trappings'. Nennius says that Urien led a coalition of British kings against the Angles, which included Gwallawg of Elmet and Rhydderch Hen of the neighbouring northern kingdom of Strathclyde. The Angles were led by Theodoric of Bernicia (*c*.AD 572/3–579/80) and were raiding westward. Urien's army pressed them back into Lindisfarne island and besieged them. The war seems to have continued against Theodoric's successor, Hussa (AD 582–92). Eventually Urien was slain in some internal squabble by a British chieftain named Morcant who seems to be a member of the Gododdin. Here, the similarity of the tradition of Mordred mortally wounding Arthur in an internal conflict has caused Arthurians to argue that Urien was one and the same person as Arthur. It could also be speculated that stories of Urien, his betrayal and killing by Morcant, were later cobbled on to the stories of Arthur.

Another poem ascribed to Llywarch Hen, but more likely just

about him as he appears to be a sixth-century northern chieftain, laments 'The Ruined Hearth of Rheged':

> Quiet the breeze, side of long slope.
> The man worthy of praise is rare.
> For Urien, grief is vain.
>
> This hearth that fine briars cover,
> Had courtesies upon it;
> To give was Rheged's custom.
>
> This hearth that pullets scratch in –
> Want did not injure it
> While Owain and Urien lived.

Immediately to the north lay the kingdom of Strath-Clòta, Strath-clyde, whose capital was Alcluyd (Dumbarton). During this period it was ruled by Rhydderch Hen (the Old), c.AD 580–612. According to tradition, two famous sons of Alcluyd were Patrick of Ireland and Gildas. We know that Rhydderch's father was named Tutagual. Joceline's *Life of Kentigern* claims that Rhydderch was baptized in Ireland and that his wife was named Languoreth. In Welsh tradition Rhydderch is known as Rhydderch Hael (the Generous). Rhydderch was strong enough to repel an attack on his kingdom by Aedán Mac Gabhráin of the Dál Riada. He was also acclaimed for his patronage of Christian foundations. It was he who invited Kentigern (Cunotigern, hound lord), who became known as Mungo, to return to the kingdom from Llanelwy in Wales, in order to rebuild Ninnian's great monastery at Whithorn after the Angles had attacked and burnt it, destroying its library. Kentigern, or Mungo, also built a foundation by the Clòta (Clyde) which he called 'a dear, green spot' (Glaschu, Glasgow). Rhydderch's death is placed in the same year as Kentigern's death.

We have a medieval confusion of tradition with Rhydderch's possible son, Constantine, becoming king. Joceline's *Life of Kentigern* refers to Constantine as succeeding his father but, being a Christian of saintly disposition, he subsequently retired to a monastery. Irish sources also mention him and his conversion and his journey to see Colmcille. But another source claims that this Constantine was the son of Padernus of Cornwall who suffered martyrdom in Kintyre in

AD 567. The confusion cannot be resolved. What is clear is that Rhydderch's kingdom eventually passed to his cousin Neithon, son of Guipno, and Neithon's grandson, Owen map Bili. Owen defeated not only the Dál Riadans but the Picts and Northumbrians, making Strath-Clòta the dominant power in northern Britain in the mid-seventh century.

To the east of Strath-Clòta was the kingdom of the Gododdin, a people known to the Romans as the Votadini. Their territory stretched between the Forth and the Tyne and they have been generally regarded as part of the southern Pictish kingdom. The settlement of Angles at the mouth of the Tweed and the emergence of Bernicia posed a direct threat to their territory. Following the war with Urien and his allies, the Bernician king Ida, and his successors, decided to strike back and seize the Celtic stronghold of Catraeth (Catterick in Yorkshire). Catraeth was a strategic position, sited on the network of roads between Bernicia and Deira and Rheged. A poem by Taliesin has Owain son of Urien, king of Rheged, being killed at Catraeth.

The plan to recapture Catraeth was apparently the idea of the ruler of the Gododdin, Mynyddawg Mwynfawr, whose capital was at Dineidyn (Dunedin and later Edinburgh). He was a contemporary of Rhydderch of Rheged in the late sixth century and his attack on Catraeth has become famous in the poem 'Y Gododdin' by Aneirin. Aneirin not only lived at the time but may have accompanied the Celtic warriors in their attack. Aneirin described how a war band of picked warriors rode southward in the attempt to recapture Catraeth from the Angles. Several interesting points arise from the poem: Mynddawg carefully chose his warriors and they were more than just Gododdin. They are described as coming from several areas, from the land of the Picts, from Strathclyde, Rheged, Gwynedd, Powys and even Elmet. They surely represented the most renowned warriors of the British Celts of the day, all united in their effort to halt the Angles. Moreover, they rode into battle as a mounted army. The Celts always preferred cavalry tactics while the Anglo-Saxons were at home as infantry.

> The retinue of Gododdin on rough-maned horses like swans,
> With their harness drawn tight,
> And attacking the troop in the van of the host,
> Defending the woods and the mead of Eidyn.

It is recorded that they comprised 300 men, a rather small band, especially when another verse maintains that the Angles comprised 100,000. No figure is to be taken seriously but one must remember that as one verse referred to chieftains in the front rank, it may well be that the 300 is meant in Celtic triad tradition and that there were actually 300 war bands. The expedition was a disaster. Of the Celtic warriors only one returned, perhaps the poet Aneirin himself, who survived to sing the battle honours. The defeat, listed in Welsh Triads as one of 'The Atrocious Assassinations of the Island of Britain', might have been the event which led to the destruction of the Gododdin as a separate kingdom and its absorption.

North again. On the islands and peninsulas of Argyll, in western Scotland, still small but rapidly spreading at this time, was the settlement of Irish from what is now Co. Antrim – Dál Riada, which had been founded by Fergus Mór, son of Erc, around AD 500. In AD 558 Conall, son of Comgall, had succeeded his uncle Gabhrán as the fifth ruler of Dál Riada and began to expand the settlement, encompassing islands such as Islay. He is credited with granting the island of I-Shona (Iona, Holy Isle) to the Irish exile Colmcille who is recorded as staying with him in AD 563 on his arrival from Ireland.

Of all the enigmatic characters of the period it is Colmcille (Columba) who has left the greatest influence on the culture of Celts and Saxons alike. He was born at Gartan, Co. Donegal, Ireland, in AD 521, where his father, Fedhilimidh, was a chieftain of the O'Donnell clan and a great-grandson of Niall of the Nine Hostages. He was called Colm (dove) Crimthain (wolf). He entered Moville, Co. Down, the monastery of Finnian, to study. His surreptitious copying of *The Gospel of Martin* caused an infuriated Finnian to take him to court and in AD 561 the Irish High King Diarmuid pronounced the world's first copyright law. 'To every cow belongs her calf, to every book her offspring book.' Therefore Colmcille's copy was also the property of Finnian of Moville. Diarmuid's finding against him was the start of a quarrel which intensified when the High King killed someone who was under Colmcille's protection. Colmcille lost his temper and he raised his clan against the High King but was defeated at a battle at Cul Drébene.

The High King, after a council at Teltown, Co. Meath, which pardoned Colmcille, decided that he was to be banished from Ireland. He was forced to leave his church at Daire Calgaich (the oak wood of Calgaich), now known as Derry, and set sail with some companions for Dál Riada. He was forty-two years old, in AD 563, when he settled with twenty bishops, forty priests, thirty deacons and fifty students on the small island off Mull, which became known as I-Shona, Iona. A missionary named Oran had already founded a monastery there but this did not prevent Colmcille from taking over. Both the Dál Riadans and the neighbouring Strathclyde British had already become Christians. For two years Colmcille stayed on the island, building his monastic centre, and only then did he begin to make missionary journeys through Dál Riada, Strathclyde and to the land of the Picts.

In AD 574 Conall, the king of Dál Riada, was succeeded by Aedán mac Gabhráin, who was to rule Dál Riada until AD 608 and make it one of the most powerful of the Celtic kingdoms. He is acknowledged as, perhaps, the greatest military commander of the period, campaigning in Ireland, the Isle of Man, the Orkneys and taking the war to the heart of the Angle settlements in Bernicia and Deira. He is said to have been one of twin sons born to an exiled Irish king, Eochaid mac Muiredaig of Leinster. Another tradition makes him a son of Gabhrán and his mother a daughter of Dyfnwal Hen, a king of Strath-Clòta. There was conflict about the suitability of his candidature for king. Here we must remember the Celtic custom of electing kings and officials. The law of primogeniture did not operate. Colmcille preferred Aedán's brother, Eoganán, but accepted the election of Aedán. Several people were slain during the struggle for power, including a son of Conall. As adviser to Aedán, Colmcille returned to Ireland with him to attend the Convention of Druim Ceit (Drumceat), Co. Derry, in AD 575, at which an agreement was worked out between Dál Riada and Ireland. Dál Riada would recognize the supreme authority of the High King, Aed mac Ainmerech, over the settlement but the High King confirmed that Dál Riada had authority over its territories in Ulster.

Colmcille was not only Aedán's religious adviser but a diplomat of the first water, arranging negotiations with Bruide Mac Maelchon of the Picts, evangelizing his people, and also exerting an extraordinary influence in Ireland, being on friendly terms with the new Irish High King, to whom he was related, and with the Strathclyde king, Rhydderch Hen. Several poems ascribed to him have survived and he is remembered as a pastor, a scholar and a man of tremendous strength of character. He was to die in Iona just after midnight on the Sunday morning of 9 June AD 597. Nearly a hundred years later (AD 688–92) Adomnán, an abbot of Iona and a worthy successor to Colmcille as both scholar and diplomat, wrote his celebrated *Life of Columba*, providing a major source of information on the Celtic Church.

With the backing of the agreement of Druim Ceit, in AD 575, Aedán of Dál Riada embarked on a campaign of consolidating his power. His first campaign was in AD 580 against the Picts over his claim to the Orkneys, which were part of their kingdom. Two years later he was attacking the Isle of Man, ousting an Ulster king who claimed the island. Then Aedán attacked a southern Pictish tribe called the Miathi (seemingly the Maeatae of Roman accounts) in a battle where he lost two sons. This territory was in Angus and Mearns. Aedán seems to have exerted overlordship over the Picts and one tradition has him as being father of Gartnait, a Pictish king who died in AD 602.

It was now that Aedán turned his attentions to the Angles to the south. In AD 598 two of his sons, Domangart and Bran, were assassinated by the Bernician Angles in unknown circumstances. Aethelfrith of Bernicia (AD 592–604) and of Northumbria (AD 604–617), whom Bede describes as 'most eager for glory', was probably the Anglian ruler who defeated the Gododdin and was now eager to grab their territory. Perhaps the killing of Aedán's sons was part of a plan to advance northward. Bede says that Aedán felt threatened by Aethelfrith's ambitions to extend Bernician borders beyond An Lomair Mòr (the Lammermuir Hills). Aedán gathered an army, which included contingents from his territories in Ulster, and met the Angles in battle at Degastan in AD 603. It was a débâcle from the Celtic viewpoint. While the Angles incurred heavy losses, the Dál Riadan army were routed. The defeat was so significant that, under Celtic law, Aedán was deemed not to have promoted the common-wealth of his people and he was stripped of his kingship. He eventually died on 17 April AD 608.

The remaining British Celtic kingdom to be identified covered the major area of Scotland, the kingdom of the Picts, reported to comprise a northern kingdom and a southern kingdom, with the southern kingdom eventually incorporating the area of the Gododdin to the borders of the Anglian settlement of Bernicia.

Ever since the Roman soldiers stationed on Hadrian's Wall nick-named the Celtic tribes of Caledonia 'painted ones', because of their use of warpaint in battle (*picti*, the past participle of *pingere*, 'to paint'), the so-called Picts have been perceived as a separate people and, as such, they have become the subject of myth upon misconception. Even today, many believe that the Picts were a non-Celtic people. The name 'Picti' was first recorded in a Latin poem of AD 297. However, they were not a new element in the tribes of Caledonia but the same Brythonic-speaking Celtic tribes, calling themselves Priteni, and uniting in tribal confederations. The place-names in the area are unquestionably Celtic, as are the names in their king lists. Moreover, most of the kings have British Celtic names given in Goidelic (Irish) form, the language in which they first were written. During the sixth century, the Caledonian tribes – we shall continue to call them the Picts for easy reference – were undergoing a linguistic change due to the expansion and Christianizing forces from Dál Riada. Therefore, when the Priteni, or Picts, appear in recorded history, they are called the *tuatha Cruthin* – this is simply Priteni in Goidelic form with the famous substitution of 'Q' for the 'P' sound which marks the difference in the two branches of Celtic. Thus *ceann* (head) in Irish becomes *pen* in Welsh. This change has caused scholars to talk in terms of Q-Celtic (Goidelic) and P-Celtic (Brythonic).

The first recorded king of the Picts was a contemporary of Aedán of Dál Riada and Colmcille. Bruide mac Maelchon (*c*.AD 556–584) was visited by Colmcille when the Irishman attempted to bring Christianity to the pagan kingdom. Adomnán, in his *Life of Columba*, says that Bruide's capital was on the Moray Firth. This has been identified as the hill-fort of Craig Phádraig where the Ness flows into the Moray Firth. According to the *Annals of Ulster*, Bruide won a battle over the Dál Riadan settlers in AD 558 and was campaigning again in AD 561. The Dál Riadans were attacking his kingdom in AD 580. So relations were not good between the two peoples.

However when Bruide died, according to the *Annals of Ulster* in AD 584, Gartnait became king and ruled until AD 602. His reign is confirmed by both the Pictish king lists and the *Annals of Tigernach*. Now his father is given as Aedán of Dál Riada in several sources, while the Pictish king lists claim his parent to have been Domelch. The significant word 'parent' has allowed scholars to accept that this was the name of his mother and indicative of the Pictish system of matrilinear succession – the theory being 'You may not know who your father was but you do know who your mother was'. Gartnait's rule over the Picts was a secure one and he was finally succeeded in AD 602 by his grandson, Nechtán (AD 602–621).

This was the situation among the British Celts of the sixth century. The Celtic areas of the island had reorganized into eleven distinct kingdoms. The settlements of the Angles and Saxons, at the same time, formed ten opposing kingdoms. After 150 years of warfare and settlement, by the end of the sixth century, by far the largest territory of the island of Britain still remained in Celtic hands.

[6]

The Saxon Consolidation

The Saxons increased their number and grew in Britain.

Nennius, Historia Britonnum (c. AD 830)

T HE Saxons of the south, having been soundly defeated at
Badon by Arthur, had been biding their time and waiting
for the right conditions before they renewed their military
expansion. When Arthur was killed at Camluan in AD 537/539, the
time was deemed right. There is, however, a record of some expansion among the West Saxons before this time. In AD 530 Cerdic and
Cynric led an expedition to the Isle of Wight where they killed many
British Celts at an unidentified place later called Wihtgaraesbyrg. We
find that in AD 534, Cerdic having died, Cynric was now undisputed
Saxon chieftain in the area and had given control of the Isle of Wight
to Stuf and Wihtgar. In spite of the claimed relationship of Stuf and
Wihtgar to Cerdic and Cynric, Bede believed them to be 'Jutes'
and the island to be settled by 'Jutes'. Wihtgar died ten years later
and was buried at Wihtgaraesbyrg.

With Arthur dead, Cynric and his West Saxons started a new
westward expansion with a series of raids and battles.

We have a brief glimpse of this expansion from the Celtic viewpoint from a *Life of Finnian of Clonard*. Finnian was an Irish abbot
(*c.*AD 549), a friend of Cadoc, one of the most important British
church leaders of the time and founder of Llancarfan. Finnian was
staying with Cadoc at the time of the new Saxon onslaught. In this
Life it is recorded that Finnian, as a 'neutral' foreigner, went as an
emissary to the Saxons and asked them to go home and not attack
the British. When they refused, however, Finnian is said to have
advised the Celts on a defensive strategy, getting them to prise loose
boulders with their staffs and send them rolling down on the Saxon
army as they marched through a narrow valley. The *Life* says: 'The

sequel was marvellous, for the high hills are said to have poured down upon the enemy, so that none of them escaped.' The Saxon records tend to be reticent about recording defeats and so do not identify this conflict.

In AD 552 Cynric was fighting the British Celts at Searobyrg, Salisbury, and defeated them. Then again in AD 556 Cynric and his son Ceawlin fought them at Beran byrg, an oval Celtic hill-fort now called Barbury Castle, five miles south of Swindon. The hill-fort was refortified by the Celts in the face of the Saxon invasion. But the Celts here were defeated and annihilated. About this time Cynric died but it was not until AD 560 that his son and successor, Ceawlin, was fully acknowledged as an influential leader among the Saxons and his West Saxon kingdom began to be a major influence in the area.

The *Anglo-Saxon Chronicle* makes mention that Aethelberht of Kent, son of Iurminric, became king in AD 565, although scholars are not agreed on the date. Three years later, the young king attempted to exert his control over the Middle Saxons. Ceawlin and Cuthwulf also claimed to be rulers of the Middle Saxons. Cuthwulf is identified by a late gloss on the *Chronicle* as brother of Ceawlin and he appears to be a co-king or general. Together, they defeated Aethelberht in battle at Wibbandune (Wimbledon, Winebeald's tun or fort) and forced him to retreat to Kent.

Six years later, in AD 571, Cuthwulf marched on the British Celts in Bedford and destroyed them. This was followed by the Saxon occupation of Aylesbury and Limbury as well as Bensington and Eynsham. Many pro-Saxon historians have found it hard to swallow that the British Celts could still be holding out in Bedford in AD 571. E. T. Leeds tried to alter the date to AD 471 while Sir Charles Oman attempted to change the opponents of the Saxons into Angles. But there is little doubt, from place-name and archaeological evidence, that the Celts still clung persistently to this area for a long while. Cuthwulf then pushed on into Oxford and no more is heard of him. Was he, with his war band, defeated and annihilated by the Celts?

Ceawlin's major expansion against the British continued. In AD 577 Ceawlin, together with his son Cuthwine (or Cutha), led the West Saxons in a series of victories culminating at Dyrham, Gloucestershire. Here he was victorious against three Celtic chieftains, Coinmail, Fairinmail and Condidan. He sacked the British cities of

Gloucester, Cirencester and Bath. These victories brought the valley of the lower Severn into the hands of the Saxons and opened the way for settlement in the west. The *Anglo-Saxon Chronicle* accords Ceawlin the position as Bretwalda.

Ceawlin also attempted to expand north across the Thames valley but, in AD 584, the British Celts defeated him at Fethanleag (probably Stoke Lyme, in north-east Oxfordshire). It is recorded that Ceawlin took much spoil. However it is also recorded that he came back to his kingdom 'in anger'. A victorious king does not return 'in anger'. Indeed, Ceawlin's son Cuthwine was killed here and we can conclude that the chronicler uses the euphemism, 'in anger', to record a Celtic victory.

There emerges at this time a significant British leader named Mouric, well attested to in Welsh sources, whose father was Theodoric, son of Budic, and who significantly bears the name of the man traditionally said to be Arthur's naval commander. His mother was sister to Urien, ruler of Rheged, the northern British king. The *Liber Landavensis* and *Life of Cadoc*, by Caradoc of Llancarfan, state that Theodoric, advanced in years, abdicated in favour of Mouric and became a *religieux* at Tintern. This was quite a normal and acceptable thing for a Celtic chieftain or king to do. Several Irish High Kings gave up office and retired to a life of monastic seclusion or religious pilgrimage. 'While Theodoric was living that life, the Saxons began to invade his country, against his son Mouric.' This is identified as the area which Ceawlin was attacking – along the lower Severn valley.

The *Liber Landavensis* takes a Christian motif of an angel prophesying a Celtic victory over the Saxons after which they 'will not dare attack this country again for thirty years'. The Celts win and Mouric pursues the enemy.

The Celtic victory fits in with a reference which occurs in a *Life of Maedoc*, otherwise Aidan of Ferns, an Irish bishop who, as a young lad, had left his native Connacht and arrived in Britain to study under Dewi Sant (David, patron saint of Wales) at his monastic settlement at Mynyw (Menevia, St David's in Dyfed). According to the *Life*, the British, gathering to face Ceawlin's Saxon army, sent to Mynyw and asked Dewi to send Maedoc to guide them spiritually. Perhaps they simply asked for a priest and Maedoc happened to be the person available. He went to join them and found they were ill prepared for battle. He prayed for victory and the British defeated the Saxons and pursued them for seven days with great slaughter. Dewi's death is placed at AD 589 and it is said Maedoc studied under him between AD 577 and AD 585. The Celtic victory over the Saxons would undoubtedly be Fethanleag and it would seem that the architect of this victory was Mouric.

Both Celtic and Saxon sources seem to concur. The Irish and Welsh sources tell of the westward movement of the Saxons during AD 577–585 and its repulse. The Saxons tell of a similar movement and a withdrawal 'in anger' in AD 584.

Ceawlin was eventually to be driven from his kingdom in AD 592 by a rival named Ceol after a 'great slaughter' at Wodnesbeorg, identified as Adam's Grave overlooking the Vale of Pewsey. Ceawlin died or was assassinated in the following year together with two leaders named Cwichelm and Crida who are not mentioned elsewhere.

Having established Wessex as a major Saxon settlement, which would one day be the dominant Saxon kingdom, Ceawlin's reign ends in confusion and disaster. Once more the Saxon expansion was checked and it was not until AD 614, exactly thirty years after the Celtic victory at Feathenleag, that the Saxons were once more on the move and defeated the British at Beandun, overlooking Axminster on the Devon-Dorset border. It would seem likely that the prophecy of the *Liber Landavensis* text was written with hindsight.

In the mean time Christianity had come to Kent. Aethelberht, who had learnt a lesson in power politics from his early attempt to encroach on West Saxon territory, had made a good political marriage to Bertha, daughter of Charibert, the king of the Franks. Now Charibert and his daughter were Christians. She came to Kent with her own chaplain, Luidhard, bishop of Senlis, and it was probably through them that Aethelberht was persuaded to allow Christian missionaries into his kingdom. For the pagan Anglo-Saxons, Christianity was something foreign, associated with the Britons. And the Britons, while eagerly propagating their faith among themselves and to other peoples, drew the line at trying to proselytize their blood enemies. Indeed, they made no attempt to do so and it would eventually fall to the Irish to play the key role in Christianizing the Saxon kingdoms.

In AD 590 the Pope, Gregory, who had himself once been asked by Benedict I (AD 574–578) to undertake a mission to convert the Saxons but had been recalled before he had even left Rome, ordered the prior of St Andrew's in Rome, Augustine, to go to Aethelberht's kingdom. Augustine landed in Kent in AD 597 with forty missionaries from Rome. The former Celtic church, dedicated to Martin of Tours in Canterbury, was once more opened to Christian worship. This was where Augustine established himself and spent several years preaching to the people of Kent with some apparent success. His centre was then dedicated to SS Peter and Paul but after his death became known as St Augustine's. In AD 601 new missionaries arrived to help him. Among them was Mellitus who was sent off to Saeberht, king of the East Saxons, who was son of Aethelberht's sister Ricula. Mellitus was given permission to establish a church in London dedicated to St Paul. Since the Saxons had captured the city from the Celts all the churches had been destroyed. Another missionary, Justus, set up a centre at Rochester among the Northumbrian Angles.

Under Augustine's instruction, Aethelberht became the first Saxon king to become a Christian and to promote literacy among his people, also issuing a law code 'after the manner of the Romans'. Bede now calls Aethelberht 'Bretwalda', implying he had authority over all the southern Saxon kingdoms.

Augustine decided to make contact with the British Celts and a meeting was arranged, probably at Aust, opposite Chepstow on the Severn. The Roman cleric had obviously spent too long among the Saxons, hearing their racist tales of the mere *welisc* or 'foreigners'. He must have known that the British were Christians and had been so for a long time. But he was apparently swayed by the Saxons' view of them and obviously felt he was going to meet with 'savages'. His feelings of superiority ooze through the pages of the chroniclers.

He arrived at the meeting place first and when the seven leading British bishops arrived he did not even rise to greet them as fellow bishops, a usual Christian custom, but remained seated, and immediately launched into a tirade of criticism. He accused them of acting contrary to Church teachings, failing to keep Easter at the prescribed Roman time and not administering baptism according to Roman rite.

The British were astounded at his attitude and amazed when Augustine wound up his lecture by demanding that they join him in preaching the faith to the Anglo-Saxons and accepting his church at Canterbury as their spiritual centre. There were many older and greater centres, with extensive libraries, in the Celtic world – Ninian's Candida Casa, for example – than the Canterbury church. Augustine must have sounded like some brash and ignorant upstart to the British bishops. They did not lose their tempers but diplomatically requested another meeting, replying that they could not abandon their customs or make decisions without the consent of their people – a significant phrase endorsing the democratic idea of the Celtic law system.

The second meeting was worse than the first. Again Augustine made no effort to rise to greet them and started to lecture the Celts on Roman orthodoxy before demanding that they submit to his authority. The British must have attempted reason and pointed out the folly of placing themselves under the ecclesiastical tutelage of Canterbury, a centre ruled by the very people who were attempting to annihilate them. How could they accept a Saxon ecclesiastical authority in the very midst of their life and death struggle against Saxon domination? Finally, the Britons said pointedly that if Augustine had not the manners to rise to greet them, as fellow bishops, how much more would he hold them in contempt if they meekly agreed to subject themselves to him.

Bede, the chronicler of this conference, shows that Augustine lost his temper and threatened that the Celts would suffer vengeance at the hands of the Saxons if they did not agree to his terms. Had he wished to win them over, that was surely the last thing to threaten them with. The conference ended abruptly.

A few months later Augustine was dead and a fellow Roman, Laurentius, was in charge of the Christian mission to the Saxons. This was somewhere between AD 604 and 610. Aethelberht of Kent died about AD 616/618. The British suspicion about the Saxon commitment to the Christian faith was proved correct. Eadbald succeeded his father, and, in accordance with pre-Christian custom, married his father's widow. This, some scholars say in an attempt to escape the fact that Eadbald was using pagan ceremony, implies that he was the son of a previous wife. However, the inescapable truth is that the Kent kingdom now resorted to its pagan religion.

In the East Saxon kingdom, Saeberht, the king, had also died; his three sons resumed the old religion and promptly expelled Mellitus, the missionary. Mellitus and his fellow clerics had to flee to the Continent. The Angles in Rochester also chased out their missionary,

Justus. Laurentius was having problems with the pagan Kent king, Eadbald, and seriously considered joining his fellow missionaries and retreating to Gaul. Bede says he had a vision of St Peter who rebuked him for his cowardice and so Laurentius made a fresh attempt to convert Eadbald and succeeded. But Eadbald did not have the same authority that his father had had and for a long time the attempt to convert the Saxons in the south foundered.

At the time the Christianizing of Kent was taking place, a new power was arising among the kingdoms of the Angles in the north.

Aethelfrith, grandson of Ida of Bernicia, had succeeded as king of the settlement in AD 592. The kingdom, attacked by the Celts led by Urien, was barely surviving. Now Aethelfrith had turned the tide of fortune with his victory over Aedán and the Dál Riadan army. The year afterwards he seized control of Deira, the kingdom of Angles to the south. The son of the deposed king, Aelle, a boy named Edwin, was taken out of Deira for safety. According to some records he was raised at the court of Cadfan of Gwynedd and baptized a Christian there by Rhun, son of Urien of Rheged. As an adult he went to Mercia, married the daughter of its ruler Cearl, a lady called Cwenburgh, and had two sons, Osfrith and Eadfrith. But his ambition was to oust Aethelfrith and he moved on to East Anglia where Raewald eventually gave him an army to help overthrow Aethelfrith. But that was not to be until AD 616. In AD 604 Aethelfrith had formed the two kingdoms, of Bernicia and Deira, into one kingdom, 'the land north of the Humber', *be northan Hymbre* – Northumbria.

Having consolidated himself in this new kingdom, by forcing Edwin's sister Acha to marry him, Aethelfrith launched himself against the British. He marched an army to Chester to confront Selyf map Cynan, king of Powys, in AD 616. According to Bede, a thousand monks from the great monastery of Bangor Iscoed accompanied Selyf's army and arranged themselves on a hillside to pray for victory over their pagan enemies. It is slightly reminiscent of the Celtic druids gathering at a battle to pray for the victory of the Celtic warriors over the Romans. Aethelfrith not only defeated Selyf's warriors but he turned his men on the monks and slaughtered all of them. This massacre presented a problem to Bede, torn between his nationalism and his faith; nationalism won and he puts these words into pagan Aethelfrith's mouth: 'If they cry to their God against us, and load us with imprecations, then, though unarmed, they fight against us.'

Aethelfrith returned to Northumbria victorious but the following year, AD 617, Edwin was to take his revenge. Edwin had secured the support of Raedwald and together they marched an army to the River Idle, Nottingham, and defeated and killed him, enabling Edwin to make himself king of Northumbria. He accepted the two united kingdoms without demur, knowing that it would give him a strong power base. Meanwhile Aethelfrith's sons, Oswald and Oswiu, with their sister Aebbe, were sent into exile. They are presumed to be the children of Edwin's sister Acha. There is another son on record – Eanfrith, the son of a former marriage, who also fled. Surprisingly, it is recorded that Eanfrith, Oswald, Oswiu and Aebbe, instead of being taken to another Saxon kingdom, went to Iona, among the Dál Riada, where they were baptized as Christians. This action was to have a tremendous influence over the future development of the Saxon kingdoms, both in the changing of their religion and in the introduction of literacy and learning into the Saxon world.

Another fascinating point arises. The German historian, Hermann Moisl, has traced a sequence of fragmentary evidence to suggest that Saxon war bands were fighting in the armies of the Irish and Dál Riadans during this period. His study, 'The Bernician Royal Dynasty and the Irish', appears in *Peritia* (Journal of the Medieval Archaeology Society of Ireland), Vol. II (1983), pp 102 *et passim*. We find that Aedán Mac Gabhráin is recorded as bringing an army of 'Saxons, Britons and the men of Dál Riada' to Ireland to fight in an Irish dynastic war about AD 604. So it appears that there were some links between the Dál Riadans and dissenting Saxons, political refugees from Northumbria at this time. When, in AD 617, the children of Aethelfrith went into exile, they did not go to Dál Riada alone: probably their loyal thanes and a small retinue or even an army went with them. Saxon war bands are recorded as fighting for the Ulster king Congal Caech against Domnall Mac Aedh of the Uí Néill. And Congall Caech was in alliance with the Dál Riadans. Most fascinating is the Irish saga *Togail Bruidhne da Derga*, the famous 'Destruction of Da Derga's Hostel', which says that three Saxon princes took part and names one of them as Osalt – this could well be the Irish form of Oswald. Certainly Wilbord, Bede's contemporary, returning from a pilgrimage to Ireland, told the Northumbrian monk that stories of Oswald's prowess and adventures as a warrior were widespread.

What is absolutely certain is that Eanfrith, Oswald, Oswiu and their sister Aebbe grew to adulthood in Dál Riada, proficient in the Goidelic Celtic language and as Christians educated in the ways of the Celtic Church.

In Northumbria, secure in his new kingdom, Edwin now made a political marriage, his first wife having presumably died. In AD 625 he married Aethelburgh, daughter of the now dead Aethelberht of Kent. Here traditions are contradictory, for if Edwin was baptized by Rhun, then Bede's contention that Aethelburgh's chaplain, the Roman missionary Paulinus, who had been preaching in Kent since AD 601, converted him is not true. Aethelburgh had come north to marry and brought Paulinus with her as her chaplain. Paulinus is said to have established a church at York. The year after his wedding, Edwin, who was to become one of the most notable of the Anglo-Saxon warlords, moved his army into the British Celtic kingdom of Elmet, defeated Ceredig, and annexed it to his Northumbrian kingdom.

By the third decade of the seventh century, the Anglo-Saxon settlements had taken over the eastern side of the island of Britain and were beginning to look a permanent feature.

Massacre, Migration or Assimilation?

A number of the wretched survivors were caught in the mountains and butchered wholesale. Others, their spirits broken by hunger, went to surrender to the enemy; they were taken to be slaves forever, if indeed they were not killed straight away, the highest boon. Others made for lands beyond the sea, beneath the swelling sails they loudly wailed, singing a psalm that took the place of a shanty. 'You have given us like sheep for the eating and scattered us among the heathen.'

Gildas (d. c. AD 570), De Excidio et Conquestu Britanniae

T HE invasion and settlement of the Anglo-Saxons had a devastating effect on the native British Celtic population. It is inevitable that, faced by a ruthless military society with an unquenchable thirst for land and conquest, the native population would be driven from the land and dispossessed. But from the nineteenth century, in attempts to cement the idea of an homogeneous 'British' nation, so essential to the development of empire, English historians have generally adopted the theory that the native Celts were pushed back into the areas of land in which they are still to be found in modern times while those left behind were rapidly assimilated into Anglo-Saxon culture. References to the massacres by Gildas, a British Celt living through the experience, have been dismissed as biased, while similar references to 'great slaughters' in the Anglo-Saxon records have been called 'exaggerations'. Even the Welsh historian, Arthur Wade Evans, has gone so far as to maintain that there was no Anglo-Saxon 'invasion' of Britain but that it was a 'gentle' settlement with the incomers coexisting happily side by side with the natives and eventually absorbing them. This idea is currently receiving a new airing from a group of archaeologists led, notably, by Nicholas Higham of the University of Manchester.

Indeed, other Celtic scholars, seeking to get the Anglo-Saxons 'off the hook', have argued that the mass migrations which undoubtedly took place were not due to the inexorable advance of the Saxons but to the raids of the Picts and Scotii (Irish). The theory has been popularized by Nora K. Chadwick in her studies.

The first authority we have on the period is, of course, the British monk Gildas (c.AD 516/18–570). Gildas wrote *De Excidio et Conquestu Britanniae* (On the Ruin and Conquest of Britain) about AD 560/62. He mentions that he had been born in the year of the battle of Badon and was then forty-four years old. He speaks with a clear unequivocal voice. The British Celts were being massacred and forced to flee from their territories because of the attack of the *ferocissimi Saxones* (the ferocious Saxons).

He expands on the horrors of massacres and, referring to the start of the mass migrations of the British Celts out of Britain, he ascribes the cause of their going clearly to the Saxon war machine. Not only was Gildas an eyewitness to the events he described, he was also one of those who migrated from Britain to spend the end of his life in a monastery he founded in Morbihan, Brittany.

Gildas grew up in the years of relative peace and security following the battle of Badon. The later *Life* describes him as a Strathclyde Briton, born at Alcluyd (Dumbarton), the son of a chieftain named Caw. He married and had two sons, Gwynnog and Noethon, accounted as missionaries and 'saints' in the Denbigh area. He went to study under Illtyd at Llanilltyd Fawr (Llantwit Major) and became a close friend of Cadoc, another of the great Celtic Church fathers, who spent some time at Lismore in Ireland. Tradition has it that Gildas was a very knowledgeable man and he is referred to as *sapientissimus* (most wise). As well as the famous *De Excidio et Conquestu Britanniae*, other works such as *De Poenitentia* (Preface on Penance) and a fragment of a letter are ascribed to him. Arthur Wade Evans has postulated a theory that *De Excidio* was actually written by a fellow monk or pupil of Gildas because he believes there are stylistic differences between this work and his other works. It is not a popular theory and there is no reason to believe that anyone other than Gildas wrote the work for which he is most famed.

Gildas must have our attention when he speaks about the causes of the migration of the British Celts to Brittany because he was one of those migrants. He made his way to Brittany about AD 555 and founded a monastery at what is now called St Gildas-de-Rhuys in

Morbihan. The abbot of the monastery in the twelfth century was the ill-fated Breton Abelard whose love for Heloise has become one of the classic tragic romances. Gildas is said to have died on the nearby island of Houat about AD 570. Before his death Gildas had visited Ireland. It is recorded that he had corresponded with many Irish churchmen such as Finnian of Moville. This visit occurred in AD 566, during the time of the High King Ainmire Mac Sétnai. There is an interesting sequel to Gildas's visit. According to the *Book of Leinster*, the provincial king of Connacht (AD 617–622), Guaire Aidne, wished to hear the saga of the *Táin Bó Cuailgne* but found that not even the chief bard of Ireland, Senchán Torpéist, knew the saga in its complete form. Senchán Torpéist decided to assemble all the poets and story-tellers of Ireland to find out who knew the complete saga but it was discovered that none knew it nor had a written copy. It was found that a 'wise man had taken it to the east in exchange of the *Cuilmenn*'. The *Cuilmenn* was the Irish name for the *Origines* or *Etymologie* of Isidorus of Seville (*c.*AD 560–636), an encyclopaedia of science and arts. Gildas was of course known as the 'wise man'. It would seem that Gildas had indeed exchanged a copy of Isidorus's work for a copy of the Irish saga during his visit to Ireland. Senchán Torpéist asked one of his pupils to go to Brittany to copy or relearn the entire saga, which presumably he did, for the *Táin*, one of the great pieces of Irish saga literature, survives in eleventh- and twelfth-century texts.

The indications are that there was a constant interchange of manuscripts between the British and Irish Celts. Indeed, the *Lorica* of Gildas appeared in an Irish version in the *Leabhar Breac* and the later work of Nennius has been preserved in five Irish manuscripts, the earliest dated to the twelfth century.

Because of his graphic account of the Saxon invasions, the massacres and migrations of the Celts, Gildas has come in for much criticism from modern historians who would make light of the events and have seized on whatever contrary evidence they could to diminish his authority.

A curious contradiction to Gildas's history comes from a Byzantine Greek historian, Procopius of Caesarea (*c.*AD 500–after 562) who was secretary to Belisarius, general of the emperor Justinian, and who wrote a *History of the Wars of Justinian* in eight books. Procopius points out that Britain, in his day, was inhabited by the Britons,

Angles and Frisians. He claims that each race was so fertile that women and children were sent in large numbers to the land of the Franks who then planted them as colonists in sparsely inhabited areas of their territory. Frank Stenton believes the reference important in that it shows that after Arthur's victory at Badon the Anglo-Saxons were confined in their territories and were unable to move into Celtic territory despite an expanding population.

The simple truth is that Procopius was miles away from the 'action' while Gildas was 'on the spot'. It becomes obvious who is the more creditable witness. However, a monk of Fulda, in the ninth century, does record a tradition that Anglo-Saxons and *Britons* joined the army of the Frankish king Theuderich as mercenaries in the war against the Thuringians in AD 531 and were then paid in land and settled in the conquered areas, so Procopius could have been partly correct.

For Nora Chadwick, the tradition of the monk of Fulda, and the mention made by Procopius, entirely dispose of Gildas and the numerous other writers who record the British tradition at first hand. But even the eighth-century Frankish chronicler, Eginhard, from whom some justification of his Germanic brethren might be expected, recorded that 'when the island of Britain had been invaded by the Angles and Saxons, a large part of its inhabitants, crossing the sea, occupied the regions of Venedi and the Coriosoletes in the remoter part of Gaul' (i.e. Armorica). The chroniclers talk of the slaughters and migrations from pressure by the Saxons and not from any other source. It makes more sense than Procopious's talk of a high birth rate causing over-population and Nora Chadwick's later theory that Irish raids produced the mass migration. Although the Irish were indeed raiding at this time and settling in certain areas of the west coast, the evidence is that they did not cause massacres and migrations. They were, after all, related by language and custom and, in Dyfed, the Irish settlement soon merged culturally with the British Celts. This was patently not true of the settlement of the Saxons.

A major point in arguing against the theory that fear of the Irish caused British migration is the fact that a great many of the British Celts fleeing their homeland actually crossed to and settled in Ireland. The fact is that there was considerable intercourse between the Celts of Ireland and the Celts of Britain from early times. During the fifth and sixth centuries particularly, British and Irish *religieux*, who have come down to us as Celtic 'saints', were constantly travelling to and fro. As we have seen, even Gildas visited Ireland, and had the Irish been responsible for the suffering he described in *De Excidio* then he must surely have made some disparaging reference to them. But he did not. At the same time Gildas's contemporary, Cadoc, is said to have gone to Ireland and 'instructed in the seven liberal arts' at Lismore. Cuby (Cybi) of Cornwall went with a kinsman named Cungar to stay with Enda on the Aran Isles. Another Briton named Cynog was allowed to establish two monasteries in Ireland, one at Gallen, near Ferbane, Co. Offaly, which the *Annals of Clonmacnoise* give as Galinne na mBretan (Gallen of the Britons), and the other at Delgany, Co. Wicklow, which the *Annals of Ulster* call Dermagh Britonum (Durrow of the Britons). The recorded interchanges are numerous. In fact, during this period relations between the Irish and British Celts were at their closest and most continuous.

The *Book of Armagh* records a fifth-century chieftain, Fedelmud Mac Loigaire, as having a British wife named Scoth Nua. They were visited by Lomman, a Briton who was a colleague of Patrick – and, of course, Patrick himself was a Briton. Ethne, daughter of the king of Munster, came to Britain at this time to marry a British king who had sent a member of his household to escort her, according to the *Life of St Tigernach*. Such incidents are recorded in Welsh myths, in *Brannwen ferch Llyr* and, indeed, in the most famous love tale of them all, when Mark of Cornwall sends Tristan to escort Iseult, daughter of a king of Munster, and bring her to his court for marriage.

Support for the fact that large bodies of Britons crossed to Ireland to escape the Saxons comes from Wrdistan, a Breton monk of Landévennec, writing his *Life of St Winwaloe* in the ninth century. He states clearly that the Britons 'who escaped the sword of the invaders [Saxons] abandoned their native land, to seek refuge some among the Scotii [Irish] and the rest in Belgic Gaul'. The seventeenth-century historian Seathrún Céitinn, who had access to sources destroyed during the Cromwellian and Williamite conquests later that century, reiterates this statement: 'Ireland was a place of refuge for the Britons whenever they suffered persecution from the Romans or the Saxons or from any other races that oppressed them.' He goes on: 'Large companies of them, with their families and followers and with their wealth, used to fly for refuge to Ireland; and the Irish chieftains used to give them land during their stay; and the children they had during their time of exile used to learn Irish.'

The proof of these contentions is to be found in the Irish chronicles, particularly the *Annals of Ulster*. That the Britons who had fled and settled in Ireland remained identifiable communities in later years is remarked by these sources. In AD 682 at the battle of Rathmore in Moylinny we find Britons fighting as a unit. In AD 702 Britons fought some of the Ulster clans in a battle at Magh Cuilinn in Ard ua nEacach. The *Annals of Tigernach* add that the son of Radhgaind, an enemy of God's clergy, fell at that battle and the name here is a British Celtic one, Ridgent. In AD 705 we find Britons recruited into the army of Cellach or Ceallaigh and fighting for the Irish king at Selg, near Glendalough, Co. Wicklow. They are referred to as *cum Britonibus Ceallaigh* (Cellach's Britons). In AD 707 the Britons are reported as having slain Iorgalach ua Conaing at a place called Ireland's Eye. In AD 797 we find Britons and Ulster clans at war together, ravaging the plains of Muirtheimme (Lough). The *Annals of Ulster* make several references to the Picts in Ireland, the last reference being in AD 809. This has been seen as a reference to a distinct people, but, as we have argued, the Picts called themselves Pretani (Britons), so were these references to British Celts from the south or specifically to those from the north of Britain?

Certainly in the ninth century, with the Viking raids and continued pressure from the expanding Anglo-Saxons, a great influx of British Celtic refugees is also recorded. If we can rely on Seathrún Céitinn, then these refugees settled and assimilated with remarkable rapidity into the Irish nation, as subsequently did the Danes, the Normans and some of the later Scottish and English colonists.

Again there is evidence that the movement to Ireland was not all one-sided. Political fugitives from Ireland are recorded as taking refuge among the British Celts. The Irish annals speak of many Irish chieftains, would-be rulers, who fled and settled. Aed Guaire is reported to have fled to Britain in the sixth century from the wrath of Diarmuid mac Cearbaill. Aurthuile, chieftain of the Cinel Eoghain, found refuge in Britain in AD 699. And Fogartach ua Cearnaigh, who was High King in AD 715–723, was also a political refugee in Britain, according to the *Annals of Ulster*, sometime during AD 712/ 713.

This closeness, this intercourse, would seem incompatible with

South-east bastion of Burgh Castle, on the Suffolk/Norfolk border, built during the Roman occupation of Britain as part of the 'Saxon Shore' defences to prevent Saxon raids.

Built in the 4th Century, the central roundel of the mosaic floor from the main room of the villa at Hinton St Mary, Dorset, which is now reassembled in the British Museum.

A Saxon war helmet reconstructed from the Sutton Hoo find. The helmet corresponds to the description of war helmets in the *Beowulf* saga.

The 8th Century iron and embellished copper war helmet found at Coppergate, York.

A reconstruction of an Anglo-Saxon building excavated at Bourton-on-the-Water, Gloucester.

The Frank Casket, carved in 7th Century Northumbria in the wake of the 'Age of Learning' inspired by the work of Irish missionaries. It is made of walrus ivory.

The Alfred Jewel made in the 9th Century. As well as portraying the king, the jewel bears the inscription: 'Aelfred mec heht gewyrcan' (Alfred had me wrought).

Offa of Mercia (757–796 AD) decided to build a physical barrier bordering his kingdom and the lands of the British Celts, inspired, no doubt, by the concept of Hadrian's Wall. Offa's Dyke can still be seen running 193.1 km from Treuddyn to near Chepstow on the Severn.

A Charter of Offa of Mercia held in the British Museum.

The Frith Stool at Hexham Abbey built as the throne for an abbot in the 7th Century, possibly at the order of Bishop Wilfrid of Ripon. It imitates a Byzantine model.

The Farne Islands off the coast of Northumbria. It is thought that a group of refugees from the kingdom of Lindsey settled on one of them and it became known as Lindisfarne.

The only surviving early manuscript of *Beowulf*, the Anglo-Saxon saga, is now in the British Library, part of the Cottonian manuscript collection.

Fragments of Cuthbert's portable altar which were recovered from his tomb and are now in Durham Cathedral.

A page from the Lindisfarne Gospels, an illuminated Latin manuscript written at Lindisfarne sometime in the 7th Century and now in the British Museum.

The battle-axe was a favourite Viking weapon. These are a selection found in the Thames dating to the Viking period, which are now in the Museum of London.

Nora Chadwick's contention that it was the Irish who forced the extensive migration of the British Celts at this time. The argument is also contradicted by the earliest sources and, moreover, by accounts written by people who were in a position to know. Mrs Chadwick argues that, according to tradition, most of the immigrants to Brittany were led by people with connections with what are now Wales and south-western Britain. Therefore, they came from areas which were not under threat from the Saxons, and their departure to seek new lands could not have been induced by the Saxon invasion. If we allow that the start of a migration away from the Saxons would logically push the British west into these areas, initially causing overpopulation and probably food supply problems, it would be seen as a rational progression in the process for the immigrants to then move on from western Britain to the Continent. It does not mean that because the migrants had associations with the west before they moved that they had always been domiciled there. After all, Gildas, one of the migrants, had associations with the west but he originally came from Strathclyde.

The conclusion is that Gildas was being truthful. The 'ferocious Saxons', moving across British territory and dispossessing the natives, were the one primary cause of the mass migration out of Britain.

The theory that large parts of the British Celtic population carried on living side by side with the conquerors and intermarried with them needs to be addressed before we follow the fortunes of these immigrants. Yet again, the leading proponent of this theory is none other than Nora K. Chadwick ('The British or Celtic Part in the Population of England', in *Angles and Britons*). Mrs Chadwick said in this O'Donnell lecture, 'I firmly believe myself that the predominant element in the population [of England] is Celtic. I am aware that proof is not possible, and therefore I may not be able to persuade you to the belief I hold.' One immediately wonders what criterion Mrs Chadwick uses to describe this predominant element as Celtic. 'Celtic' is a linguistic and cultural definition and not a racial one, and in most of her work, she fully subscribes to this view. Here, however, she seems to abandon it and to fall back on some other definition, which can only be the illusory one of 'race'.

Mrs Chadwick too easily dismisses one of the most damning pieces of evidence for the non-assimilation of the native Celts into the

Anglo-Saxon population: the fact that nothing survives in pre-Norman Conquest English of a Celtic language apart from a few place-names and a few words pertaining to religion. I make no apology for repeating Dr Mario Pei's succinct argument: 'One might imagine that the Celtic of the original Britons would have supplied a fertile field for loan-words to the Anglo-Saxons. Such is emphatically not the case.' He points out that there are in English, apart from place-names, only about a dozen Celtic words assimilated during the period of the Anglo-Saxon conquests. 'The reason for this seems to lie in the scantiness of social relations between the two races, the English considering the Celts as inferior and their own race and tongue as superior.' Dr Pei talks of the 'bitter racial and linguistic animosity that had marked the ... clash between Saxons and Britons'. Pei adds that the numerous Celtic loan-words in modern English demonstrably arrived by Celtic immigrant populations into England in the eighteenth and nineteenth centuries.

Mrs Chadwick thinks this argument in support of an extermination of the native population is fallacious. Her theory is that the Saxons did not accept any Celtic loan-words into their language because the British Celts 'were in a less-advanced stage of culture'. This is palpable nonsense even if we accept that curious judgemental criterion – by what yardstick does one define an 'advanced' or 'less-advanced' culture? English is replete with loan-words brought into it from numerous cultures across the face of the earth which Mrs Chadwick would presumably regard as 'less-advanced'. Furthermore, was the Celtic culture really in a 'less-advanced' stage than the Anglo-Saxon? The reverse is surely the case. The British Celts were highly literate; not only were they writing in their own language but using both Latin and Greek as a *lingua franca*. They had transferred from centuries of oral tradition to writing and were producing a literature which is second to none. Even their artwork had a centuries-old tradition at this time, producing a form which was to be copied and adapted by the Anglo-Saxons. Celtic metalwork, weaving and scholarship had European reputations. The attempt to paint the Britons as primitive and pastoral is curious for someone of Mrs Chadwick's knowledge and reputation in the field of Celtic scholarship. She makes no attempt to justify her assertion but simply states it. Emotional support for her contention overcame her normally careful scholarship.

If there had been intermarriage between Celt and Saxon then we would have had a situation comparable to what occurred in France. The Franks, cousins of the Anglo-Saxons, had conquered most of Gaul and intermarried, accepting Christianity almost immediately and absorbing a significant Gaulish vocabulary in the language which has now become French. The Académie Française grudgingly admits to about 500 Celtic loan-words surviving from this period, but Georges Dottin (*La langue gaulois*, Paris, 1920) suggests that a far larger Celtic vocabulary survived through Low Latin and that both Gaulish and Latin equally created the French language. Aware that this example did not support her theory, Mrs Chadwick tried to maintain that 'Gaul ... had a more highly developed civil and religious system of institutions, the ecclesiastical based on the civil. The incomers naturally adopted this in a large measure as a matter of convenience.'

Mrs Chadwick fully supports the bizarre theory of Arthur Wade Evans (in *Welsh Christian Origins*) that there never was an Anglo-Saxon 'conquest' and that the Anglo-Saxons 'peacefully' established themselves in eastern Britain. Much of the argument rests in trying to dismiss Gildas or rubbish his arguments. Mrs Chadwick suggests 'the survival of a native British population carrying on its arts undisturbed by the political changes'. Even Mrs Chadwick, presented with the indisputable facts that the Anglo-Saxons were pagans and illiterate, compared with the literate and Christianized Britons, is hard pressed to explain why, if the Britons were carrying on undisturbed, the Christian Church disappeared in the areas occupied by the Saxons. She admits that 'undoubtedly the native British institutions disappeared before the new ones imposed by the Anglo-Saxons in this part of the country'. Her explanation is that the Anglo-Saxons simply stopped patronage and wealth to the Christian communities. The easier and more plausible argument is that the native British churches disappeared because there were no native Britons in the areas to support them: that these populations had been driven out, one way or the other, by the pagan Saxons. Indeed, in archaeological terms nothing Celtic survives after the Saxon settlements in these areas – no Celtic burials, no Celtic agricultural systems distinct from the Saxon open field system, indeed, nothing at all to show the existence of 'the survival of a native British population carrying on its arts undisturbed by political changes'.

We can safely assert that, in the face of Saxon attacks, large sections of the Celtic population were exterminated while others decided to seek homelands in safer areas. As we have seen, many pressed westward, reinforcing the populations in those areas; others decided to move on to lands where there was more living space. Some crossed the sea to Ireland; other bands crossed to the Continent. Some settled on the Rhine where they established the 'town of the Britons', Brittenburg; others went to Gaul where a number of places called Bretteville are to be found; others moved south to north-east Spain, and more made the most lasting and significant settlement in the Gaulish Celtic peninsula of Armorica – whose name was changed to 'Little Britain', Brittany, because of the extent of the settlements.

We will follow the migrations to the Iberian peninsula first. Iberia had once been predominantly Celtic, settled as far back as 1000 BC, but the Roman Empire had eventually altered the language and attitude of the people. As I have demonstrated in *The Celtic Empire*, the fight to bring the Celts of Iberia under the *pax Romana* was a long and savage one. But traces of the Celtic-speaking population seem to have disappeared by the second century AD. Therefore, the theory that the new migration of Celts in the fifth and sixth centuries reinforced a native Celtic population is not credible.

The migration to this area took place at an extremely early period, starting in the mid-fifth century – perhaps even before the mutiny of the Jutes – at the time when southern Britain was trying to fight off the Saxon raids. Orosius Paulus, a cleric and historian born in Braga in the AD 380s, mentions, perhaps with some significance, that the new Celtic settlers came from Ireland. Orosius certainly knew where Ireland was and, indeed, quotes Aethicus of Istria who went to Ireland to examine the Irish libraries. There is no doubt, however, that the newcomers were Britons for we know they had British names, a British Celtic language and customs. But perhaps the explanation is that they came *via Ireland*. And this would be in perfect accord with the Irish and British records showing a movement of British Celts fleeing to Ireland.

The British settlers began arriving on the northern seaboard, mainly in Asturias, between Lugo and Oviedo. King Thiudemir ordained a Council of Lugo in AD 567. This Council recognized the British settlers as a separate division of the church administration. 'To the See of Bretoña belong the churches which are among the

Britons, together with the monastery of Maximus and the churches which are in Asturias.' The monastery was that of Santa Maria de Bretoña at Pastoriza near Mondonedo.

We learn that in AD 527 the name of the bishop of the Britons was Mahiloc – clearly a British Celtic name. He signed the *acta* of the second Council of Braga. The Britons were still a recognizable community in AD 633 when they were represented at the fourth Council of Toledo where they accepted Roman rule and gave up their individualist Celtic practices. In a *Life of St Fructuosus of Braga*, who died c.AD 655 and who must not be confused with his namesake at Tarragona who died in AD 259, the church of Bretoña was described as Celtic in practice until the fourth Council of Toledo. In AD 646 and 653 the British sent delegates to the seventh and eighth Councils of Toledo and in 675 they attended the third Council of Braga. By the ninth century the area was being ravaged by the Moors. While the name Bretoña survives as late as AD 1156, in a *Privilegium* of Alphonse VII, it is clear that, as a distinct cultural community with its own language, the British Celts had vanished by the ninth century, merging into the Romance-speaking population of what is now Galicia.

It is true that there are some identifiable remnants of Celtic culture in local folklore and music, and several words of Celtic origin in the Romance language of Galicia, which is closely akin to Portuguese. But recent claims that Galicia is still a Celtic country are sheer fantasy.

The most famous and lasting of all migrations of Britons during this time is, of course, that to Armorica. According to Dr John Morris, there were, in fact, three distinct migrations to Armorica, with the first settlement taking place during the time of Magnus Maximus. This tradition was put forward by Geoffrey of Monmouth in the twelfth century; he says that Magnus Maximus instructed Conan Meriadoc to take large numbers of civil and military to create 'a second Britain' in Armorica. The tradition was refuted by Dom Antoine de Galois (*Réfutation de la fable de Conan Meriadoc*, Rennes, 1902). But Geoffrey does echo Nennius's tradition that Maximus took soldiers to Gaul who 'are the Armorican Britons, and they never returned to this day'.

According to Dr Morris, the second mass migration to Armorica took place in the late fifth century, following the mutiny of the Jutish mercenaries; this is, of course, well attested by Latin sources. The third and final mass migration took place during the middle of the sixth century, in the years following the death of Arthur.

With the Germanic tribes such as the Franks (who would eventually give their name to the country), the Alamanni and the Thuringians pouring over the Rhine into Gaul, the face of Romano-Celtic Gaul was changing. The peninsula of Armorica, 'the land by the sea', had not been seriously affected by the Franks; indeed, it had remained fairly remote from Roman rule during the Romanizing administration. Zosimus tells us that in AD 409 the Armoricans, 'encouraged by the example of the insular Britons, had thrown off the Roman yoke'. The anonymous *Gallic* or *Gaulish Chronicle* refers to a Celtic chieftain named Tibatto (*c*.AD 435) who attempted to maintain an independent Armorica but was captured and slain two years later.

There is an interesting point to be considered which not only makes Zosimus's reference to the British influence in Armorica intelligible but also makes the success of the British settlements in Armorica more understandable. Julius Caesar reported that the rulers of Celtic tribes in Gaul also ruled septs of the same tribes in Britain, particularly among the Belgae. For example, Commios of the Atrebates of northern Gaul claimed authority over the Atrebates of southern Britain. In the sixth century, Cunomoros (Mark) of Kernow (Cornwall) also ruled in Kernev (Cornouaille) in Brittany. This dual kingship in both Gaul and Britain is underscored by references in the later *Vitae Sanctorum*. The Celts of Gaul and Britain not only had a close trading relationship with one another but had been intermixing, with tribes crossing back and forth between the Continent and Britain over many centuries, so that many shared the same rulers and traditions in common. I believe that in this state of affairs lies the answer to the question posed by scholars as to how the British Celtic immigrants, during the fifth and sixth centuries, migrated to Armorica and managed to 'dominate' the peninsula in such a short space of time without any violent protest by the native Armoricans who had not only prevented total Roman domination of their land, as elsewhere in Gaul, but had kept the Saxons and Franks, who were attacking their coastal settlements, from forming any permanent bases there.

Mrs Chadwick is inclined to seek another answer, having admitted: 'Not only is it incredible that the Celtic immigrants could have succeeded otherwise in entirely "dominating" the country which the Saxons had failed to penetrate in force; but it is equally incredible that the Romans could have permitted their penetration and occupation unopposed, even as far as the very borders of Gaul.'

Her answer to the problem is to accept a suggestion put forward by Professor Ferdinand Lot, that the Saxons had simply depopulated the coastal areas of Armorica and the British Celts then settled in the now uninhabited regions. This ignores the question of why the Saxons or their Frankish compatriots did not seize the opportunity of settling in the country they had depopulated, something they were doing with effective speed in Britain and Gaul. The rich coastal towns and settlements would surely have been valuable prizes. Mrs Chadwick, however, prefers this rather tenuous theory against Professor Lot's second suggestion that the British Celts settled by force. There is no evidence for either of these suggestions, but at least some evidence for the theory I proposed: that, speaking the same language and related by culture, often under the same ruler who governed on both sides of the sea, the natives accepted the new immigrants without any cultural, economic or military backlash. Their arrival might well have been seen as desirable and welcome against the attacks of the Germanic peoples such as the Saxons and Franks.

If we accept Dr Morris's plausible argument of three migrations, we will find that the Chadwick theory of settlement in uninhabited areas is even less likely. Again, we must return to our earliest authority on the migration, Gildas. And Gildas is reinforced by an eighth-century Frankish monk of Poitou, Ermald Le Noir, in a panegyric to Louis the Pious, confirming that the British had fled before the Saxons and that the people of Armorica had taken pity on the refugees from motives of humanity and because they were both Christians. He adds, however, that the Britons were not grateful and 'had made themselves supreme throughout the country'.

Again, we must bear in mind that the languages of Gaul and Britain were scarcely distinguishable from each other. Yet Abbé François Falc'hun, in his essay 'Le Breton, forme moderne du Gaulois', Annals de Bretagne, 1962, argued that the Breton language which emerged after the migrations was a form of Gaulish and was not simply an importation by the British Celts. Professor Kenneth Jackson immediately responded by arguing that the British language and culture swamped the indigenous Armorican culture. The British settlers did, indeed, rise to positions of prominence over the Armoricans.

'It is highly doubtful whether Gaulish still existed anywhere as late as the fifth century.' This is a strange slip for Professor Jackson to make because we have the evidence from Sidonius that it was only in the late fifth century that 'the leading families of Gaul' were trying to throw off 'the scurf of Celtic speech'. Clearly, Professor Jackson overlooks this evidence.

That Brittany, emerging from Armorica, began to acquire numerous British place-names does, however, suggest that the settlers did become dominant, and traditions of 'saints' of the sixth century in Brittany point to these Christian missionaries as being British in origin. Even our much maligned friend Gildas became one of the leading churchmen in Brittany. What also becomes clear is that there was constant intercourse between the British Celts and Brittany, just as there was between the British and Irish Celts. Rulers seem to continue an old Celtic tradition, demonstrated in Julius Caesar's time, of ruling kingdoms in both countries. In the *Life of St Leonorus*, we find that his kinsman was Rhiwal, who 'took possession of Little Britain and ruled jointly on both sides of the sea, and continued in that rule until his death'.

That intercourse between the Celts of Britain and Brittany continued on a close and regular basis right down to the Reformation. Particularly in Cornwall, from the lay subsidy rolls and parish registers of the early sixteenth century, we find large numbers of Bretons living in Cornwall, speaking the same language as the native Cornish. But the Reformation also brought in the decline of Cornish as well as changes in religious practice and gradually the centuries-old intercourse between Brittany and Cornwall ceased.

The sixth-century religious leaders seem to have enjoyed a principal role in the new settlements but, as Mrs Chadwick concedes, most of the religious leaders were also secular leaders and chieftains of their tribes.

Among these immigrant leaders was the abbot bishop, Samson, whose *Life* was written within half a century of his death, c.AD 565, making it by far the earliest biography of a British Celtic saint and therefore of more value than *Vitae* written many centuries afterwards. Samson, born c.AD 490, had grown up during the Arthurian period and was educated at Illtyd's school in Glamorgan. He, too, had visited Ireland, then Cornwall, before moving on to Brittany where he became the leading churchman of the British migrants and adviser to Judual, king of Domnonia (Domnonia in Brittany, not Dumnonia in Britain – though it may well be possible that he ruled the two kingdoms). He acted as emissary between Judual and Childebert I, king of the Franks. He also founded the monastery of Dol, which eventual became Brittany's premier religious centre. Judual, incidentally, was imprisoned by the famous Mark Cunomoros who was later reported as killed while fighting Clothair of the Franks.

It is of interest, though a digression, to mention another of these sixth-century British/Armorican church leaders – Meriadoc, or Meriasek as he is known in Cornwall. In Breton tradition he comes down as a bishop of Vannes. In Cornish tradition he is said to have been a Breton who was a missionary in Cornwall and is now revered as the patron saint of Camborne whose people were known as 'merry-geeks' or 'merry-jacks' until recent years. He became the hero of the only surviving example of a medieval saints' play, *Beunans Meriasek* (Life of Meriasek), written in a vernacular language. The only surviving copy was transcribed by Father Ricardus Ton (Dominus Rad. Ton) in 1504 when he was a priest at Crowan, near Camborne. It was written for a performance over two days.

In the *Lives* of the 'saints', or early Celtic churchmen, which have survived, we find that many of these churchmen-cum-chieftains moved their entire tribes to the new country. Early in the sixth century, a British chieftain called Francan fled to Brittany with his wife, three sons and all his followers. Of the sons, one – Jacut – set up a monastery near St Malo (St Jacut de la Mer), while another – Winwaloe – became one of Brittany's best-known saints, Gwennole or Guénolé.

By the middle of the sixth century there are three kingdoms distinguishable on the Armorican peninsula. The first is Domnonia on the north of the peninsula, taking its name from the British kingdom of Dumnonia, and referred to in the *Life of St Samson* as one of the first British settler kingdoms to rise to prominence. Then comes Cornouaille in the south-east, again the name Kernev arising from Kernow in Britain, and, incidentally, underscoring my argument that Cornwall was always seen as a separate kingdom from Dumnonia. Thirdly, the rest of the country to the south which was known as

Bro Érech, with its capital at Vannes. It was the ruler of this land, Waroc'h II (*c*.AD 577–94), who united Brittany, helped by attacks from the east by the Franks which caused the new kingdoms to unite to face the aggression. Gregory of Tours, bishop and historian (*c*.AD 538–*c*. 594) has much to say of Waroc'h in his *History of the Franks*. Armorica, incidentally, under the old Roman Gaulish administration, formed part of the province of Lugdunensis III, whose ecclesiastical head was the bishop of Tours. As bishop of Tours from AD 573 to 594, Gregory was well placed to know about the British settlement there. But the British settlers were reinforcing the movement for independence in Armorica and strengthening Celtic church practices as opposed to those of Rome. As may be expected, when Gregory writes about the Breton ruler, he does so with hostility. He paints Waroc'h as a violent man. But Waroc'h is merely defending his country from Frankish invasion.

Waroc'h was succeeded by his son, Canao, who defeated another Frankish army near Vannes. In AD 635 Judicael of Brittany managed to conclude a treaty with Dagobert of the Franks agreeing the political frontiers of the Breton kingdom. For over a hundred years Brittany was left to develop peacefully. But the Frankish rulers started to claim overlordship of Brittany again and commenced military action. Pépin Le Bref (the Short) attempted to invade in AD 753 but was turned back by an enthusiastic defence and not until AD 799 did Charlemagne succeed in temporarily subduing the country. In AD 818, four years after Charlemagne's death, the Bretons, under a new king, Morvan, seized the opportunity to drive the Franks out. But Louis the Pious put himself at the head of an army and invaded. He brought with him the chronicler, Ermald Le Noir, who was then able to learn at first hand the Breton traditions for the migration which he duly transcribed.

Louis's conquest was also short-lived and soon Wiomarc'h (AD 822–825) was leading Breton resistance once again. Louis led a second invasion and defeated Wiomarc'h. At this point a Breton chieftain named Nominoë persuaded the Frankish ruler to recognize him as 'duke' of Brittany on the understanding that he would govern things for the Franks. There is an old Celtic proverb: he who is not strong must be clever. Nominoë was an astute political leader. He used his time to consolidate Brittany, allowing her to recover from the years of ravages of the Franks and strengthen herself. In AD 840 came the time he had been waiting for. Louis the Pious died and his three sons started squabbling over the Frankish empire. Charles the Bald took most of France, Louis took Germany east of the Rhine and Lothar held the middle kingdom from Holland to the Rhone and further to Rome itself.

Nominoë declared Brittany independent. Charles the Bald led a large army of Franks to assert their claims. Nominoë and his Bretons met them at Ballon and on 22 November 845, the Bretons defeated the Franks. In AD 846 Charles recognized Nominoë as king of Brittany. Later French histories denigrate the title to 'duke' to justify political and cultural claims over Brittany. But in spite of Frankish plots and Norse raids, Brittany was to remain independent until the French finally defeated the Breton armies at Aubin du Cormier in 1488 and Francis II of Brittany was compelled to accept French overlordship. In 1532 France enforced the union of crowns. Brittany retained its autonomy, with its own parliament, within the French kingdom until the parliament was abolished in 1790 in the wake of the French Revolution.

Today, in spite of concerted attempts to eliminate its language and culture, Brittany remains an integral part of the Celtic world, still with some 800,000 native-speakers of Breton. No official survey of speakers of the language is allowed by the French government but this figure was estimated by *Le Monde de l'Education*, Paris, in September 1976. Brittany therefore remains the inheritor of 3000 years of a Celtic cultural continuum.

[8]

Cadwallon and Penda

Dark is Cynddylan's hall tonight
With no fire, no light.
Grieving for you overcomes me.

Anon, ninth-century Welsh

FROM the end of the sixth century and through the seventh, the British Celts had resolutely played no part in the educating and Christianizing of their enemies and must have looked askance at the activities of their cousins from Ireland. We know that there was close communication between the British and Irish Celts, particularly in ecclesiastical matters for, as bishop Dagan had informed Canterbury, they adhered to the same religious practices. British Celts went to Ireland and Irish Celts regularly came to the British territories.

In Cornwall we find sixth-century traditions of many Irish missionaries, such as Gwinear who landed with a group of followers at the mouth of the Hayle, only to be met by a local ruler named Tewdrig (Tudor) who put several of them to death. Henry Jenner has argued that Tewdrig was unlikely to be a pagan at this time but was merely resentful of foreign missionaries coming into his territory. But other Irish missionaries fared better, such as Ia (of St Ives), daughter of a Munster chieftain who won the patronage of a local ruler named Dinan. There are six inscriptions extant in Cornwall in Ogham, the first form of Irish writing, but bilingual in Latin. Five of them are near the Camel which would seem to be the main point of Irish entry. Two other inscribed stones in the Camel area are of interest because, while not in Ogham, they carry Irish names and are dated to the same period. The Irish missionaries also moved eastward into the territory of Dumnonia for at Ivybridge, south Devon, we find a sixth-century Ogham stone commemorating an Irishman named

Suaqqucos. The stone has two other inscriptions to Irishmen, Fanonus and Sagranus.

Ogham inscriptions also occur in quantity in Wales with the bulk of them, some fifty, in Pembrokeshire alone – this, significantly, being the area of the settlement of the Dési. Other inscriptions occur in Scotland and, of course, the Isle of Man. As already argued, the period of the sixth to seventh centuries was one in which the relations between the Irish and British Celts were at their closest and most continuous. Not only was there ecclesiastical interchange but there is evidence of British Celts being appointed to bishoprics in Ireland and vice versa. Aedgen the Briton, for example, is recorded as bishop of Kildare, and Colmán the Briton as abbot of Slane. There was also an interchange of political refugees and their retinues. The conclusion is that the British Celts, being in such constant communication with the Irish, surely, at some stage, would have held discussions on the efficacy of converting the Saxon enemy. One wonders exactly what the British Celts' view of the Irish experience with the Saxons was. For the British Celts, the struggle against the Saxons continued.

It was Aethelfrith who had united Deira and his own Bernicia into the single kingdom of Northumbria in AD 604. He had renewed the attack on the Celtic territories of the north, perhaps in retaliation for the raid of the Gododdin. In AD 603 he had defeated Aedán mac Gabhráin of the Dál Riada at Degastan. Not until AD 613/616 did he take his army and, moving across Celtic territory bordering Rheged and Elmet, he attacked the kingdom of Powys, arriving with his forces at Carlegion (Chester), on the River Dee, a river coincidentally dedicated to a Celtic war-goddess. The British Celts had taken up defensive positions, commanded by Selyf, son of Cynan of Powys. Cynan does not appear to have been present – perhaps he was not even alive. Cynan was eulogized by Taliesin for his military victories against the Saxons and described as a descendant of Cadell, who Nennius claimed had taken the kingship of Powys from Vortigern. Selyf, sometimes recorded as Solomon by the Saxons, and known to the Celts as 'serpent in battles', was slain by Aethelfrith. The Saxon king had opened the battle, as we have seen, by the slaughter of one thousand Celtic monks.

From the Celtic viewpoint, it was this Saxon massacre and military victory at Chester which had now brought the Saxons to the shore of the Irish Sea and effectively divided the Celts of what was to become Wales from the Celts of the north. This need not mean that communication was entirely cut off nor that the Saxons immediately occupied the land. Elmet continued to be a Celtic kingdom for at least another ten years, and as for Powys, it did not submit to Saxon conquest, for Eiludd, Selyf's brother, replaced him as king.

Edwin of Northumbria, who had now replaced Aethelfrith, resumed the attack on the British Celts in AD 625 when, according to Nennius, he annexed Elmet, defeating its last Celtic ruler, Ceredig. Elmet seems to have been quickly settled by Anglo-Saxons and once again, from their almost immediate disappearance following that annexation, we can only conjecture as to the fate of the indigenous Celtic population. Then Edwin turned on Gwynedd. Cadfan ab Iago was still king. If Edwin had indeed been fostered at his court as a youth in exile, which we find in later traditions, then it is interesting to speculate on his reasons for the attack. He may have been raised with Cadfan's own son, Cadwallon, who was to become his implacable enemy and slayer. The *Annales Cambriae* claim that it was not Paulinus who baptized Edwin but Rhun map Urien of Rheged. Edwin, it was claimed, was raised as a Christian with the Celts of Gwynedd, a tradition with which Nennius concurs. But Saxon traditions have it that it was Paulinus who converted Edwin when he married the Christian Aethelburgh of Kent. John Marsden, in his masterful account, argues that the two traditions could both have been right. Edwin could have been baptized into the Celtic Church, an event important enough to have been recorded by the Celts, but he may not have seen it as in any way significant enough to stop him from worshipping the numerous gods of his fathers. And to Paulinus's perception, Celtic Christianity was heretical anyway and he would not have recognized anyone so baptized as being other than a pagan.

In AD 625 Cadfan ab Iago, the king of Gwynedd, died. An inscribed stone from the mid-seventh century from Llangawaladr, Anglesey, commemorates Cadfan as 'wisest and most renowned of all kings'. Could his death have prompted Edwin's decision to invade Gwynedd? Bede is boastful. Edwin's 'earthly power increased until he held under his sway all the kingdoms of the Saxons and Britons in the land of Britain. A power more extensive than that of any previous Saxon king . . . he also made the Mevanian islands subject to the Saxons.' Bede goes on to identify these as the Isle of Man

(Ellan Vannin) and the island of Anglesey (Ynys Mon), both called Mona in Latin. From Anglesey, the new king of Gwynedd, Cadwallon, had been pressed back into the island of Glanauc, the tiny isle of Priestholm off the eastern tip of the island, where he was besieged by Edwin's army. According to the *Annales Cambriae* the siege broke when Cadwallon was able to seek political asylum in Ireland where he waited for an opportune moment to return to Gwynedd.

In the Welsh Triad 'Three Fettered War Bands of the Island of Britain' we find a Belyn of Llyn (the Lleyn peninsula) fighting Edwin at Bryn Edwin (Hill of Edwin) in Rhos. This must have been at about this time, either before Cadwallon was forced to seek refuge or just after he had fled. Who Belyn of Llyn was we do not know, but presumably he was a local Gwynedd chieftain.

Cadwallon was undoubtedly possessed of a keen analytical political mind and turned to the dissensions within the Saxon kingdoms as a means of help. Cwichelm, of the West Saxons, had sent an assassin, Eumer, to kill Edwin but his attack was foiled by Lilla, a thane of Edwin's who received the blow of Eumer's dagger instead of the king. The same night Edwin's wife bore him a daughter, Eanflaed. The Saxon tradition has Edwin, as a token of thanks, declaring that Northumbria would become Christian. He then made a retaliatory attack on Wessex and, according to Bede, 'there slew five kings and many of the people' in revenge. Clearly, his fellow Saxons did not like Edwin. But, in the wake of Edwin's decision, a mass baptism of Northumbrians followed his escape from the assassin's knife, with Paulinus officiating at Cataracta, in Deira, and Ad Gefrin in Bernicia. Both are British Celtic place-names. Cataracta seems to be Catraeth while Ad Gefrin, the 'hill of goats', was identified as the area of the great pre-Roman Celtic hill-fort on Yeavering Bell. This was in the most fiercely contested frontier zone between the British Celts and the Angles during the sixth century. Does the survival of the name mean that, at this time, British Celts were still in occupation here, or was it merely the name which survived? The theorists of intermarriage would claim that it meant Britons were living peacefully side by side with the Angle settlements but it is tenuous evidence for such an argument.

Cadwallon could see that Edwin had many enemies among his own people. But it was in the kingdom of Mercia that Cadwallon saw his main chance for help. Penda, son of Pybba, had become king and his power was in the ascendant. In AD 628 he had attacked the West Saxons and defeated them, annexing, as his reward, the small kingdom of the Hwicce of which Wessex claimed overlordship. This was on the the Severn with a royal residence at Gloucester. Through aggressive warfare Penda had extended the borders of Mercia to the north and Nennius claims that he did this as a means of preventing Edwin's designs for the conquest of Mercia. Nennius believes that Edwin had demonstrated his designs to annex Mercia early in Penda's reign, which might well account for his implacable dislike of Edwin.

According to Reginald of Durham, writing a *Life of Oswiu*, Cadwallon came back from 'Armorica' and conquered Penda, forcing him into an alliance. This conquest of Mercia seems unlikely and is perhaps an excuse for explaining how the Angles of Mercia came to be in an alliance with the 'mere' Celts. The British Celtic sources are explicit.

Canu Taliesin also confirms the *Annales Cambriae* in stating that the alliance began on Cadwallon's return from Ireland and was based on a mutual enmity of Edwin:

> When Cadwallon came
> Over the sea of the Irish
> He thanked the high creator.

Both Celtic and Saxon sources agree that Cadwallon had been able to raise an army from Gwynedd to attempt to wipe out the shame of his previous defeat by Edwin. The *Red Book of Hergest* says that Cadwallon 'fought . . . fourteen great battles for fairest Britain and sixty skirmishes'. Finally the British Celts and Mercian Saxons joined forces for a last battle. They met up with Edwin's army in AD 633 at Hatfield Chase. To British sources the battle was known as that of Meicen.

Edwin was defeated and slain with his son Osfrith. His army was scattered. The *Red Book of Hergest* says the battle was sited around Cefn Digoll in Powys. Whether this is another battle or a confusion of place is hard to judge. The same battle is called in a Welsh Triad 'The Three Discolourings of the Severn'.

> Cadwallon when he went to the battle of Digoll,
> The armies of the Britons with him,

> And Edwin on the other side,
> And the armies of the Saxon with him,
> And the Severn discoloured from source to mouth.

A further British source claims that Cadwallon refused to parley with 'Edwin of the great treachery' which implies that Edwin was not to be trusted in negotiations. Bede says:

> A fierce battle was fought on the plain called Haethfeld [Hatfield Chase] in which Edwin was killed; the date was the fourth of the Ides of October, in the year of our Lord 633, and Edwin was forty-eight years old. His entire army was slain or scattered. Also in this war, one of his sons, Osfrith, a warlike young man, fell before him, while the other, Eadfrith, was forced to desert to Penda, who later murdered him in contravention of an oath, during the reign of Oswald.

Victorious, Cadwallon and Penda marched into Northumbria. Bede pointed out that while Penda still worshipped Woden, Cadwallon, a Christian, 'had the temperament and character of a barbarian'. Significantly enough, Bede, relating the devastation of Northumbria which followed, is not so much concerned with the conduct of Penda and his men as with that of Cadwallon who, he says, ravaged the Northumbrians as if he meant to exterminate them. 'For a long time [he] spread havoc throughout their lands, intending to extirpate the entire Saxon race from the land of Britain.'

Following Edwin's death, his widow Aethelburgh of Kent fled with her children and loyal thanes together with the missionary Paulinus back to Kent.

The *Annals of Tigernach* have a terse record of the battle: 'The battle of Edwin . . . he was conquered by Cadwallon, king of the Britons, and Penda the Saxon.'

For Northumbria, a year of anarchy followed in which Eanfrith tried to claim the kingship only to be defeated and killed by Osric, petty king of Deira. Soon afterwards Cadwallon 'caught Osric unprepared and destroyed him and his entire army'. Cadwallon's Celtic army obviously occupied most of Northumbria and Bede says this period 'even today . . . remains an ill-omened year and hateful to all good people'.

The internal dispute about the Northumbrian succession was settled a year later and the new Northumbrian king, Oswald, son of Aethelfrith and Eanfrith's brother, met up with Cadwallon at Deniseburn. This was the period in which Irish missionaries were converting Northumbria to Christianity and we will deal with this development as a separate subject in the ensuing chapters. Oswald told Ségéne, the abbot of Iona, that before the battle, he had seen a vision of Colmcille and knew that he would be victorious. He had his entire army kneel and pray and afterwards the place was called Hefenfelth, which is Heavenfield, near Hexham. Here Cadwallon of Gwynedd was defeated and slain and his army scattered.

In Celtic record Nennius calls it the battle of Cad-y-gual (Battle of the Wall). Both Bede and Nennius agree that it was Oswald who personally slew Cadwallon. Both Adomnán and Bede agree that Oswald launched his attack at night, under which element of surprise he gained the advantage.

An early bardic poem laments Cadwallon who is celebrated as 'the most brilliant lord king' who destroyed York and was 'a man like Maelgwyn'. The *Red Book of Hergest* has an interesting comment: 'From the plotting of strangers and iniquitous monks, as the water flows from the fountain, sad and heavy will be the day for Cadwallon.' This plotting of 'strangers and iniquitous monks' is undoubtedly a comment on the role of the Irish Celtic monks of Dál Riada in supporting the enemies of the British Celts.

Cadwallon's son Cadwaladr now became king of Gwynedd but little is known about him except that in later tradition, particularly in the tenth-century poem *Armes Prydein Vawr*, he is regarded as the promised deliverer who would one day return to lead the Celt in a victorious campaign against the Saxon. In other words, Cadwaladr was seen in the same terms as later generations of Celts viewed Arthur. What did Cadwaldr do to achieve such a reputation? Nennius records that he died in the great plague of AD 664 while the Harleian annals claim he died in the lesser plague of AD 682. The only other thing known is that he endowed the church of Llangadwaladr (Cadwaladr's church) near Aberffraw on Anglesey.

To have such a subsequent reputation, Cadwaladr must have achieved some military renown in his lifetime but no record of it remains. If we may make an informed guess, it is likely that Cadwaladr continued his father's alliance with Penda for, according to Reginald of Durham, Penda had Celtic allies with him when he finally defeated and killed Oswald of Northumbria at the battle of Maserfeld (Oswestry) on 5 August AD 642. We have an interesting aside by Reginald in which he implies that Penda, after the defeat of Cadwallon, had fled to 'Armorica' (Brittany) for refuge. It seems an odd place for the Saxon king to go. 'There, Penda assembled large forces of "the heathen".' Brittany was, of course, Christian. Penda's war is recorded in both British and Irish records. It would seem more likely, from these accounts, that Oswald had made a pre-emptive strike on Mercia, driving Penda into Powys or Gwynedd. Regrouping his army, Penda struck back and achieved the victory. Maserfeld became known as Oswaldes-treow (Oswald's Tree, Oswestry) where Penda had the body hung up for display. Oswald's head was eventually retrieved by his brother, Oswiu, and taken back to Lindisfarne where it was preserved in the coffin of Cuthbert, which is why the saint is often depicted as carrying Oswald's head.

A British source gives Cynddylan ap Cyndrwyn, a chieftain of Pengwern (Shrewsbury), which was in eastern Powys, as one of the British Celtic leaders present at the defeat of Oswald. If the source is correct then we can probably date his subsequent death in a Saxon attack to the period following Penda's defeat at Winwaed in AD 655.

After Oswestry, Penda was raiding deep into Northumbrian territory and put the royal Northumbrian residence at Bamburgh to the torch. Soon after, Penda was considered Bretwalda of the southern Saxon kingdoms. His son Peada was king of the Middle Angles, another son Merewalh had formed a kingdom called the Magonsaete (parts of Hereford and Shropshire). Aethelhere of East Anglia and Aethelwold of Deira were in alliance with him and there was no demur from Wessex after he had defeated it in his earlier wars.

Penda now poised himself for a *coup de grâce* against his old Northumbrian enemy, leading a grand alliance of 'thirty legions'. Nennius brings out an important fact. Penda was accompanied by many British Celtic rulers. Cadwaladr must have been dead by the date of the battle because Nennius says Penda was accompanied by Cadafael ap Cynfedw, as king of Gwynedd. The Welsh Triads claim that Cadafael was one of three kings whose lineage was 'sprung from villeins'. Cadafael means 'battle chief' or 'battle seizer'. However, when Penda marched his army to face Oswiu at a place called Winwaed (possibly on the Went near Leeds), Cadafael decided to withdraw his British Celts on the very eve of battle, thus earning the pun in Celtic records as 'battle shirker'. At this crucial moment, Aethelwold, the petty king of Deira, who had made an alliance with Penda, also decided to stand aloof from the battle.

Penda and Aethelhere of East Anglia were killed and Oswiu of Northumbria not only achieved the victory but was recognized as the Bretwalda of all the Saxons. Additionally, Oswiu began to make inroads into the kingdom of Powys.

It has been argued that it was at this time that some of the poems associated with the name of Llywarch Hen, in reality a sixth-century British Celtic warrior from Rheged, were actually written – in particular the lament about Cynddylan's Hall. Heledd, sister of Cynddylan, laments over the Saxon invasion and destruction of her brother's territory. If Cynddylan of Pengwern was one of the Powys chiefs present at Oswald's defeat then this destruction could only have taken place during a retaliatory invasion by Oswiu after the victory at Winwaed.

> The court of Pengwern is a raging fire . . .
> The hall of Cynddylan is dark tonight
> Without fire, without bed,
> I weep a while, then fall silent.

Cynddylan has been killed, the people have been driven off the land.

> Dark of roof is Cynddylan's hall
> After the Saxon destroyed
> Cynddylan and Elfan of Powys.

With the British Celts dispossessed of Pengwern (Shrewsbury) the Saxons quickly moved into this area of eastern Powys and started their settlements. This was the time that the rich farming lands of eastern Powys were lost to the Celts.

Mercia and the land of the Middle Angles now became a province of the Northumbrian kings and remained so until Wulhere, Penda's son, came out of hiding and made himself king of Mercia. He then began to Christianize Mercia and exert his influence over his neighbours to the south. While he doesn't appear on Bede's list of Bretwaldas he was certainly strong enough to invade Northumbria in AD 674 at the head of an army drawn from all the southern kingdoms in order to check Northumbria's territorial ambitions. He was, however, defeated and died the next year.

About this time a sub-kingdom of Mercia became prominent for a while, ruled by two brothers, Eanfrith and Eanhere, and called the Hwicce. The Hwicce had become part of the Mercia overlordship after Penda had wrested it from Wessex as part of the spoils of a battle at Cirencester in AD 628. Some scholars believe that the kingdom was originally formed when the land was granted to a Bernician war band who had taken service with Mercia. However, there is no supporting evidence for this. The royal residence of the Hwicce was in the town which the British Celts had once called 'the bright and splendid place' – Glevum (Gloucester). The territory spread from Gloucestershire and incorporated Worcestershire and part of Warwickshire. Wichwood Forest is probably the only surviving memorial to the kingdom, for it transmutes from Hwiccewudu. The Hwicce accepted the overlordship of Mercia during the kingdom's comparatively short existence. Eanfrith and Eanhere, mentioned by Bede, appear to have been succeeded by a king called Osric before the end of the century.

The Hwicce were, of course, a frontier settler people, facing the British Celts to the west, across the Severn, and also to the south in Somerset which was still part of Dumnonia. Though the annals are silent, there must have been a period of continuous warfare during the Hwicce settlement as the Celts struggled to retake the lands from which they had been dispossessed.

Another son of Penda, Aethelred (AD 675–704), succeeded his brother to the kingship of Mercia in AD 675 but although he married a Northumbrian princess, Osthryth, daughter of Oswiu, relations between Mercia and Northumbria remained as bad as ever. In AD 679 Aethelred defeated his wife's brother Ecgfrith in a battle at the Trent, bringing another period of Northumbrian supremacy to an end. The Mercians still bore great enmity toward the Northumbrians. Osthryth had joined her husband in helping the Christianization of the Mercians and founding monasteries at Bardney and Lindsey. In AD 697 the Mercian *ealdormen* and thanes turned on the queen and murdered her, apparently merely because she was Northumbrian. During this time, AD 691–702, the Mercian king and his queen had given shelter to Bishop Wilfrid, driven out of Northumbria by

Aldfrith. Aethelred seems to have been one of the more peaceful Mercian kings and he eventually retired to join the religious order he had endowed at Bardney in AD 704, the place where his wife had been buried. The kingdom was left to his nephew Coenred, a son of his brother Wulfhere.

[9]

The Celtic Church

To journey to Rome
Great hardship, no gain;
The Master you seek in Rome,
You'll find at home –
Or search in vain.

Anon, ninth-century Irish

THE traditional explanation of the development of the phenomenon known as 'The Celtic Church' is that the insular Celts were cut off from Roman influence by the constrictions of the Saxon invasion and thereby evolved their own forms of Christianity. I have leaned towards this easy explanation in *Celtic Inheritance* (1985). Now, on more informed reflection of the evidence, I find I am not convinced that it was the Saxon incursions which separated the Celts from Roman influence.

Our chief sources for this period are a class of documents known as *Vitae Sanctorum* (Saints' Lives). It has become the custom to designate all the missionaries and teachers of the early Church as 'saints', a distinction showing that they were men and women of eminent virtue. The lives of these saints, written by monks, some identified and some unknown, have survived or been reworked over the centuries until late medieval times. The earliest saint's life we have is that of the sixth-century Samson of Dol, written within half a century of his death. Other *Lives* do not survive from before the ninth and tenth centuries. One interesting point arises from these lives of both Irish and British Celtic missionaries: there are numerous references to pilgrimages to Rome or attendance at Roman synods or councils during the period in which the Celtic Church was developing. Therefore, there must have been continual intercourse with Rome, and if there was such intercourse then the Celts must have been well aware of the reforms that were being undertaken in Rome and have consciously rejected them.

The development of the Celtic Church lies in the reason why this rejection took place.

The evidence is that the Christianity practised by the Celts was similar in expression to the Eastern Orthodox Church which had also begun its schism with Rome at this time. After the councils of the fourth century, the churches in the east had rejected the bishop of Rome's claim to be the leader of all Christianity as well as the infallibility of his pronouncements. Could the Celtic Church, in the extreme west, have been part of that same movement? I believe that it was.

We have dealt briefly in Chapter One with some of the differences between the Celtic Church and Rome. Let us now examine the main disparities which were to be such a 'bone of contention' during the next century. Rome looked to Simon Bar-Jonah, Christ's disciple, who was nicknamed 'The Rock' (*cephas* in Greek and *petrus* in Latin), and is more popularly known today as Peter, as the founder of the Church after Christ. The Celts, however, cited the authority of John, son of Zebedee and brother of James. Jesus confided his mother to John's care, a fact which appealed to the mother-goddess-orientated Celts, and tradition was that John was the unnamed disciple whom Jesus loved. This was the argument also put forward by the theologians of the Eastern Orthodox Church.

One visible difference between the Celtic clergy and Roman clergy at this stage was that while the Romans adopted what they described as the tonsure of St Peter, shaving the head on the crown as symbolic of the crown of thorns, the Celts used what they called the tonsure of St John, shaving a line from ear to ear. The Roman argument was that this was merely a druidic practice which had been maintained, and it was thus regarded as 'barbaric' by Rome.

The Celtic sabbath ('day of repose') was celebrated on a Saturday, the last day of the week and Jewish holy day. The Romans had now begun to observe Sunday, the *first* day of the week, as their sabbath, it being symbolic of the Resurrection. More often than not, until the seventh and eighth centuries, the services were conducted in Greek, not Latin, by the Celtic clergy. Greek was, of course, the original language of the Christian movement after its break from Judaism. Greek was the language of the Byzantine rites of the Eastern Church.

In fact, the Celtic services had much more in common with Orthodox services than with Rome. The Eucharist, bread and wine, was given by the celebrant who stood facing the altar, not behind it. The wine was given by a deacon. When the blessing was given, the Celtic priest raised the first, third and fourth fingers to represent the Trinity. The Roman priest held up thumb, first and second finger. The blessing in the Celtic Church was given before communion and the breaking of bread was at the end of the service. As in the Orthodox Church, the Celtic bishops celebrated the mass, so called by Rome from the Latin *missa* (dismissal) but called the 'offering' in the Celtic and Eastern Churches, in crowns and not in the mitres worn by Roman bishops.

The Celtic Church emphasized active participation in the worship by the people; while the deacon led the congregation in prayers, the people would respond with psalms and hymns. The deacon fulfilled an important link between priest and people. Celtic bishops were under the authority of abbots. The clergy could, of course, marry but this was not unique because it was only in the eleventh century that Rome expressly forbade its clergy to marry. Pope Leo IX (1002–1054) launched a programme of clerical reform, discouraging priests from marrying. In the Celtic world there were mixed monasteries in which the *religieux* of both sexes lived and worked. Of course, in the Eastern Church today, the clergy can still marry. Confession was not obligatory but voluntary and could be made in public or to a chosen 'soul friend'. Absolution did not follow immediately, and sometimes a penance could last some years.

The most famous difference between the Celtic Church and Rome was the dating of Easter. The rules governing the Christian calendar were originally agreed at Nicaea in AD 325 with the years reckoned from the year of the birth of Christ. Rome altered its computations during the time of Pope Leo I (AD 440–461) when the 'Alexandrian computation' was adopted in AD 444. Amendments were added by Victorius of Aquitaine during the time of Pope Hilary (AD 461–468) and more were adopted following proposals by Dionysius Exiguus during the pontificate of Felix III (IV) in AD 527. The last time Rome seriously altered the calendrical system, which now affects the entire Christian calendar, was in 1582 when Pope Gregory XIII ordained that ten days be dropped and the years ending in hundreds be leap years only if divisible by 400. The Gregorian Calendar was eventually adopted throughout the Christian world, by England in 1752, and by the Eastern Orthodox world this century.

The Celts saw the early amendments taking them further and further away from the original dates and rendering the commemorative ceremonies and anniversaries arbitrary and without meaning. Celtic computations remained those inherited from the early Council of Arles in AD 314, attended by four British Celtic bishops, and were based on the Jewish lunar calendar which allowed Easter to fall, as did the Passover, in the month of Nisan. This was the seventh and spring month of the Jewish calendar (March/April) in which the Passover fell at the full moon. Under this method, the first Easter had been on the fourteenth day of Nisan. Using this calculation, the Celts celebrated the festival on whatever Sunday fell between the fourteenth and twentieth days after the first full moon following the spring equinox. They would do this even if Easter then fell on the same day as the Passover.

The early Christians adopted the name of the Passover festival as the name for the commemoration of the death of Christ because he had been executed at that time. Paul, in his epistle to the Corinthians (5:7), had referred to Christ as their 'Passover lamb' or sacrifice. So the Christians celebrated the Jewish Passover in memory of Christ's execution and called it, in the Latin calendar, Pasca from the Hebrew Pesach (Passover). To the Celts, it became a little nonsensical when, in AD 325, the Council of Nicaea declared it unlawful to celebrate a Christian festival on the same day as a Jewish one. After all, Christ, a Jew, was known to have been executed during that particular Jewish feast. The Christian Easter then became an arbitrary date for the commemoration and not one with any relevance to the actual anniversary. Seen from this point in time, it could well be argued that the Celtic dating of Easter was far more accurate than the later reformed calculations.

If we argue that the Celts became imbued with the same ideas as the Eastern Orthodox Church, simply because these were, in fact, the original concepts of the Christian movement before the decisions of the Council of Nicaea, in AD 325, began to change the attitude of Rome, then we must also take into account another aspect – intercourse with another Celtic country which was clearly part of Eastern Orthodoxy. Galatia stood on the central plains of Asia Minor in what is today modern Turkey. The Celts, at the time of their eastern expansion in the third century BC, had established their 'Common-wealth of Galatians' and been recognized by the surrounding Hellen-ized kingdoms. Indeed, their state presents us with our first information on how a Celtic state was governed. In 25 BC Galatia had eventually been conquered and became a Roman province. But Galatia was not cut off from the rest of the Celtic world. In Ancyra, capital of Trocmi, one of the three Celtic tribes to settle Galatia, stood a monument from around AD 14 which mentions the names of two British Celtic kings. St Jerome (Eusebius Hieronymous, c.AD 342–420) visited Ancyra (Ankara) at the beginning of the fifth century and was able to report that while educated Galatians used Greek to communicate with the surrounding Hellenistic world, among themselves they still spoke Celtic and, moreover, he likened their Celtic language to that spoken by the Treverii (of Trier) in northern Gaul. Jerome knew what he was talking about, for he had lived in Trier. The Gaulish Celtic language was mutually understand-able with British Celtic.

The Galatians were the first Celts to be converted to Christianity, sometime between AD 40 and 50 when Paul of Tarsus, a city in Cilicia bordering on Galatia, visited Pessinus, the chief city of the Tolistoboii. The Galatians received a permanent place in Christian history through Paul's famous letter to them in which he reveals the reasons for his argument with Christ's disciple Peter. The Galatians subsequently developed, at least outwardly, as part of the Eastern Church; however, because of the close relationship between all parts of the Celtic world, no matter how far removed from one another, it is more than likely that travellers from Galatia were in contact with western Celts, in Gaul and in Britain, reinforcing their differ-ences with Rome. Pelagius was certainly in that part of the world during his later travels.

The argument that these differences with Rome came about through the isolation of the Celtic Church in Britain and Ireland is no longer tenable.

We have previously generally accepted the idea that the Celtic Church became isolated from Rome after the Saxon invasions. Before the Saxon invasions, the British Celts, and indeed the Irish, were well represented in Rome and were regarded as leading theologians. Likewise, the Gaulish Celtic Christians also had a tremendous influence, such as Hilary of Poitiers. Pelagius, Fastidius, Faustus,

Celestius, Ninian and others were well known in Rome. The British Celts were praised for their supportive attitude against what became known as Arian heresy. Arius of Alexandria (d.AD 336) had, following the teachings of the original Nazarene sect of Christians, propounded the doctrine that Christ was not consubstantial with God. Hilary of Poitiers, a Gaulish Celt who had written the first tract on the Trinity (c.AD 315–373), was the chief opponent of this idea and at Nicaea Arius was banished from Alexandria. Hilary was the first native Celt to become an outstanding figure in the Christian movement with *De Trinitate* regarded as his greatest contribution. As a Celt, Hilary, like Pelagius, was imbued with his own culture which had mystic traditions concerning trinity and the concept of triune gods. How much of that belief permeated his writings on the new Christian concepts?

During the time of the Saxon invasions a host of Celtic Christian missionaries were working not only among the Celtic population of Britain but also in Ireland and Gaul. Some of these were, by their traditions and dedications, people of tremendous influence in building up the Church.

Among them we find Dyfrig (Dubricius), who was born about the same time that Hengist and Horsa mutinied against Vortigern. He is said to have been born at Moccas ('moor for swine') in Hereford, founding a college there before encouraging a monastic settlement on the holy island of saints, Enlli or Caldey Island, where he died on 14 November AD 612. Later traditions have him as the bishop who ordained Arthur and founded the monastery at Llandaff.

Another famous missionary was Illtyd who, according to the *Life of Samson*, was from Armorica and came to Britain as a soldier of fortune, fighting against the Saxons in the army of Poulentius, a chieftain in the Glamorgan region. Cadoc urged him to take up religious work, into which he threw himself enthusiastically, founding Llanilltyd Fawr (Llantwit Major) and giving his name to many other dedications. His dates are given as AD 425–505 and, according to the *Life*, he was 'the most learned of all the Britons in the Old and New Testament, and in every kind of philosophy, that is geometry and rhetoric, grammar and arithmetic and in all the arts of philosophy'. He was 'by descent a most wise man, a Druid, and a fore knower of future events'. Not for the first time, an early Christian missionary was seen by the Celts as a druid, one of the pre-Christian priesthood. Among the famous pupils of Illtyd were Samson, born about AD 480, ordained by Dyfrig in AD 504, who studied at Caldey Island and then at Llanilltyd. He taught in Dumnonia, in Cornwall, and then moved on to Dol, in Brittany, where he is acknowledged as a founding father of the Breton Church.

These church leaders were in contact with Rome. And, most significantly, for my opening argument, Samson is recorded as a leading participant in the Council of Paris in AD 557. His attendance there is another of the records of communication between the Celtic and Roman Churches.

Pol Aurelian was another pupil of Illtyd, son of a local chieftain, whose *Life* was written by the monk Wrmonoc at Landévennec, working from earlier sources, and completed in AD 884. Pol Aurelian worked in Cornwall before moving on to Brittany where he became bishop of Léon. Historically, one of the most famous pupils of Illtyd was undoubtedly Gildas. But perhaps the most widely known pupil was Dewi Sant (St David), son of a chieftain of Ceredigion who also studied at Ninian's Whithorn foundation and with Finnian of Moville. He worked in Dumnonia before returning to the land of Mynyw, now St David's peninsula, Pembroke, where he founded St David's. This became a major centre of the Celtic Church while Dewi Sant has become the patron saint of Wales.

Tradition has it that Dewi Sant went on a pilgrimage to Jerusalem with a friend called Teilo around AD 540. On their return they stayed with Samson at Dol, in Brittany. The Celtic Christians were constantly travelling and at no time were they ever isolated.

Hundreds of shadowy figures of these early missionaries flit across the historical canvas of the fifth and sixth centuries but the traditions and dates are often in contention. Irish saints as well as British Celtic saints move through the country, educating and establishing churches, monastic centres and great seats of learning among the inhabitants. The monks in these monastic foundations, with their literacy in Greek, Latin and Hebrew, also became the recorders of what was, until this time, a sophisticated oral tradition by which the genealogies, histories, origin myths and sagas of the Celts had been passed down from time immemorial. Now, freed from the religious proscription of the druidic priesthood forbidding knowledge to be committed to written record, the new *religieux* set to work with enthusiasm. From this period the Celtic languages came to be written.

Apart from the early inscriptions, Irish literary survivals begin in this sixth century. There is evidence that Ireland was literate before then in the work of a Christian writer of the third or fourth century named Aethicus or Ethicus of Istria, the triangular peninsula between the Gulf of Venice and Kvarner, which was conquered by Rome in 177 BC. Aethicus wrote a Cosmography of the World (*Cosmographia Aethici Istrii*), part of which was inserted by Orosius Paulus in his *History Against the Pagans*, composed in seven books, about AD 417. It states that Aethicus left Spain and 'he hastened to Ireland and remained there some time examining their books'. He called the Irish books '*ideomochos*', implying that the literature was particular to Ireland and quite new and strange to him. Aethicus would, of course, consider anything not in the strict Greek or Latin tradition simply as 'barbaric'. As an example he speaks slightingly of Spanish works. But what sort of libraries of books was he examining in Ireland in the third or early fourth century?

In early Irish literature we hear of the Tech Screptra, the great libraries of books, many of which were destroyed during the Viking raids. And in stories such as *Baile Mac Buain* we learn of libraries holding 'rods of *fili*', books consisting of bark or wands of hazel and aspen on which histories and sagas were carved in Ogham. There are countless references to figures in Irish myth writing poetry, messages and stories on 'Ogham wands'. Could these have been the books Aethicus saw in Ireland during his visit? There is no reason why not. We have no surviving evidence but it is natural that only the stone-carved Ogham inscriptions, which we do have, would have survived rather than wands of wood. We also know that the language of the Ogham inscriptions was already an archaic form of the language when it was written.

Or could it be that the Irish had already begun to write in Greek or Latin characters by this time? The bilingual texts in Ogham and Latin show that such characters were in use certainly by the fifth century. The Continental Celts were recording their language with Greek and Latin characters in memorials by the fourth century BC, with longer texts surviving from periods soon after, such as the text written in Latin cursive on a lead tablet found in 1983 in L'Hospitalet du Larzac, Aveyron, southern France. Dr H. D. Rankin has already demonstrated that many Celts were literate at this early 'Classical' period, presumably ignoring the druidic proscriptions; in fact, they are now regarded as among the foremost of Latin writers because they chose to write in Latin as a *lingua franca* just as, in later years, insular Celts, Irish and British also chose to write in Latin as the language of scholarship.

But even accepting the date from which clear Irish literary remains survive, Calvert Watkins, Professor of Linguistics at Harvard University, has pointed out that 'Irish has the oldest vernacular literature of Europe'. He correctly points out that both Greek and Latin were used as a *lingua franca* among diverse peoples, while Irish was a *lingua materna*. Irish, certainly with the exception of Greek and Latin, is possessed of a literature which is older than that of any other European people. A wealth of manuscript books still survive, in spite of attempts at destruction by the Vikings and, later, the English. Among the references to Tech Screptra, great libraries, in Ireland, are indications that books were preserved in many languages. Had it not been for the fact that a large number of works in Greek, Latin and Hebrew were preserved in Irish libraries, then the writings of many classical scholars would have been lost by the time the Renaissance swept through Europe. Old Irish, of course, became the parent of both Scottish and Manx Gaelic as well as Middle and Modern Irish.

British Celtic literary remains also date from the sixth century, although the surviving manuscripts are from a later period. British Celtic is the parent of Welsh, Cornish and Breton, diverging from the time of the Saxon invasions. The evidence is that by the end of this century British Celtic was a flourishing literary language. The sixth-century poems we identify as 'Welsh', such as those of Taliesin and Aneirin, were, of course, composed in what is now southern Scotland in British Celtic.

Christianity had reached even the Isle of Man, called Mona by the Romans (and thus confused with Ynys Mon, or Anglesey). It would seem that the island was called after the Celtic ocean God, Manannán Mac Lir in Irish or Manawydan fab Llyr in British Celtic. The islanders had spoken the British form of Celtic until they were settled by groups moving from Ireland. In support of this theory, the stone from Knoc y Donee in Andreas is quoted in which British Celtic names are recorded. There are five Ogham inscriptions on the island. It seems most likely that Christianity was introduced through the Irish settlements and there are many place-names and dedications associated with Irish missionaries of the sixth century. There is a cult of Patrick, of Brigit, Brendan, Conchan and even Colmcille. Also, interestingly, is a cult of Ninian, preserved in the corruption of St Trinian in Marown.

Small churches or keeills (*cille* in Irish) have been found in great profusion on the island – some 200 keeill sites in all. But by the seventh century we find one monastery rising into pre-eminence: Maughold. According to tradition, Macaldus was an Irish brigand who was converted by Patrick. He was sent to the island and became its bishop, succeeding Romulus and Conindrus, of whom nothing is known. He founded his monastic settlement and this became the island's great centre of learning. From the site of the monastery comes one of the first Christian crosses found on the island, Irneit's Cross Slab, dating to the second half of the seventh century. It records the name of Irneit, who seems to have been the abbot of the monastery. The famous Calf of Man Crucifixion is dated to the sixth century. This is particularly interesting as it depicts a Celtic view of the crucifixion with Christ alive, head erect and elaborately robed as an eastern Mediterranean figure, again showing a closer similarity to the Eastern Orthodox Church than to Rome. A similar rendition of the crucifixion appears in the *Lindisfarne Gospels* of later date.

There are no literary memorials for the Manx language, as opposed to its parent Old Irish, until much later although we have no reason to suppose that the Manx were lagging behind the other Celtic peoples in setting down written records. In all probability they were either confused with Old and Middle Irish texts or destroyed by the initial ravages of the Norse who were eventually to conquer the island. The medieval Latin work known as *The Chronicle of the Kings of Man and the Isles*, from the opening rubric – '*Incipiunt cronica regum mannie & insularum & episcoporum . . .*' – dates from the twelfth century.

To return to our contention: during this time, the period when it is generally claimed that the Celtic Church was in isolation, we find numerous references to a sustained intercourse between it and Rome, even between the fledgeling Irish Church over which, according to Patrick's *Confessio*, the British Celtic bishops were claiming jurisdiction. Docco (also known as Congar) was a British Celt (AD 400–473) who is mentioned as writing the first Irish Christian liturgy. Rome was the instigator of sending Palladius to Ireland while

Patrick's work was known and approved of by Leo I (AD 440–446), which implies communication. We find Ibar, pupil of the British Celt Mocteus, who taught in Louth, arriving in Rome with three other Munster Irishmen and being consecrated bishops there in AD 460. Enda, abbot of Killeany (d. AD 530) who studied at Rosnat, identified as David's foundation in Pembroke, is reported as going to Rome with two companions, Ailbe and Puteus, travelling first to Britain and then to Rome. We find an embassy to Rome of Irish and British churchmen, led by Finnian of Clonard and Erlatheus, bishop of Armagh, at the end of the fifth century.

One interesting point emerges in view of the fact that Abingdon is now shown to have been one of the earliest Saxon settlements in Britain. Towards the end of the fifth century, perhaps during the very period of the Jutish uprising, a *Life* of an Irish monk named Aben from Leinster records that he stopped at the former Romano-British town on his way to Rome. The *Life* says, correctly, that he found, among the British, a pagan Saxon settlement and so he established a religious foundation on the 'hill of Abendoun' in which some 300 monks were gathered. Eilert Ekwall, while agreeing that the original Abingdon was on a hill (Boar's Hill), thinks the name derived from a woman's name, Abba's dun. But the *Vita Abbani* seems to be confirmed by medieval English traditions, and archaeological evidence shows a very early Saxon burial ground. The late medieval English monks of Abingdon, whose religious house had been transferred from the hill to the riverside in the seventh century, and who were inclined to give scant regard to the work of the early Irish monks, had a tradition that Aben of Ireland founded the monastery 'in the time of the British'. Aben then journeyed on to Rome.

What becomes apparent from all the sources is regular communication between British and Irish Celtic churchmen and Rome and the representatives of Rome, without break, from the fourth century through to the end of the sixth century, the period in which it was supposed that the Celts were cut off from Rome. The development of the Celtic Church was therefore due not to isolation from Rome, but to the conviction that Rome's reforms were wrong, that Rome was 'revisionist' and not adhering to the true dating of Easter. Like the Eastern Orthodox Church, the Celtic Church stuck firmly to the original computations of Arles and the earliest ritual practices. The

Celts staunchly defended those practices against the edicts of Rome as did the Orthodox Church.

It was, then, with firm conviction, and not out of ignorance or naïvety, as has been suggested, that Columbanus of Ireland was able to take on the wrath of Pope Gregory I (AD 590–604) and lecture him about his mistakes in theology and the government of the Roman Church. Columbanus spoke with the same authority which the Eastern Orthodox Church still maintains. While arguing that the Christian movement was one movement, he pointed out that the learned men of Ireland and Britain thought that the calendrical computations of Victorius of Aquitaine were a nonsense. Columbanus, significantly, adds that the Celts followed the computations of the eastern theologian, Anatolius of Laodicea, which, some scholars claim, were actually concocted in Britain around AD 490. There seems little hard evidence for this belief and the idea probably arises from attempts by Rome to denigrate the computations. But the most interesting point made by Columbanus in his letter to Pope Gregory is that he wishes the Pope to pronounce against the Roman dating of Easter and therefore implies that he accepts the Pope's authority. So, unlike the Eastern Church, the Celtic clergy were not contemplating a complete schism with Rome.

Columbanus had set up monastic settlements at Annegray, Luxeuil and Fontains. He had amazed the Frankish world by striding into the court of Thierry II of Burgundy and denouncing him for his loose living and then turning on his formidable grandmother, Brunhilde, and rebuking her for her immorality. Shortly afterwards, inevitably, the Irish monks of Luxeuil were told to leave the country. Columbanus moved on, founding new monastic settlements with growing numbers of missionaries from Ireland and Britain, and even converts from Northumbria and from the Frankish territories.

Columbanus became a prominent Christian figure in Europe, concerned not only with ecclesiastical matters but with politics and literature. He delighted in making parodies of ancient Greek and Latin writings and several examples of these survive, including a boat song most likely composed on his journey across Lake Constance.

> The wind raises blasts, wild rain-storms wreak their spite
> But ready strength of men subdues it all –
> Heave men! And let resounding echo sound our heave!

One of Columbanus's companions, Gall, who had trained at Bangor, Co. Down, decided to establish a monastery south of Lake Constance, in modern Switzerland, which still bears his name (St Gallen). The monastic settlement there became an Irish centre for many years. An Irishman named Moengal was abbot there as late as AD 850. The monastery of Gall contained a priceless collection of manuscripts written by Irish scribes, such as the eighth- or ninth-century *Gospel of St Gall* which is considered equal in its illumination to the more famous *Book of Kells*, as well as a ninth-century *Priscian Grammar* containing lyric verses in Irish in the margins. The monastery was suppressed in 1797.

Columbanus continued over the Alps to Lombardy when he established the famous monastic settlement at Bobbio in AD 612. He was to die there three years later. Bobbio continued until its suppression in 1803. The library of Bobbio became celebrated for its wealth of early Irish manuscript books, which were eventually scattered to libraries in Florence, Vienna, Paris, Milan, Turin and the Vatican.

A flood of Irish missionaries swept through Europe during these years, establishing their own monastic settlements as far east as Kiev in the Ukraine, south to Taranto in southern Italy, and north to Iceland and the Faeroes. Not only did they found monasteries, they were also appointed as bishops of towns and cities by local rulers. An Irishman became archbishop of Rheims in AD 744. They became advisers, teachers and doctors of medicine to kings and princes. Few European countries were exempt from Irish monastic foundations and influences. These foundations followed the Celtic Church traditions. From them, the Irish produced a mass of works of literature, theology and general scholarship which promoted a 'Carolingian learning'. Diciul wrote the first and best geographical study of the age – *De Mensura orbis terrae* – in AD 825, while Clemens the Irishman dedicated his *Ars Grammatica* to the emperor Lothar. But undoubtedly the most considerable scholar of this European movement was John the Irishman, known as Eriugena, an idealist, poet, mystic and philosopher writing in the late ninth century, who is considered the foremost philosopher of the western world between Augustine of Hippo and Thomas Aquinas. We shall return to Eriugena in our study of Asser in Chapter Fourteen. Some fourteen works by Eriugena have been identified, including – perhaps an inevitable work from a Celt – 'On Predestination', written *c*.AD 851, and Eriugena's most famous discourse 'Periphyseon or the Division of Nature', written in AD 864–866.

The Irish had become the foremost travellers and geographers during the 'Dark Ages'. Diciul's work was widely consulted and so was the work of his fellow Irishman, Dungal, who wrote a cosmography. Their voyages to and settlements in the Orkneys, Faeroes and Iceland are well attested, proving a knowledge of building and sailing ocean-going ships that could weather the great Atlantic storms. Native Irish literature now produced a fascinating class of tales known as the *immramma* or voyage tales: accounts of marvellous journeys of which the most famous are the voyages of Connla, Bran, Maelduin, Snedgus and Mac Ríala, Ua Corra's Sons and the Wanderings of Colmcille's Clerics. The sixth-century southern Irish abbots, Ailbe and Ibar, are reported to have sent voyagers out to seek a land to the west, the 'Land of Promise', to which the pious might emigrate. Adomnán records the explorations of Cormac Ua Liathain in the northern ocean.

Somewhat separate from the highly colourful 'fantasy' voyage tales is *Navigatio Sancti Brendani Abbatis*, The Voyage of Brendan the Navigator. The work survives from the early tenth century but it was suggested by Professor James Carney that this is a copy from a version composed around AD 800 which, in turn, comes from a much earlier source. According to Professor Carney, the story, in more primitive form, existed during Brendan's own lifetime – indeed, he came across a reference which asserted that Brendan himself wrote the original text. This surviving work was written in Latin and became extremely popular during the late Middle Ages. Some 120 Latin manuscript copies survive from the period.

Brendan was born in Kerry *c*.AD 489 and died *c*.AD 578. He had studied under bishop Erc of Kerry and under the famous Enda. He was reputed to be a traveller, attending a meeting with Colmcille in Iona, being appointed as abbot of Llancarfan in Wales, and going on to Brittany, where he tutored Malo. There are also intriguing references placing him in the northern islands, perhaps the Orkneys or Faeroes. The *Navigatio* commences with Brendan in his abbey at Clonfert being visited by a monk named Barrind who tells him that he and an abbot named Mernoc had made a long voyage to the west, discovered a land and spent fifteen days there before returning home.

Brendan picks fourteen monks and sets them to work building a boat.

The fascinating thing about the story is that it lacks the usual Irish fantasy detail and describes in technical detail how the boat was built and how Brendan and his men navigate it throughout the voyage; it describes the islands on which they land, the time taken to get there, the tides and experiences which bring them to the land in the west. Did the Irish, who certainly reached Iceland before the Norse, also journey on to reach America centuries before Leif Eriksson in AD 1000? Intrigued by the wealth of technical references in the work, Tim Severin organized a team to build a ship, based on the technical details from the manuscripts, and set sail from the west coast of Ireland on 17 May 1976. He followed the details of the journey carefully, travelling through the Hebrides, the Faeroes and on to Iceland, and then towards Greenland, across the Davis Strait, finally landing on the coast of Newfoundland on 26 June 1978. Severin proved that the voyage *could* have taken place as the manuscript recounted, given the Irish knowledge of ship-building and navigation at the time.

I think it is an excusable diversion out of our period to mention that not only the Irish have a claim to have reached the American continent before the Genoese, Christopher Columbus, in 1492. Leif Eriksson's Vinland voyage in AD 1000 is attested to in Norse saga literature. However, there is a second Celtic claim, this time from Wales. Tradition has it that Madog, or Madoc, son of Owain ruler of Gwynedd in the mid-twelfth century, went on an expedition and landed on the American coastline in about 1170. The story is that Madog and his followers settled and intermarried with the Mandan Indians of the upper Missouri area. The story of Madog was very popular in the Elizabethan age although no conclusive contemporary proof has been offered. It was seriously examined in 1967 by Richard Deacon, who made a comparison of Mandan words and Welsh, finding numerous similarities (*Madoc and the Discovery of America*, pp. 228–9). Professor Gwyn Alf Williams examined the story and its sources with a more studied and analytical eye in *Madog: the Making of a Myth*, 1979. Nevertheless, the Madog legend was so firmly believed in the 1790s that the 'Daughters of the Revolution' raised a monument to his landing.

If the Irish monks were able to make voyages across the Atlantic, and we know they already had religious settlements in the Faeroes and Iceland by the beginning of the eighth century, a hundred years before the Norse settlements, then their journeys through Europe and their numerous religious establishments were merely child's play by comparison.

But the days of the Celtic Order of Christianity were numbered in Europe. Almost predictably, it was a Saxon convert who became known as the 'hammer of the Celtic Church'. Wynfryth was a West Saxon, born about AD 675. His birthplace, given as Crediton, is suspect, for it places Crediton, a few miles north-west of Exeter, in the hands of the Saxons over forty years before they reached Exeter and defeated Geraint of Dumnonia. Whether he was converted by Celtic monks or by missionaries from Rome, Wynfryth took to the religious life and changed his name to Boniface. He became ardently pro-Roman and in AD 718 he was in Rome receiving a commission from Pope Gregory II to work among the Germans. Ironically, it is Boniface who has become known as the 'apostle of Germany' despite the numerous and influential Irish missionaries who were working among the Germans before him.

Boniface was concerned at the extent and influence of the Christian Celts in Europe. He urged the Frankish king Pépin Le Bref to suppress the Celtic foundations and expel the Irish missionaries. His most famous conflict was with Fearghal, otherwise known as Virgil of Salzburg (d. AD 784), who had left his monastery at Aghaboe in AD 740 to become part of the Irish *peregrinatio pro Christo*. Boniface twice complained about Fearghal to Rome, angered by his adherence to the Celtic rituals. On the first occasion the Pope, Zacharias (AD 741–752) supported Fearghal. Undaunted, Boniface tried again to remove the Celt by denouncing Fearghal's works on cosmology which the Pope was reported to have found 'shocking'. However, it is far from certain what Fearghal's speculations were and he was afterwards consecrated a bishop of Salzburg at the insistence of Pope Paul I in AD 767. At Salzburg, Fearghal, as Virgil, was venerated and he was subsequently canonized by Pope Gregory IX in 1233. It would seem that Boniface was a prisoner of his cultural dislike of things Celtic coupled with the belief that Bavaria was his personal fiefdom. One of his complaints was that Fearghal was sowing hatred between Odilo, the king of Bavaria, and himself.

In AD 754 Boniface was attacked by brigands when on a journey

in Dokkum, modern Holland, and was slain. His extensive correspondence is one of the sources of the history for this period. One
letter to Cuthbert, archbishop of Canterbury, gives a fascinating
social comment on the time. Boniface asked that Cuthbert should
'forbid English matrons and nuns to make pilgrimages to Rome.
Many of them die, and few keep their virtue. In most towns of
Lombardy and Gaul, most of the whores are English. It is a scandal
and disgrace to the English Church.'

While it would take an entire book to study the extent and influence of the work of Irish missionaries in Europe during this period,
that extent and influence are important when considering the role of
Irish missionaries among the Saxon kingdoms. Their work through
the Saxon kingdoms must be seen as part of that great *peregrinatio
pro Christo* which seized the Irish missionaries at the end of the sixth
century and early in the seventh, a movement which can be said to
have continued unabated, even after the Anglo-Norman and subsequent English conquests.

At the end of the sixth century, the Irish missionaries stood ready
to tackle what was to prove the thankless task of converting and
educating the Saxon kingdoms.

The Conversion of the Saxons

So Oswald sent to the Irish elders, among whom he and his family had received the sacrament of baptism when in exile, and asked them to send him a bishop, who would teach and minister to the English people that he ruled so that they might learn the blessings of the Faith.

Bede,
Historia Ecclesiastica Gentis Anglorum

WHEN the Jutes, Angles and Saxons began their landings in Britain, and made their settlements, they were pagans and illiterate. They obviously had some oral traditions of their history and beliefs for when, after being Christianized, they began to write their origin myths, they traced themselves back to a hero called Sceaf – but later Christian influence caused him to be born in Noah's Ark. According to the *Anglo-Saxon Chronicle, 'se waes gebren on thaere earce Noés.'* He left the ark and floated in an open boat which was eventually washed up on the shores of Scandia (Scandinavia) and there the Angles, with their cousins the Saxons, developed.

They worshipped a pantheon of gods: Woden (the equivalent to the Norse Odin) was the chief god and he proliferates in English place-names. Other place-names refer to Grim, and Grimr was another name applied to a certain aspect of Woden when he was wearing a hood. They worshipped Thunor (equivalent to the Norse Thor), the god of thunder, whose memory is also to be found in numerous place-names. The god Tiw, the god of the sky, is remembered and Frig, mother of gods and men – a Mother Earth figure. Two more goddesses represented aspects of Mother Nature – Hretha and Eostre – probably in her youth and in her vernal guises. And there were several other gods, such as Seaxneat, whose function we do not know. Place-names incorporating words such as *ealh* (temple), *hearh* or *hearg* (sanctuary), *weoh* (idol, shrine, sacred spot) are found in many parts – *ealh* as in Alkham, Kent, *hearh* (Harrow on the Hill), and *weoh* most widely distributed in places like Wheely Down (Hants), Weedon (Bucks), Weeford (Staffs) and Wyham (Lincolnshire).

Like their Norse cousins, the Anglo-Saxons probably believed in a selective afterlife: an afterlife only for those who died heroically, weapons in hand, in battle. Above all, they constituted a warrior society and so they believed in Waelheall (the Norse Valhöll or Valhalla) to which, according to a reference in a tenth-century text, the warrior heroes would be borne by a *waelcyrge* (Norse – *valkyrja* or Valkyrie).

Following their conversion to Christianity, the Saxons clung to remnants of their old pagan gods, so that the festival celebrating the resurrection of Christ was named Easter after the goddess Eostre whose festival was held at the spring equinox. The Celts had, of course, adopted the Roman form *Pasca*, which word remains in their languages: *Y Pasg* (Welsh) and *Cáisch* (Irish). (In the latter form we must remember the Goidelic change of P into Q.) Similarly, the Saxons rejected the Latin names of the weekdays, which the Celts had also accepted, and they used the names of their former gods such as Tiw (Tuesday), Woden (Wednesday), Thunor (Thursday) and Frig (Friday).

While, in later times, history being written from the perception of the conqueror, the Celts become uncivilized and warlike, the reality is that the violent tenor of Anglo-Saxon life was horrific in comparison with Celtic society. Although we have already touched on this aspect, it is wise to underscore what the Anglo-Saxon scholar, Dr Page, sees as a matter of prime importance in understanding Saxon society. When the Saxons were not at war with the Celts, they were constantly clashing with each other. Murder of kings, slaughter of entire populations, burning of fortresses, villages and settlements and general brutality marked the early Saxon way of life. This is not to suggest that Celtic society was purely peaceful or that in Saxon society all one could expect was sudden death. But the Saxons lived in closer contact with violence; blood feuds were an established feature of everyday life, as were the death penalty and a variety of mutilations of the body.

Even after the Saxons were converted to Christianity, prescribed punishments for certain trespasses were the cutting off of hands, feet, nose, ears, upper lip or tongue, blinding, castration and scalping, not to mention branding and scourging. It is fascinating that scalping occurs in early Saxon society as a punishment. During the seventeenth-century Cromwellian conquest of Ireland, English soldiers were given a reward of five pounds for the head of an Irish rebel. Because heads weighed heavily, most soldiers brought in scalps. The method was transferred soon after to the English colonies in America where the native Americans (Indians), thinking that scalping bore some deep religious symbolism for the white man and anxious for their own spiritual development, adopted it. Again, as the conquerors write history, so now the American Indians are blamed for the origination of scalping! The Saxons also offered execution by means of hanging, beheading, stoning, burning, drowning and the breaking of the neck. Christian Saxons preferred mutilations for, while the sinner lived and suffered, in their eyes, the soul was given time to repent.

By comparison, the death penalty was carried out in Celtic society only in extreme cases. Banishment or imprisonment on some lonely island were options but the main concept of all Celtic law was that punishment involved compensation and loss of what we would today call civil rights. In the Celtic order of things, taking the Brehon law system as our example, there were six basic social categories or 'classes' but it was possible for a person to rise from the lowest order of society to the highest, and likewise to fall. At the bottom of Celtic society was a group which many commentators have called 'slaves' but it is wrong to attempt to find an analogy in the feudal order of things. 'Non-freemen' is a better translation. This class was subdivided into three. The lowest were cowards, who had deserted their people in time of war, prisoners of war and hostages. Also within this group were the habitual law-breakers. It is interesting to compare the Celtic punishment of placing a criminal in this class with the recent example in French law where a penalty of civil degradation was passed by the Chambre Civique, that is a loss of civil rights. For a criminal to wind up in this 'non-freeman' group simply meant that he had lost his rights, was prohibited to practise any craft or profession or rise to any rank in society, and had no voice at the tribal assembly. In comparison with the pagan Saxons, and, indeed, the Christian Saxons, Celtic society was effectively humane, preferring to prevent the offender from taking a full part in society until he had redeemed himself by making a contribution to the community. Should he not be able to redeem himself and die a 'non-freeman', then it was up to his offspring to make the redemption. However, the third generation was automatically freed with full citizenship.

We have already discussed the comparative class structure among the Saxons in Chapter Three.

Another important comparison between Celtic and Saxon society was that, as with most other societies, the Saxons often put to death the sick, handicapped and elderly. Indeed, even in such civilizations as those of Egypt, Assyria, Babylonia, Greece and Rome, there was little provision for the ailing poor. Only in the fourth century did St Fabiola (d. AD 399) found a hospice for the sick and needy in Porto, near Rome. In Celtic society, however, there was a long tradition of hospitals and medical practice which were open, free of charge, to everyone in society, with the inclusion of the payment of 'sick maintenance' to those whose sickness prevented them from supporting their families. So not only was everyone in Celtic society assured of treatment and hospitalization, but society would not let them or their dependants lack food or means of livelihood. In Ireland, this practice was particularly prevalent, and Irish physicians, during the period under discussion, were acclaimed throughout Europe. Europeans found it prestigious to go to Ireland to train in Irish medical schools. The most acclaimed school of medicine during this period was that founded by Bracan Mac Findloga at Tuaim Brecain (Tomregan), Co. Cavan, in the fifth century. In AD 860 we find the death recorded of one of its professors, Maelodar Ó Tinnri, 'the best physician in Ireland and beyond'. Irish physicians continued to be highly regarded throughout Europe down to the time of the English conquest of the seventeenth century. Jan Baptiste, Baron Van Helmont of Vilvoorde (1580–1644), the famous chemist, physiologist and physician, wrote that Irish medical men were considered far better than any others in Europe in their knowledge and training. The oldest surviving Irish medical textbooks date from the early fourteenth century and they constitute the largest collection of medical manuscript literature, prior to 1800, surviving in any one language. Both the Irish Brehon laws and the Welsh laws of Hywel Dda are very explicit on medical practices.

Interestingly, we find that the story of the origin of the *Book of the O'Lees* (a medical text written in 1443, in forms resembling the pattern of astrological figures) is similar to a Welsh tale. The book was said to have been given to O'Lee by Otherworld folk from Hy-Brasil. In Welsh myth, the Meddygon Meddfai are also given an Otherworld book of medical knowledge and thus become the greatest physicians in Wales.

In these different social attitudes between Celt and Saxon we see another basis for mutual antagonism. War to the Saxon was a way of life for the warrior class, war to the Celt was undertaken in defence or for retribution of a wrong by a neighbouring people. With any war against fellow Celts, the conflict was often a bloodless one, for both peoples, believing in the same symbolism, could undertake symbolic raids. For example, sacred trees were talismans of all tribes and clans. A tree would stand in the centre of a territory and a tribal raid by a rival clan would simply be for the purpose of destroying the tree and thus demoralizing the enemy. Not so with the Saxons, who would not only destroy the warriors but the entire village settlement including its women and children.

As a result of the viciousness of this type of warfare, Adomnán (*c.*AD 624–704), the former abbot of Iona and confidant of the kings of both Celts and Saxons, brought forward a 'Law of Innocents' which was designed to protect non-combatants – the elderly, women and children and clergy – from the savagery of the Saxon type of total warfare. The 'Law of Innocents' was promulgated at the Synod of Birr, in Ireland, in AD 697, and witnessed by fifty-one kings and provincial rulers as well as forty leading churchmen. It was made binding throughout the Celtic realms. Alas, this earliest form of a 'Geneva Convention' was not generally recognized among the Saxons.

Dr Page in *Life in Anglo-Saxon England* comments on the conditions in Saxon society: 'It is not surprising that the life of Anglo-Saxon man, often poor, nasty and brutish, was often also short.'

Not only was there a military clash, then, between the Celt and Saxon, as between any group of aggressive invaders and the natives they seek to dispossess, but there was a cultural clash and nowhere was this more evident than in the religious differences between the two peoples. There is an irony when Bede, writing in his *Historia Ecclesiastica gentis Anglorum*, in AD 731, echoes Augustine of Canterbury's criticism of the British Celts for making no attempt to convert the Angles and Saxons to Christianity when they invaded Britain. How do you convert a people who are attempting to annihilate you? The Saxons were out to dispossess and drive out the Celts. The Celts were, therefore, in no mood to argue the finer points of religious theology with them.

During the pontificate of Benedict I (AD 574–578) the fact that the Saxons were pagan caused concern in Rome and it was decided that a monk from the monastery of St Andrew's, on the Coelian Hill, Rome, should be sent to the lands of the Saxon in Britain. The monk's name was Gregory. However, before the mission could get underway, more urgent matters arose and Gregory was appointed papal agent to Constantinople. Then in AD 590 Gregory himself was elected as Pope. As we have discussed, he appointed Augustine to take a mission to the Saxons.

While Augustine and his missionaries did have some degree of initial success among the Saxons, it was not lasting. Augustine's autocratic and pro-Saxon attitude, when calling upon the British Celts to help him in the work of conversion, caused no dialogue at all to arise between the Celtic Christian bishops and Augustine's missionary group from Italy. While the Saxons continued slaughtering Celtic monks, such as the massacre of a thousand of them at Chester in AD 616, there was little hope of British Celtic missionaries attempting to preach among the Saxons. And their attitude seemed justified when the Saxon kingdoms threw out some of Augustine's missionaries and resorted to the former gods.

However, the Irish Celts had not suffered from contact with the Saxons in the way their British cousins had. They were more inclined to be open-minded and in AD 610 Dagan, bishop of Inverdaoile, Wexford, was authorized by the Irish bishops to visit Canterbury and have discussions with Augustine's successor, Laurentius, who, on the death of Augustine, had become archbishop of Canterbury and head of the mission to the Saxon kingdoms. Dagan was one of the leading churchmen of Ireland. He had already visited Rome and taken the monastic Rule of St Molua to Pope Gregory (about AD 604) for his approval. Dagan wanted genuine discussions with Laurentius on the differences between the Celtic Church and the Roman practices now established at Canterbury. Reading between the lines, we find the Irish bishop was much upset by Laurentius's superior attitude towards the Celts and, during the discussions, he appears to have walked out, even refusing Laurentius's hospitality. Bede quotes a letter sent by a furious Laurentius to the Irish bishops. From it we hear that 'the Irish in no way differ from the Britons in observance'. Laurentius also confesses in this that the mission from Rome had come 'to this island, which is called Britain, without possessing any previous knowledge of its inhabitants'. When they found that the British Celts followed customs which were dissimilar to those of Rome they obviously decided that they were heretics and now found the Irish to be the same. At the same time, Laurentius makes it clear in his letter that he knew of Columbanus's arguments on theology and practice with Pope Gregory.

A few years after this first clash between the Irish bishops and the Roman missionaries at Canterbury, the Saxons began to revert to paganism, rising up and turning on the missionaries. Both Mellitus and Justus fled the country. Laurentius was on the verge of flight but decided to stay on and managed eventually to convert Eadbald of Kent. Paulinus, who had been a member of the second mission to arrive in Kent in AD 601 to help Augustine, had also remained in Kent.

In Northumbria the former deposed prince Edwin had toppled the usurper, Aethelfrith, driving his sons into exile, reportedly 'in Ireland', although more probably, from subsequent events, in the kingdom of Dàl Riada and the island of Iona. In AD 625 Edwin decided to remarry and a political marriage was arranged with Aethelburgh, the sister of Eadbald of Kent. Aethelburgh was now a Christian and Paulinus was her personal chaplain. When the bridal party set out on the journey north, Paulinus went with it, not only to act as Aethelburgh's chaplain but to attempt to bring Christianity to Northumbria. According to Bede, he did so, converting Edwin and then building the first Saxon church at York.

Yeavering was the royal residence where Paulinus baptized his converts in the River Glen. Edwin became a hero to Bede, our first English historian, and became venerated as a Christian saint, presiding, according to Bede, over a 'Northumbrian Golden Age'. His daughter Eanflaed became abbess at Whitby to which she took her father's remains after he was slain.

To the British Celts, and, indeed, many of his fellow Saxons, Edwin was simply a power-hungry and ruthless warlord. We have discussed his campaigns against the Celts as well as the fact that he may already have been converted to Christianity while growing up in exile in Gwynedd.

Edwin was killed in AD 633, by which time Paulinus was regarded as bishop of Northumbria, working in Bernicia in the north as well as Deira in the south. Edwin's enemies were numerous and in AD 633 the Mercian ruler, Penda, had made an alliance with the British Celts, specifically with Cadwallon of Gwynedd, to destroy him. Together they launched an attack on Northumbria and defeated Edwin, who was slain at the battle of Hatfield Chase. With Edwin's death, his widow, Aethelburgh, and her children fled for safety back to Kent. With her went Paulinus, giving up his missionary work among the Northumbrians. Obviously, in Paulinus's perception, the safety of the temporal rulers was more important than continued preaching of heavenly rulers. Was there a return to paganism now that the Christian king, Edwin, was dead? Bede glosses over this question. Paulinus, on his safe arrival in Kent, became bishop of Rochester and lived there until his death in AD 644.

Eanfrith, son of Aethelfrith whom Edwin had deposed, now returned from exile and attempted to seize power in Bernicia only to be slain by a relative of Edwin called Osric, a petty king of Deira. A year later, Eanfrith's brother, Oswald, seized power. Oswald, it is reported, had been baptized a Christian among the Irish – presumably by the monks of Iona. Oswald was immediately put under pressure by Cadwallon of Gwynedd but defeated him. We have discussed the political aspects of this conflict in Chapter Eight. Oswald, now firmly in control of Northumbria and, according to Bede, regarded as the Bretwalda of the Saxons, saw that he was the Christian ruler of a non-Christian people. Oswald, with his brothers and sister, spoke Irish fluently and he had been brought up in the Celtic Church, so it was to Iona that he turned rather than to the precariously surviving Roman mission at Canterbury. Canterbury was a small and isolated voice among the Saxon kingdoms who were still mostly pagan. Moreover, in Oswald's eyes, Canterbury was in the territory which had given refuge to the relatives of his former enemy, Edwin. Oswald now made his most important decision, according to Bede, and that was to send to Iona for Celtic missionaries to teach in Northumbria.

The abbot of Colmcille's famous foundation on I-Shona, the holy island, was Ségéne. He was the first abbot not to have served as a monk during Colmcille's lifetime but he was a close kinsman and nephew of Laisran, the third abbot, and he was to play a central part in transmitting the oral traditions of Colmcille to Adomnán who wrote a *Life* of the saint. Ségéne had known Oswald during his exile on Iona and is recorded as listening to Oswald recount how he had seen a vision of Colmcille just before the battle with Cadwallon at Hexham in AD 634. This means that he met the Northumbrian king again sometime between that date and AD 642 when Oswald died.

Ségéne and his monks held strictly to Celtic custom and after being pressed by an Irish monk, Cummian, to abandon the Celtic dating of Easter in favour of Roman computations, Ségéne wrote to Pope Severinus (AD 640) to explain his reasons. By the time the letter reached Rome, Severinus had died but John IV, Pope-elect, succeeding Severinus in August AD 640, replied. But the monks of Iona stuck firmly to their liturgy and practice. Iona now had established sub-houses on Rathlin and in many other parts of the Celtic world and was emerging as an authoritative centre of the Celtic Church. It was around AD 635 that Oswald of Northumbria requested Ségéne to send a mission to his people.

Ségéne sent a monk named Colmán who, after a short stay, withdrew, reporting that the mission was too difficult. Colmán, according to Bede, was a man of stern temperament. 'Although he preached among the English for some time he met with no success, and the people were unwilling to listen to him. He therefore returned home and announced at a meeting of the elders that he had been able to make no headway in teaching the people to which he had been sent, for they were an intractable people of stubborn and uncivilized character.'

Colmán was replaced by Aidan mac Lughar, who was a prominent churchman and a more imposing person than Bede paints. He established his church near the royal court of Bamburgh, on an island he called Inis Medcoit. This was Lindisfarne which had been named, according to Bede, after a settlement of people from Lindsey. Lindisfarne was an ideal site, cut off from the mainland by high tide, and therefore a safe haven for the missionaries among the pagans. Aidan appears very efficient. He chose twelve people as his disciples, after the Celtic fashion. Among them, demonstrating the equality of male and female in Celtic society, he chose Aebbe, the half-sister of Oswald, who had been raised at Iona and spoke Irish, and Oswald's own daughter Elfleda, who also spoke Irish and was raised among the Christians of Dál Riada. But his most famous female disciple was Hild (AD 614–680), sometimes referred to as Hilda. It seems that Hild and her sister Hereswith had originally been baptized by Paulinus, according to Bede. Hereswith had married a brother of Anna, king of East Anglia, and borne him a son who was to be the future king Ealdwulf. She then entered a Frankish monastery at Chelles. Hild was going to join her but Aidan persuaded her to join him and become abbess of Hartlepool. In AD 657 she moved to Streoneshalh (Whitby). In AD 664, when the Synod at her abbey decided to follow Roman custom, she accepted its decision although she tended to Celtic usage throughout the rest of her life. A famous son of Whitby was Caedmon, now acclaimed as the first Saxon religious poet.

Aidan began to have success. He was not able, at first, to speak Saxon, and so relied on those of his followers who did as well as on Oswald himself. According to Bede:

In all matters Oswald listened humbly and joyfully to the bishop's advice, and showed great concern to build up and extend the Church of Christ within his kingdom. The bishop was not fully conversant with the English language, and on many occasions it was delightful to watch while he preached the gospel, and the king himself, having acquired a perfect knowledge of Irish during his long exile, acted as interpreter of heaven's word for his *ealdormen* and thanes.

Oswald also brought Christianity to Wessex by marrying again, this time to Cynegburga, daughter of the Wessex king Cynglis. Oswald, having also defeated Cynglis in battle, insisted that a condition of the peace should be that he accept Christianity; Oswald became his godfather. Cynglis was now the first Christian ruler of Wessex. Aidan sent missionaries to instruct the Wessex king in the new faith. According to Bede:

From that time many missionaries from Ireland began to arrive, who preached the word of the faith with great zeal to the English kingdoms ruled over by Oswald, and to those who believed, such of them as held the rank of priest, administered the grace of baptism. Churches were built in various places, and the people gladly flocked together to hear the word. By the gift of the king, estates and lands were granted for the establishment of monasteries, and English boys together with their elders were given systematic instruction by Irish teachers and taught to observe the disciple of a Rule.

When Oswald was slain in battle in AD 642, Aidan was deeply affected but the Northumbrian successor, Oswiu, Oswald's brother, continued the Celtic Christianization policy.

Aidan died in AD 651 and was replaced as bishop to the Northumbrians by Finán who had been one of Aidan's companions from Iona. Finán was a highly active missionary. He baptized Peada, king of the Middle Angles, before he married Alhflaed, Oswiu's daughter. He then sent Cedd, a Northumbrian convert, to preach to the Mercians with two other Northumbrians, Adda and Betti, plus an Irishman named Diuma. Cedd and his companions moved on while the Irishman, Diuma, became first bishop of the Mercians in AD 655. Cedd established missions not only in the land of the Middle Angles but in the land of the East Saxons, founding communities at Tilbury, Bradwell-on-Sea and St Peters-on-the-Wall.

There now occurred some dissension within the Celtic Church: a monk called Ronan 'who, though Irish by race, had learned the true rules of the church in Gaul and Italy', says Bede, urged Finán to accept the Roman method of calculating Easter. Finán was as fierce in his defence of Celtic custom as had been Ségéne. When Finán died in AD 661 he was succeeded by Colmán. This was not the same Colmán as had originally been sent to Northumbria. The name was a popular one as is illustrated from the *Life of St Carthage* (Cathach Mochuda of Lismore, d. AD 637). This recounts that a score of Irish monks were working by a stream when one cried, 'Colmán, get into the water!' Twelve monks jumped in.

Colmán had been dispatched from Iona on the death of Finán by the abbot Cumméne Find (AD 657–69). Cumméne Find was a leading Celtic theologian and had written a book, which only survives in passages, on the miraculous powers of St Colmcille, in which he defended Celtic liturgical practices. Colmán was also a staunch defender of the Celtic system. The dispute between Celtic and Roman practice was growing in Northumbria.

The catalyst for the confrontation between Celt and Saxon on religious matters was to be Wilfrid, born in AD 633 of a noble Northumbrian family, and educated under Aidan on Lindisfarne. Wilfrid decided to visit Canterbury and spent a year there before travelling on to Rome. But at Lyons he left his travelling companions and stayed in the house of Aunemunduss, the bishop of Lyons. He was there for three years before proceeding to Rome. By the time of his return to Northumbria he was fully converted to the Roman rites and practices but he was not ordained as a priest. He therefore gained the support and friendship of the petty king of Deira, Alhfrith (AD 655–664), who gave him the monastery at Ripon. Eata, then abbot of Melrose, and his assistant, Cuthbert, had been sent to establish the monastery but, because they held to the Celtic custom, Alhfrith sent them away. But the new abbot, Wilfrid, was not an ordained priest. So Alhfrith also arranged for Wilfrid's ordination by Agilbert, a Frank who had been preaching in Wessex. Wilfrid now emerged as the main spokesman of the opposition to the Celtic liturgy. Those that supported the Roman system quickly rallied around him.

In AD 644 the Irish Celtic Church missionaries were at the height of their influence among the Saxon kingdoms. However, the end was in sight. Wilfrid and his pro-Roman supporters had convinced Oswiu the Northumbrian king that a special council should be held to debate the matter once and for all. The advocates of both Celtic and Roman order would come together at Hild's abbey at Whitby and argue their case. The main debate was between Colmán, on behalf of the Celtic practices, and Wilfrid, on behalf of Rome.

The debate narrowed down to one focal point – did Rome have greater authority than Iona or any other Christian centre? Wilfrid's argument was that the Gospel of Matthew, 16 v.17, unequivocally stated that Peter would build Christ's Church and have the keys to the gates of heaven. According to tradition, Peter had died in Rome and therefore all Christians should look to Rome as their centre.

Colmán was unable to refute the Biblical passage, nor did he argue the tenuousness of the evidence that Peter was ever in Rome or point to Paul's letter to the Galatians which clearly described the quarrel between Paul and Peter, showing that the Church in Rome and its theology were the result of Paul's work rather than that of Peter. Instead, Colmán merely pointed out that the Celtic Church took its authority from John, the disciple to whom Christ entrusted the safety of his mother and family, the emphasis being on the 'family', for were they not all the family of Christ? John, therefore, was their protector and mentor. Oswiu, acting as sole judge, eventually delivered his decision. If Peter had been told by Jesus that he would be the builder of the Church and hold the keys to the gates of heaven then it was Peter who had the greater authority and was the person whom Christians must obey. Peter, according to Roman claims, had died in Rome; this was accepted by all Christians and, indeed, a church dedicated to him had been founded there. Christians had to follow where Rome led. Henceforth, in Northumbria, the rule of Rome would apply.

Colmán was unable to accept continuation in the office of bishop of Northumbria under such conditions. He led the monks of Lindisfarne, and those other Northumbrian foundations who supported the Celtic order, both Celt and Saxon, back to Iona and eventually from there to Ireland where he founded a settlement on the island of Inishboffin, off the west coast of Mayo. In one of those ironies of history, a thousand years later, Oliver Cromwell attempted to imprison all Irish priests on Inishboffin, little realizing that Saxon monks had once sought shelter there. Conditions on the island were harsh and eventually Colmán's followers were resettled on the mainland of Mayo which was referred to by the Irish, because of this, as 'Mayo of the Saxons'.

Among those Celtic-trained monks who decided to adopt the Roman customs was Cuthbert, who had trained at the monastery of Melrose (Moel Ros, the bare promontory), whose prior was an Irishman named Boisil. In fact, Cuthbert's initial adherence to Celtic custom had created a mystery about his background. Two traditions survive. One tradition has it that he was a Northumbrian who was converted as a boy during the time of Finán. The second tradition is that Cuthbert, despite his name, was an Irishman, born at Kells, originally named Mo-Uallog, and was descended from a High King, Muirchertach Mac Ercae Maic Eogain (c.AD 507–536). He had first joined the monks of Iona before being sent to Northumbria and Melrose.

Cuthbert is certainly known to have travelled widely, preaching to the Strathclyde Britons as well as to the Northumbrians. When Boisil died he became prior of Melrose.

After Whitby, both he and Eata agreed to follow Roman custom and when Eata was made abbot of Lindisfarne, succeeding an Irishman named Tuda, who had also agreed to follow Roman rule, Cuthbert accompanied him as his prior. From AD 676 to 685 he became a hermit on the Inner Farne, but then he was asked to be bishop of Hexham. Cuthbert did not want to go, so Eata decided to allow Cuthbert to be abbot of Lindisfarne while he himself went to Hexham. But two years later Cuthbert resigned to continue life as a hermit. He died on the Inner Farne in 687. It was only twelve years after his death that a cult rapidly developed when it was said that his body was found to be incorrupted. *Lives* were quickly composed, including two by Bede, one in verse and one in prose.

After the council at Whitby, Wilfrid had been chosen as Northumbrian bishop, with his see at York, in acknowledgement of his being advocate for the winning side. However Oswiu, in spite of his judgement at Whitby, was still pro-Celtic, and shortly afterwards decided to take the opportunity of Wilfrid's temporary absence in Gaul to appoint Chad as his bishop. Theodore, the new archbishop of Canterbury and a friend of Wilfrid's, had just arrived to take office and deposed Chad, confirming Wilfrid as bishop. But Theodore, a Greek from Tarsus and therefore a neighbour of the Galatian Celts, began to feel a sympathy for the Celtic point of view. At a Synod of Hertford in AD 673 he drew up ten rules designed to form a meeting ground for the two schools of thought, but nothing came of the attempt to repair relations.

Oswiu died in AD 670 and his son Ecgfrith succeeded him. Almost immediately Ecgfrith quarrelled openly with Wilfrid and chased him from the kingdom. Eata now became bishop of Northumbria. This time Theodore did not interfere to reinstate Wilfrid.

While popular history sees the Synod of Whitby in AD 644 as the end of Celtic influence in ecclesiastical matters among the Saxon kingdoms, it was nothing of the sort. Not until the mid-ninth century did a Synod of Chelsea declare that no Irish monks or priests should be allowed to preach to the Saxons. Long after Colmán and his monks departed to Ireland, many other Irish monks and educationalists came to the Saxon kingdoms to teach and Bede records that 'many nobles as well as common sort of the English race' went to Ireland to study in the famous Irish monasteries, universities and schools of medicine.

Irish missionaries were arriving directly from Ireland as well as from Iona. After Finán had converted Peada, son of Penda, of Mercia, the Irish bishop, Diuma, began to preach throughout Mercia. He attracted other missionaries from Ireland and was succeeded as bishop of the kingdom by one of them, named Ceallach. A third Irishman, named Jaruman, became bishop of Mercia until AD 667 when he was succeeded by Chad, the famous brother of Cedd, Caelin and Cynebill, all of whom had been trained under Aidan. Aidan thought Chad was such a promising pupil that he sent him to Ireland to finish his education. Chad established the See of Mercia at Lichfield, close to the royal residence at Tamworth, but his Celtic practices often brought him into conflict with Theodore of Canterbury. Canterbury was now recognized as the supreme ecclesiastical authority over the Saxon kingdoms. Chad's Irish austerity and humility contrasted strongly with the Roman pomp and dignity now being exercised.

In the land of the East Saxons, Chad's brother Cedd had been made bishop and converted Sigeberht and his people to Christianity. Cedd was also to support Colmán in the dispute with Rome. Totally disheartened when the Celts lost the argument, he retired to the seclusion of his foundation at Lastingham and died within a few years. The thirty-four priests he had ordained vowed to end their days at the shrine of their teacher but this left the East Saxons under pagan influence again. The new bishop of Northumbria, Eata (AD 678–686), who had taken over when Wilfrid was expelled, had been trained by Aidan, and sent the Irish missionary Jaruman to the East Saxons to reclaim them for Christianity.

Irish missionaries were at work in East Anglia, which kingdom was ruled by another Sigeberht, the son of Raedwald. During his brother Eorpwald's reign, Sigeberht had been driven into exile in Gaul. There he had come under the influence of Columbanus, who had worked as a missionary in Britain before moving on to Gaul and then Italy. Sigeberht was converted by Columbanus and returned to East Anglia to become king in AD 630/1. He brought with him a Gaulish Celtic bishop named Felix, who established his monastic centre at Dunwich, now almost wholly destroyed by the incursion of the sea. Felix died in AD 648 and is remembered at Felixstowe. He was buried at Dunwich but a later shrine was built at Ramsey abbey.

At the same time as Sigeberht returned to East Anglia with Felix, a group of Irish missionaries arrived led by Fursa (sometimes called

Fursey). Among them were Foillan, Ultan, Gobban and Diciul. Foillan and Ultan are described as Fursa's brothers. Fursa was said to have been born on an island in Lough Corrib where the ruins of Killursa (Cill Fursa) stand, dated to about AD 575. Sigeberht welcomed the Irish missionaries and gave them lands at Burgh Castle, in modern Suffolk, which for twelve years became the centre of their mission. Sigeberht was so impressed by Fursa and his teachings that, within a few years, the East Anglian king resigned his kingship and joined him as a monk, leaving the kingdom to his kinsman Ecgric. When Penda of Mercia attacked the kingdom in AD 636 the people demanded Sigeberht come out of the monastery and lead them. While Penda was driven off, both Ecgric and Sigeberht were killed. However Anna succeeded to the kingdom and he continued the policy of Christianizing his people.

In AD 645 Fursa gave the monastery to his brother Foillan, and went to live with Ultan in a hermitage. He eventually went on to Gaul and shortly afterwards, Foillan and Ultan followed him. Diciul, another of Fursa's band, had left the land of the East Angles about AD 645 and travelled to the kingdom of the South Saxons. Here he converted the king, probably Aethelwalh (d. AD 685), establishing his church at Bosham, from where he evangelized the people. Diciul paved the way for Wilfrid, driven out of Northumbria, who arrived thirty years later to establish his mission at Selsey. It is Wilfrid, rather than the Irishman Diciul, who is regarded as the apostle of Sussex. Again we see in this lack of credit the subsequent attempt to refrain from acknowledging the major role of the Irish in the conversion and education of the Saxon kingdoms.

Irish missionaries also had great influence in the West Saxon kingdom. After Cynglis had been converted, Aidan had sent his missionaries from Lindisfarne into the kingdom. Then Pope Honorius I had sent Birinus, a Roman, to preach the Roman liturgy. Birinus established his centre at Dorchester and also laid the foundations for monastic centres at Winchester, Salisbury and Wells. When Birinus died, Agilbert, a Frank who, according to Bede, had lived a long time in Ireland and was trained in the Celtic Church, became bishop to the West Saxons. Agilbert's cousin, Audo or Adon, was a friend of Columbanus. In spite of this background Agilbert became convinced of the correctness of adopting the Roman rituals.

Agilbert (AD 668–90) was not a fluent Saxon-speaker and this caused problems not only in Wessex but also when he was asked to put the Roman case at Whitby. He therefore had to choose pugnacious Wilfrid, whom he had ordained at the request of Alhfrith of Deira, as the advocate to speak for him. He eventually left Wessex, having been affronted by the discourtesies of the king, and died at Jouarre. However, before he left he was visited at Dorchester by an old friend from Ireland, Moeldubh (Mailduff). This Irish monk decided to settle and teach the West Saxons and he persuaded Agilbert to allow him to build a monastic centre near Ingelborne. Pupils were reported to have flocked to him from all over Wessex and they called his place Mailduff's Burgh, which was eventually corrupted into Malmesbury. It is from William of Malmesbury, its most famous son, that we hear the story of its founder.

Among Moeldubh's pupils was Aldhelm, who was later to write a famous letter to Geraint of Dumnonia, rebuking the Celts for still adhering to the Celtic Church rituals.

The Irish Celtic contribution to the conversion of the Anglo-Saxon kingdoms to Christianity cannot be underestimated. The nineteenth-century historian, the Comte de Montalembert (*The Monks of the West*, London, 1896), commented: 'Ireland was regarded by all Europe as the principal centre of learning and piety. The Anglo-Saxons were the one of all nations which derived most profit from the teaching of the Irish Schools.' To Ireland, English Christendom, literacy and learning owed an immeasurable debt; a debt, as I have pointed out elsewhere, sadly repaid with bloodshed and conquest and the near-destruction of the Irish nation.

Perhaps the most culturally influential of the Saxon kings was Aldfrith, king of Northumbria AD 685–705. He was undoubtedly one of the most literate, peaceful and successful of the Saxon monarchs. He was the son of Oswiu who had married, presumably while in exile among the Dál Riadans, Fín, daughter of the northern Uí Néill High King of Ireland, Colmán Rímid, to whom Adomnán dedicated his book *De Locis Sanctis* (The Holy Places). Colmán Rímid is recorded as providing the ransom for the release of Irish prisoners taken by Ecgfrith in his raid on Ireland in AD 684. Aldfrith had been born at Druffield, north Humberside, but was taken as a youth by his mother to her own country for an education where, as Flann Fín, he became an accomplished poet in Irish. Three of his compositions remain extant. One reference maintains that he was 'Adomnán's pupil'. The records indicate that he was surprised when his half-sister, Aelfflaed, abbess of Whitby, on Cuthbert's advice, recalled him to Northumbria to repair the damage to the shattered kingdom. At the time he was living at Lisgoole on the west bank of Lough Erne, engaged in his poetical studies.

Having been recalled to Northumbria on the death of his half-brother, Ecgfrith, Aldfrith ushered in a golden age of learning and literacy among his fellow Northumbrians. He was able to heal the rift which had opened up due to Ecgfrith's attack on Ireland and negotiate the release of the Irish prisoners with Adomnán, the abbot of Iona. Alcuin of Northumbria, abbot of St Martin at Tours, AD 796–804, described Aldfrith as 'a man from the earliest years of his life imbued with the love of sacred learning, a scholar of great powers of eloquence, of piercing intellect, a king and a teacher at the same time'. Alcuin was also educated in Ireland and contributed much to the Carolingian scholarship. His most important contribution is regarded as being made to Frankish history but he also composed a verse history of York, its bishops, kings, saints and scholars. He had been in charge of the direction of the scholars at York in AD 767 before Charlemagne invited him to join the Frankish royal court. His correspondence has become of particular value to historians of the eighth century. What tends to be overlooked is that Alcuin, one of the most renowned of Saxon scholars, was educated at Clonmacnoise in Ireland under Colcu, the *fer-leiginn*, or chief professor, there. Colcu was regarded as one of the most important scholars of his day and is referred to as 'Colcu the Wise'. There is extant a prayer written by him. Alcuin, in his letters, addresses him as 'Most holy father' and calls himself 'son', sending Colcu presents for charitable purposes from himself and from Charlemagne.

To the period of Aldfrith of Northumbria belong the Irish-influenced *Lindisfarne Gospels*, regarded as one of the masterpieces among the illustrated manuscript books. It was written by Eadfrith, bishop of Lindisfarne AD 698–721, in the mixed Celtic-Roman usages still practised at Lindisfarne.

To the same period belong Bede's *Life of Cuthbert*, commissioned by Eadfrith, whose cult Aldfrith promoted through his bishop, and also the *Codex Amiatinus*. Stone crosses appearing at this time, such as the seventeen-foot-high Ruthwell Cross, show the use of Celtic motifs indicating the Celtic influence still prevailing at the time.

More controversially, some scholars maintain that it was Aldfrith who was the originating force, if not the actual author, of *Beowulf*. Dating from Aldfrith's period, it is an epic of 3200 lines and the earliest extant composition of such length in Anglo-Saxon or indeed any Germanic literature. It contains the origin myth of the Angles and is set in the 'original homeland' before the invasion of Britain. It is the nearest thing approaching saga and myth in Anglo-Saxon. The saga includes a fifty-line fragment called 'The Fight at Finnes-burgh', in which 'Finn', king of the Frisians, having married Hilde-burh of the Danes, attacks her brother Hnaef and his followers while they are his guests. Hengest then slays Finn and returns Hildeburh to the Danes. According to C. W. von Sydow in his *Beowulfskalden och nordisk tradition* (1923), the *Beowulf* poet was well acquainted with the Irish sagas and had possibly studied at an Irish school. His arguments, supported by Professor Gerald Murphy in *Duanaire Finn* (1953), point to several close similarities between *Beowulf* and the early Irish saga *Táin Bó Fraoch* in which Fraoch sets out to woo Finnbhair and has to fight a water monster – as, indeed, Beowulf has to fight the water monster, Grendel. There are, in fact, nine points which coincide closely in the stories.

Beowulf has long been accepted as a Northumbrian composition of Aldfrith's period. Therefore, knowing what we do of Aldfrith's Irish education and of the continued presence of Irish monks and scholars, and Irish-trained monks and scholars, in the Northumbrian kingdom at this stage, we cannot find it inconceivable that this great Anglo-Saxon classic was inspired from the Celtic source.

When the Norse began to raid Lindisfarne and the Northumbrian coast later in the century (AD 793) and Northumbria itself was turned, in part, into a Danish kingdom, a large number of the Celtic books and Celtic-inspired books must have been lost with their art-work in the destruction that followed. At the time of this raid Higbald (AD 781–802) was bishop there and received from Alcuin a letter of sympathy and encouragement in his ordeal. Alcuin had once con-demned Higbald for allowing poems celebrating pagan Saxon heroes to be sung during meals – perhaps an early reference to the *Beowulf* saga? It was not for another century that the community of Lindis-farne, established by Aidan, moved from the island, taking the relics of Cuthbert to Chester-le-Street.

By the ninth century the work of Christianizing and educating the

Anglo-Saxons, undertaken in such large measure by the Celts of Ireland, was complete. Now the Saxons were beginning to display the same racial intolerance towards their teachers that they had always displayed to their British Celtic neighbours. Soon Irish monks and teachers were unwelcome in the Saxon kingdoms. Once eager to learn from Ireland, the great repository of learning in the Europe of the so-called 'Dark Ages', the Saxons began to develop a hostility which was to mark their subsequent relations with Ireland, to the extent that the debt they owed Ireland was forgotten. In AD 816 at the Council of Celchyth (Chelsea), held under the jurisdiction of archbishop Wulfred of Canterbury (AD 805–832), it was decreed that no one of the Irish nation should be permitted to exercise any religious authority within the Anglo-Saxon kingdoms.

It was Wulfred who made reforms at Canterbury and centralized the Anglo-Saxon Church, turning it into a recognizable 'business' in which the church lands were organized into large estates, administered from central manor houses, dues and services were rendered and bishops were regarded as temporal princes. The Council reaffirmed that church matters should only be dealt with by churchmen and no kings could interfere in areas of church jurisdiction. No wonder Wulfred felt that the Celtic tradition sat uncomfortably in the Anglo-Saxon Church of his vision. The Celtic social system, where the concept of absolute private property was alien and where no such law as primogeniture was recognized, was totally at odds with the Anglo-Saxon system. In the Celtic areas the church lands had been granted by the tribe or clan to the *religieux*. Under common ownership by the tribe or clan, the church lands could not be owned but merely used, and disposal, even the disposal of goods and chattels, was regulated by the tribal assembly. This concept was a point of argument between the austerity of the Celtic churchmen and the opulence and feudal attitudes of Rome.

Towards the twelfth century the evidence is that, as many Celtic *religieux* returned to their own lands after missions in other parts of Europe, they brought back concepts of ownership with them, and that even the Celtic Church began making inroads in the restrictions imposed on appropriation of the land by the tribal system. The influence of the Danes in Ireland certainly began to alter Irish attitudes, but attempts to change the Celtic system here were generally unsuccessful before the Anglo-Norman invasions in 1169. Indeed, the

attempt by leading members of the Irish hierarchy, such as Maelmae-
doc Ó Morgair (b. 1005), to adopt the Roman feudal systems within
the Irish Church was one of the prime causes of the invasion. Mael-
maedoc (St Malachy) paid two visits to Rome and his advice, and
that of his successors, was behind the issuing of Pope Adrian IV's
Bull Laudabiliter in 1154/5, confirmed by Pope Alexander III, which
gave Henry II the Church's blessing to invade Ireland and 'enlarge
the bounds of the Church'. The Synod of the Irish bishops at Cashel,
during the winter of 1171/2, was quick to welcome the Anglo-
Norman invasion as signalling the final *rapprochement* with Rome,
and, in using the invasion to make an end to the Celtic social system,
they also welcomed the extinction of an independent Ireland.

At this juncture, an unbiased observer might again remark on the
irony of the situation. The Celts brought Christianity to the pagan
Saxons, brought education and literacy, taught even their kings,
organized their historical records, and helped to establish their law
system (as we shall see from Chapter Fourteen), only to be subsequently repaid by centuries of aggressive warfare, conquest and the
near-annihilation of their languages and culture. English culture has
been left sadly imbued with an anti-Celtic prejudice that has
attempted to convey the impression that the Celts were primitive,
savage, culturally worthless and racially inferior. This becomes the
very foundation of the dishearteningly popular 'Irish joke' while the
Welsh are painted as people not to be trusted – to 'welch' on someone
is to cheat or betray them. 'Taffy was a Welshman, Taffy was a
thief,' ran the nineteenth-century childhood rhyme. Jean-Paul Sartre
commented: 'How can an élite of usurpers, aware of their mediocrity,
establish their privileges? By one means only: debasing the colonized
to exalt themselves, denying the title of humanity to the natives, and
defining them simply as absences of qualities – animals not humans.
This does not prove hard to do, for the system deprives them of
everything.'

[11]

Saxon Expansion

In Llongborth Geraint was slain.
Heroes of the land of Dumnonia,
Before they were slaughtered, they slew.

Anon, ninth-century Welsh

D URING the late seventh century and the early eighth, the
most eminent Anglo-Saxon scholar of the age lived and
worked. Bede was born near Jarrow about AD 673 and, when
he was only seven years old, his parents decided he should enter a
religious life and gave him to Benedict Biscop (Benedict the bishop),
who had founded a monastery at Monkwearmouth. Benedict had
once been a member of Oswiu's personal bodyguard. About AD 666,
he had made a pilgrimage to Rome and then decided to enter the
religious life. It was the first of many visits to Rome and he became
a convinced adherent of Roman practices, becoming abbot of
St Augustine's at Canterbury. He was charged with conducting Theodore to Britain as the new archbishop. Ecgfrith of Northumbria
eventually gave Monkwearmouth to Benedict for the creation of a
major centre in AD 674. He made another journey to Rome, returning
with several valuable books with which to stock the library of his
foundation.

The young Bede proved an enthusiastic pupil and was passed into
the care of Ceolfrith whom Benedict had appointed abbot of a new
religious foundation at Jarrow. Ceolfrith (AD 642–716) had been
raised in Celtic customs but eagerly adopted the new Roman forms
and was particularly enthusiastic to spread literacy among his people.
He enlarged the library at Jarrow which included the *Codex Amiatinus*, now the oldest surviving Latin text of the Bible and in the
Bibliotheca Laurensiana in Florence. It was intended as a gift for the
Pope. In AD 716 Ceolfrith set off for Rome, taking the book with

him, but he died *en route* at Langres, in Burgundy. An anonymous *Life*, written shortly after his death, says that earlier a plague had ravaged Jarrow and only the abbot, Ceolfrith, and one small boy were left alive. The small boy must have been Bede.

Bede has become famous for his *Historia Ecclesiastica gentis Anglorum*, completed in AD 731. It was widely read at the time and no fewer than five eighth-century copies still survive. Without this work, we would know little of Saxon thinking and internal events during this period. But Bede's work was much wider and more varied than that of an historian. He wrote *Lives* of the abbots, a history of his own monastery, two *Lives of Cuthbert*, one in prose and one in verse, and two works on the reckoning of time, *De Temporibus* and *De Temporum Ratione*, which had considerable influence at this time. They are tracts on the reckoning of Easter and, of course, Bede supports Rome in this matter. His 'Letter to Ecgberht' composed in AD 734 is also an important document, being a critique of the failings of the Northumbrian Church in the years following its abandonment of Celtic practices.

During the period of Bede's life, the Saxons continued their expansionist campaigns against the Celts and the Northumbrian scholar was a witness to the last days of the British Celtic kingdom of Dumnonia.

Ine, son of Coenred, succeeded Caedwalla as king of the West Saxons in AD 688. He made it a policy to continue the western expansionist settlements in the territory of the Celts of Dumnonia. In AD 710 he was fighting against Geraint who would appear to be one of the last, if not the last, king of Dumnonia. Ine had been pressing into the Celtic kingdom from the first days of his succession and when he issued a series of laws, in about AD 695, they demonstrated that Celtic populations had been incorporated into his kingdom. The *welisc* or Britons were provided with a definite place in the West Saxon scheme of things and a tariff of *wergelds*, or compensation payments, for taking a Briton's life was included in the new laws. These ranged from payment of fines for the killing of British Celtic slaves of between fifty and sixty shillings, to compensation of 600 shillings for the slaying of a landed Briton with five hides, being 500 acres. Obviously, ownership of five hides clearly marks a person of substance. One of the categories in the laws is defined as a British horseman in the Saxon king's service, whose compensation was placed at 200 shillings. This indicates that the West Saxons were employing British cavalry mercenaries in their wars. But were these Celtic mercenaries employed in the wars against their own people or in the internal squabbles of the Saxons such as Ine's attack on Kent? In AD 694 Ine exacted a *wergeld* from Wihtred (AD 690–725) for the slaying of Mul, brother of Caedwalla of Wessex. Kent had been conquered by Caedwalla but it was not a permanent conquest.

It becomes clear, then, that the British populated the western sections of the territory over which Ine claimed kingship. The inclusion of British Celts in the details of *wergelds* has been seized upon by the 'intermarriage theorists' as proof that Celt and Saxon did live 'happily' side by side, but we are talking of a period over 200 years after Gildas's evidence for the massacres and migrations of his day. Only at this time and only in Wessex, whose borders were fluctuating from year to year, is there such a reference. The extent of the Wessex frontier and its rapid fluctuations can be seen by the grants of ecclesiastical land given by Ine. In AD 704 he endowed Sherborne and made over to it two clearly Celtic monasteries at Congresbury and Banwell. Sherborne also acquired five hides of land by the River Tamar and it has been suggested that the gift was given by the Dumnonian king to prevent further West Saxon aggression.

In AD 706 Aldhelm was appointed bishop of Sherborne. He had studied both at the Irish foundation of Malmesbury and at Canterbury. His first teacher was the Irish scholar Maildubh, who had founded the monastery. Ine had now given him charge of the West Saxons' ecclesiastical area 'west of Selwood' with Sherborne as its centre. Aldhelm had a cathedral church built there which William of Malmesbury admired during a visit.

Aldhelm wrote a tract on the matrimonial customs of the Saxons, which were contrary to the teachings of St Paul. In *De Virginitatae*, written for abbess Hildelith and the nuns of Barking, Aldhelm produced a new philosophical approach to the problem. He was also a skilled poet in Latin and English, fond of Latin riddles, and his works became popular in pre-Conquest England. Aldhelm also became part of the diplomatic process, and was used by Ine in the period preceding his final onslaught on Celtic Dumnonia to justify such expansion.

The Saxons were certainly in occupation of Taunton by this time and the major part of Somerset was in their hands. Just how much of western Devon was left to the Dumnonians is difficult to say.

But Geraint was clearly 'king of Dumnonia' and not, as some have suggested, 'of Cornwall' which, as we have already argued, was a separate Celtic kingdom. About AD 708/9, bishop Aldhelm wrote to the British king and addressed him as '*Geruntio regi, simulque cunctis Dei sacerdotibus per Domnoniam conversantibus*'. This letter was actually an attack on Celtic Church customs and a demand that Geraint change to the Roman method of dating Easter. Geraint's refusal to give up his adherence to the Celtic Church, I would argue, was to be used as an excuse for Ine to launch his attack. Geraint and the Celtic position were, of course, regarded as heretical by Canterbury and Rome.

In AD 710/711 Ine, with the participation of his kinsman Northelm (Nonna), king of the South Saxons (d. *c.*AD 725), launched a series of attacks on the remaining territory of Dumnonia. Geraint is said to have fallen in a battle at Langport in Somerset and 'A Lament to Geraint', attributed to Llywarch Hen, survives from the ninth century. Sir Ifor Williams has shown that the poems ascribed to Llywarch Hen, who was a sixth-century chieftain in Rheged, were actually written about him and not by him in the seventh to ninth centuries. This makes sense of finding a lament to the eighth-century Dumnonian ruler among them.

The Dumnonia king list, dated to the fourteenth century (Jesus College, Oxford MS 20, now in the Bodleian Library), is not very helpful in showing what happened to Dumnonia in the years following Geraint's defeat. Rachel Bromwich believed it was copied from an authentic ancient source while Arthur Wade Evans believed it was compiled in the twelfth century merely to show the claim of Morgan ap Owain, king of Morgannwg, to trace a descent to the kings of Dumnonia. So we find that Geraint has a son Cado, whose son Peredur becomes father of Theudal whose daughter forms the basis of Morgan ap Owain's maternal ancestry. But it is uncertain whether Cado and Peredur ruled in Dumnonia or became political refugees in Cornwall or Wales.

The Saxons moved into Exeter and then beyond, using it as a base to make raids into the land of the Kern-wealhas, or Cornwall. At this time Dumnonia had ceased to exist as an independent political unit but there was still a large Celtic population living in the city of Exeter until AD 931, when they were driven out – and, indeed, a Celtic population living in the area west of the city to the River

Tamar. At this time, however, Cornwall emerged as the last independent kingdom of the 'west *welisc*'.

The resistance to the West Saxon expansion became more resolute
as Ine and his successors pressed nearer the Tamar. In AD 721/22 he
was defeated by the Cornish near Camel, according to the *Annales
Cambriae*, having pushed his army well inside Cornish territory.
By this victory over Wessex, the Cornish were able to retain their
independence for another two centuries. A few years after this defeat,
Ine of Wessex resigned his kingship in order to spend the rest of his
days in Rome in religious contemplation. A kinsman called
Athelheard (AD 726–740) became king but did not seem to follow
Ine's aggressive policy against the Britons because he was too busy
dealing with a new threat from Mercia. The Mercians had invaded
Wessex and won a battle in AD 715 at a place called Wodensbeorg,
the site of Ceawlin's defeat in AD 592. Ine had apparently eventually
checked this aggression but, during Aethelheard's reign, the Mercians
were claiming overlordship of Wessex again.

Another twenty years passed after the British victory at Camel
before Athelheard's successor Cuthred (AD 740–756) fought two
fierce battles against the Britons of Cornwall. More time passed
before it was reported that Cynewulf (AD 757–786) 'often fought
great battles against the Britons'. Cornwall stubbornly protected its
independence against Wessex.

Bede must have watched the rise of Mercian dominance in the
person of its new king, Offa, with some concern, perhaps even as
much concern as the British Celts. In the development of the western
British Celtic kingdoms, those which were to become known as
Wales, the reign of Offa, king of Mercia, came to play a crucial role,
for Offa was to build a physical barrier, perhaps after the inspiration
of Hadrian's Wall, to delineate a border for all time between his
kingdom and the *welisc* or foreigners.

The fortunes of Mercia had fluctuated in the mid-eighth century.
The Mercian king, Ceolred (AD 709–716), according to Boniface,
had been 'thrown down from the regal summit of this life and over-
taken by an early and terrible death'. He had robbed Saxon churches
and committed 'fornication' with Saxon nuns. That Boniface points
this out affirms that such actions committed against the Celts were
not considered 'sins'. With his death Aethelbald, a descendant of
Eowa, brother of Penda, who had been driven into exile during

Ceolred's rule, returned to become king. As an exiled adventurer wandering the Fens near Crowland, Aethelbald had been befriended by Guthlac (*c*.AD 673–714). As a youth Guthlac had fought in the army of Ethelred of Mercia but had decided to enter a religious life and lived as a hermit on the River Welland in the Fens. However, his hermitage was not total for his sister, Pega, lived nearby and was with him when he died. She died five years afterwards on a pilgrimage to Rome. It is claimed that Guthlac had prophesied Aethelbald would become king of Mercia and the greatest of the Saxon kings.

Bede, a contemporary, was writing his *Historia Ecclesiastica gentis Anglorum* at the time. While his Northumbrian nationalism did not allow him to name any Mercian in his Bretwalda lists he does mention that by this date Aethelbald of Mercia had authority over all the Southern Saxon kingdoms. A charter of AD 736 styles Aethelbald as 'king not only of the Mercians but also of all the provinces'. In fact, it is from this time that we find the formula '*gens Anglorum*', from which the name 'English' derives, being applied to all the Anglo-Saxon kingdoms. But while both Angles and Saxons now began to call themselves 'Aenglisc', in Celtic eyes they remained Saxons.

Aethelbald seems to have acquired his position of prominence through conquest. He issued coins bearing his image in a crowned war helmet (*cynehelm*). But it was obvious that he was neither liked nor respected by the other Saxon kingdoms. Boniface, a West Saxon, fiercely denounced Aethelbald as he had Ceolred and claimed he had seized the lands of the Saxon Church and committed fornication with nuns. Finally, in AD 757 Aethelbald wound up being assassinated by his own bodyguard at Seckington (Warwickshire).

Mercia immediately fell into an internecine war over the successor. A claimant named Beonred was defeated by another claimant, Offa, a descendant of one of Penda's brothers. During this period the Mercian overlordship had crumbled. Wessex regained its lost territories. The *Annales Cambriae* also record a victory of the western British Celts in AD 760 at Hereford. But Offa, now the main claimant for the Mercian throne, had no time to deal with the Celts. He was too concerned to secure his own position and restore Mercia's dominance over the Saxons. One of his first actions was to assert his lordship over the small kingdom of the Hwicce at Gloucester. By the time Offa came to power the four sons of Oshere had inherited the kingdom. Oshere had styled himself 'king of the Hwicce' without qualification, and appeared to be Osric's successor. In AD 777 Offa was styling the rulers of the Hwicce simply as 'under-kings' and '*ealdormen*' subject to himself. After AD 794 there are no more references to the Hwicce and it becomes an integral part of the Mercian kingdom. Offa's authority was now supreme in Mercia.

Offa was now able to turn his attention elsewhere. In AD 764 he took an army against Eanmund of Kent and fought at Otford. It seems that Offa lost this battle, for over the next ten years, until AD 785, Kent remained independent of Mercia. Offa, however, meanwhile asserted his rule in Sussex and fought a battle near Hastings in AD 771. King Osmund of Sussex acknowledged Offa as his suzerain lord in the following year. Sussex was never again to be regarded as a separate kingdom. Cynewulf of Wessex managed to prevent Mercian incursions until he was defeated at Bensington in AD 779 and thus had to give up Wessex territory on either side of the River Thames. Cynewulf was killed in AD 789 and Mercia completely subordinated Wessex for a while. In AD 794 Offa turned on Aethelberht, king of East Anglia, and ordered his murder. Little is known about the reasons for this assassination except Offa's hunger for dominance. Aethelberht was well respected by his people and subsequently became venerated as a Christian saint with a dedication in Hertford.

Offa was now styling himself Bretwalda and ruler of all the Saxon kingdoms south of the Humber. More significantly, he used the title *rex Anglorum*, king of the English. Where force could not prevail, Offa resorted to politics and married one of his daughters, Aelfflaed, to Aethelred, the king of Northumbria in AD 790. Presumably Offa was seeking to extend his authority into Northumbria, the only Anglo-Saxon kingdom not paying him allegiance. However, Aethelred was murdered on 28 March AD 796, and Offa himself was dead within the year.

A sign of Offa's importance was his negotiations with European leaders such as Charlemagne, king of the Franks. In AD 796 Offa, just before his death, concluded a trading agreement and a marriage alliance with Charlemagne. The Popes, Adrian I and Leo III, regarded him as the most important of the Saxon kings. Papal legates, such as George of Ostia and Theophylacht of Todi, attended his courts. Offa reformed the coinage and produced the first silver pennies used among the Saxon kingdoms.

But Offa is best remembered for the great wall he built to hem in the British Celts of the west.

In AD 778 Offa had made a military expedition as far as Dyfed. Another raid followed in AD 784. His final attack in the area led to a battle at Rhuddlan by the Clwyd in the year of his death. But it was sometime after his expedition of AD 784 that Offa conceived the idea of building a frontier which can still be seen today. This consists of 120 miles of massive earthworks from the Severn estuary at Sedbury near Chepstow, snaking northwards to the estuary of the Dee at Prestatyn. There are parts where the density of woodland prevented building but the wall was effective nonetheless. To the British Celts it became Clawdd Offa and to the English it was known as Offan Dic, Offa's Dyke. Another series of earthworks which ran from Basingwerk to Morda Brook, south of Oswestry, has been claimed to have been built earlier by Aethelbald and not Offa. If so, then the original idea of the dyke belongs to Aethelbald. Offa was merely completing the work of the king he had succeeded. Offa's Dyke was to become regarded as the fixed boundary between Celt and Saxon in this area.

The building of this frontier wall seemed arbitrary and, as Nora Chadwick points out, in the north the frontier actually sliced through British Celtic territory and 'cut off a large portion of the old kingdom of Powys – the richest portion'. But on the eighth-century monument known as Eliseg's Pillar, we find that Eliseg ap Gwylog, king of Powys, had managed to retake 'the heritage of Powys . . . from the power of the Saxon'. Given that Eliseg's great-grandson died in Rome about AD 850, we could place Eliseg in Offa's time. Did he overrun Offa's Dyke to the east and regain that lost part of Powys as far as Pengwern (Shrewsbury) for a time? Or was he merely consolidating Powys as far as Offa's threatening ramparts? From this time, however, the great fortifications hemmed in the western British Celts, effectively severing them from their kinfolk in south-west Britain and from the former kingdom of Rheged, now reduced south of the Solway Firth to Cumbria, but still independent and under its own kings. The Celts of Cumbria were now calling themselves 'Cymry' (compatriots) and their land 'Cymru' which the Saxons pronounced as Cumbria.

The modern shape of England was beginning to emerge.

[12]

The Triumph of the Picts

Ecgfrith, the king, rashly led an army to ravage the kingdom
of the Picts . . .

Bede,
Historia Ecclesiastica Gentis Anglorum

I T is from Bede that the north British kingdom of the Picts first
emerges into written record. There also survives a Pictish king
list in Latin covering thirty-four monarchs from Bruide Mac
Maelchon (AD 556–84) to Drust son of Ferat (AD 845–48), after
which Cináech Mac Alpín (Kenneth MacAlpin) is listed as ruler of a
united Dál Riada and Pictland called Alba, the name by which
modern Scotland is still known in Scottish Gaelic. But, as we will
see, Cináech Mac Alpín was not the first king to rule jointly over Dál
Riada and Pictland. There are no native Pictish records, in spite
of popular notions to the contrary, although there is an intriguing
reference to Pictish literacy in the eighth century. However, if any
distinctive Pictish annals or manuscript books were produced and
survived from this period, then they undoubtedly fell foul of the
destructive and Anglicizing zeal of the Scottish Reformation, which
plundered whole libraries of Gaelic books. The earliest work we have
from the land of the Picts is the *Book of Deer*, named after the
monastery near Aberdeen where it was compiled. This is dated to
the ninth century and is of tremendous importance as a Scottish
national treasure because of its eleventh-century glosses in a language
clearly Scottish Gaelic as opposed to its Old Irish parent. The manuscript is now in Cambridge University Library.

Almost from their emergence into history, the Picts have been
cursed by myth-makers so that their image has become truly distorted. Bede is the first to expand the myth, painting the Picts as a
distinct people with their own language, who came from Scythia,

went to Ireland, asked for land, and were sent on to Scotland. He is unknowingly recording the origin myth of the Gaels, for Míl (Milesius), the ancestor of the Milesians (or Gaels), was a Scythian in the service of king Reafloir of Scythia. His wife Scota (eponymous ancestor of the Scots) and his sons invaded Ireland, drove the Tuatha Dé Danaan underground and settled there. Scota's son Goidel or Gael became the progenitor of the Gaels. So, already, the Picts shared their origin myth with the Gaels of Dál Riada in Bede's time. Bede says that when the Picts went to Ireland and asked for land, the Irish sent them on to northern Britain. He adds that the Picts came without women and so married Irish women; because of this 'they chose a king from the female royal line rather than the male'. A twelfth-century Norwegian chronicler was more prejudiced about the Picts and described them as 'little more than pygmies in stature' who 'lurked through fear in little underground houses'.

The reality was that the Picts were nothing more than the northern tribes of British Celts who, in fact, clearly called themselves British or – the original word – Pretani. When they changed from speaking a Brythonic Celtic language to Goidelic Celtic, the name became Cretani and thence, with the Goidelic aspirate, Cruithin, and it was as the Tuatha-Cruthin that they regarded themselves by Bede's time. To show how they arrived in northern Britain, a new origin myth made one, Cruithne, into an eponymous ancestor of the people; one annalist explains: 'Seven of Cruithne's children divided Alba into seven divisions: the portion of Cat, of Cé, of Círech, of Fiobh, of Moireabh and of Fótla and of Fortriu. And it is the name of each man of them that is his own land.' This is obviously a later explanation of Scotland's provinces at the time of the tenth century which were called An Mhaorine ('stewardries'), each governed by Mormaers – mór-mhaor.

Cat was Caithness; Moireabh was Moray; Fótla was given as Athfhótla, hence its Anglicization into Atholl; Círech was Angus and Mearns – and in Mearns we see the survival of the word Mhaorine; Cé was Marr and Buchan; Fíobh is still easily recognizable as Fife; and Fortriu, sometimes Fortrenn, was a synonym for Ireland and covered Strathearn (Strath-Éireann).

As we have seen, the Roman soldiers manning Hadrian's Wall nicknamed the northern British Celts 'painted ones', Picti, because they used to daub themselves in battle. They were not the only people to use warpaint. The nickname first emerged in a Latin poem in AD 297. However, particularly after Bede, generations of scholars have tried to argue that the Picts (we shall continue to call them by their nickname) were a separate people from the rest of the Celts. Professor Kenneth Jackson points out that the Pictish king lists give Celtic names, most of which are British Celtic although they are often recorded in Goidelic Celtic forms. It is clear that a language change was taking place in the years following the sixth century, with the British Celts adopting the Goidelic Celtic of the Dál Riadans. So far as records show they were quickly absorbed into the Gaelic scheme of things.

In AD 638 the Northumbrians, under Oswald, had struck northwards and it was this year that their first assault on Dinas Eidyn, the capital of the Gododdin, is recorded. We must firmly discount the myth created by Symeon of Durham who mistranslated the name of the town as 'Edwinesburgh', thus causing many to think Edwin and his Angles founded the city. The *Annals of Ulster* record Oswald's attack as a siege (*obsessio Etin*). It would seem that the Northumbrians were successful in this campaign and captured the plains of Manaw around Dinas Eidyn. In AD 642 Oswiu succeeded his brother as king and commenced a conquest of Rheged, pushing back the frontiers of the British Celtic kingdom. While the Dál Riadans were welcomed in Northumbria in their role as educators and Christian missionaries, the Northumbrian warriors were determined to extend their conquests over the Picts. Yet, curiously, Talorgen, who became the king of the Picts in AD 653, was the son of Eanfrith and therefore Oswiu's nephew. He ruled for only four years and was succeeded by Gartnait, son of Domhnull. By AD 669 Oswiu had exerted authority over the Picts and he nominated puppet kings to rule and pay him tribute. These puppet rulers were Gartnait and Drest. At the same time the Northumbrian abbot Wilfrid was declared bishop of the 'Northumbrians *and* Picts'. But Oswiu died in AD 670 and the Picts took the opportunity to break free of Northumbrian overlordship.

Ecgfrith, son of Oswiu, had become ruler of Northumbria following his father's death and he was an ambitious ruler, keen for power and conquest. He began to attack the Celts of Rheged again who were forced to retreat from large areas of their territory. They were pushed from the Dent, in the West Riding of Yorkshire, and the Ribble valley, in what is now Lancashire, 'which the British clergy deserted when fleeing from the hostile sword wielded by the warriors of our own nation,' writes Stephanus Eddius (d. *c.*AD 720) in satisfaction. Eddius's *Life of St Wilfrid* is regarded as the first commemorative biography in Anglo-Saxon England. Ecgfrith is even recorded as launching an assault on Ireland in AD 684, an attempt bitterly condemned by Bede. Bede describes the Irish as 'a harmless race that had always been most friendly to the English'. The raid was conducted by Ecgfrith's *ealdorman*, Beorht, who returned with sixty Irish prisoners.

Ecgfrith had also turned his attention north of the Tweed and rekindled the ambitious ideas of his father. Following the death of Oswiu, the Picts had made some internal changes. Their king, Drest, who had been a puppet of Oswiu, was promptly expelled. Bruide Mac Bili had been accepted as leader of the Pictish resistance to Northumbria. A poem attributed to Adomnán says Bruide was the son of a Strathclyde king, Bili son of Neithon. His brother, therefore, was Owain Mac Bili of Strathclyde. The Irish annals record a series of incidents by which Bruide united the demoralized Pictish kingdom, even exerting his overlordship on the Orkneys, which the Dál Riadans claimed.

Ecgfrith attacked the Picts in AD 672 and there was a massacre. Eddius Stephanus says that two rivers were filled with Pictish corpses 'so that, marvellous to relate, the Northumbrians, passing over the rivers dry-shod, pursued and slew the crowd of fugitives'. But Ecgfrith was not in a position to follow up his victory, for Northumbria was being attacked by Wulfhere, son of Penda, who had been busy re-establishing the dominance of Mercia south of the Humber into Essex and Sussex, even conquering the Isle of Wight. Wulfhere attacked Northumbria in AD 674 and Ecgfrith had to return to defend his kingdom. The Northumbrian king eventually emerged victorious but needed time to recover from the Mercian onslaught.

It was ten years before he could return to the idea of the conquest of the Picts. Not until AD 685 did Ecgfrith and his Northumbrians invade the kingdom of the Picts once more. Even his bishop, Cuthbert of Lindisfarne, had warned the king against the advisability of such an invasion, probably hearing how powerful and organized Bruide now was. Cuthbert is even claimed to have foretold Ecgfrith's death. The most important victory of Celt over Saxon since Mount Badon was achieved by Bruide at Nechtansmere, which has been identified as Dunnichen Moss, south of Forfar in Angus. The date was Saturday, 20 May. The mighty Northumbrian king, Ecgfrith, was slain and the Anglo-Saxons pushed back beyond the Lammermuir Hills. While they did not give up their territorial ambitions over the Picts, nonetheless, this was the last serious threat to the Pictish heartland.

Nennius called the battle 'Gueith Lin Garan', 'the fight at the pool of the herons'. Irish sources record 'the battle of Dún Nechtain' named from the nearby fortress which survives in the modern placename of Dunnichen. Symeon of Durham and other English historians call it 'Nechtansmere' or 'the lake of Nechtan'.

The *Life of Cuthbert*, written twenty years after the battle, suggests the time of the victory was 3 p.m. Cuthbert was with Ecgfrith's queen, Iurminburg, as she waited for news of her husband. When the report came that he had been slain she retired to live in a convent. According to the reports, Ecgfrith's body was taken from Nechtansmere to Iona, from whose monastery the Northumbrians had been Christianized. Here the would-be scourge of the Celts was buried by some of the very Celts he was seeking to destroy. The Irish bard, Riagal of Bangor, wrote:

This day the son of Oswiu was killed with green swords.
Although he did penance, he shall lie in Iona after his death.
This day the son of Oswiu was killed, who had the black
    drink . . .

John Marsden has written: 'It is almost impossible to over-estimate the cataclysmic impact on the kingdom of Northumbria of the defeat at Nechtansmere . . .'

The result was that Ecgfrith's half-brother, Aldfrith, became king of Northumbria and reigned there for twenty years – twenty years of peace and prosperity and high artistic attainment. For Aldfrith, as we have seen, combined the best of Celt and Saxon, being the son of Oswiu and of Fín, daughter of a northern Uí Néill High King of Ireland.

Aldfrith's return brought to Northumbria a 'golden age' of learning, as we have already discussed in our survey of the conversion of the Saxons to Christianity. One of his first actions was to release the sixty Irish prisoners, taken as slaves, during Ecgfrith's raid on Ireland in AD 684. In repayment Aldfrith was given a copy of one of Adomnán's own books – *De Locis Sanctis* (On Holy Places).

Aldfrith's son Osred was declared king on the death of his father in AD 705. As the child was only eight years old, he was merely a puppet in the hands of the old Northumbrian military caste represented by his aunt Aelfflaed, abbess of Whitby, supported by the pugnacious Wilfrid, who became his foster father, and Beorhtfrith, who became his 'regent', the head of the government, until he came of age. Beorhtfrith seems to have been the son of Beorht who led the raid on Ireland in AD 684. There was much opposition among the Northumbrians, who had prospered under Aldfrith and did not wish to see a return to the wars of conquest. Eadwulf, a son of Aethwold of Deira (c.AD 652–655), was the focus of opposition. He was declared king and expelled Osred and his supporters. They fled to Bamburgh where Beorhtfrith, rallying support, then defeated and expelled Eadwulf in his turn.

Bede enthused that Osred was a new Josiah. But the boy, sadly in view of the greatness of his father, grew up as a despot 'driven by the spirit of wantonness', according to Boniface. He was accused of killing many Northumbrian nobles, forcing others into exile or compelling them to take religious vows and cut themselves off from secular life. In AD 716 Osred was murdered and Coenred, son of Cuthwine, claiming descent from Ida, the first historic king of Bernicia, became ruler.

During this time, the war between Northumbria and the Picts was renewed.

Bruide Mac Bili of the Picts had died in AD 693. He had been succeeded by Taran, son of Entifidich who, in AD 697, was expelled from his kingdom and fled to Ireland, to be succeeded by the eldest son of Derile, another Bruide. Bruide and his two brothers, Nechtán and Cináed, were powerful figures in Pictland.

The Northumbrians had begun their attacks even while Aldfrith was on the throne. The records imply that the attacks were made without Aldfrith's consent and arose from a group of militant Northumbrian thanes, smarting from the defeat of Ecgfrith and looking for revenge. They disobeyed the strictures of Aldfrith, and, led by Beorht, took matters into their own hands. They invaded the land of the Picts only to be defeated again by Bruide, and Beorht was slain.

The year after Osred became king of Northumbria, Nechtán

succeeded his brother as king of the Picts. With the young Osred being used as a figurehead for Northumbrian military ambitions, the hostilities were 'officially' opened again. The Northumbrians attacked the Picts on the plains of Manaw, surrounding Dinas Eidyn (Edinburgh), in AD 711. It is recorded that there was a great slaughter of Picts. The site is indicated as being between the River Avon near Linlithgow and the River Carron near Stirling. Here, it seems, Beorhtfrith managed to avenge the death of his father Beorht. It was the first Northumbrian success over the Picts since AD 672. As Beorhtfrith is not mentioned again one wonders if he was slain here or in some subsequent skirmish.

Nechtán's brother, Cináed, was slain in AD 713, in the ensuing warfare. But soon after, Northumbria and the Picts agreed on a peace treaty.

Nechtán now emerges as someone concerned about the arguments between the Celtic Church and Rome. The Synod of Whitby in AD 664 had, of course, passed the Picts by. They had been converted by monks from Dál Riada and from Strathclyde, and adhered to Celtic practices. But Nechtán had obvious heard of the debate and wanted clarification of the Roman view. He sent emissaries to Ceolfrith, the abbot of Monkwearmouth and Jarrow (AD 688–716), who was the teacher of Bede. He wanted to know about the differences between Celtic and Roman religious practices. He seems to have adopted Roman custom in AD 716, the very year Ceolfrith set out on his pilgrimage to Rome, taking the *Codex Amiatinus* as a gift for the Pope, and dying *en route* at Langres, Burgundy on 25 September.

At this time, however, and perhaps more importantly for Nechtán's conversion to Roman orthodoxy, Adomnán, the former abbot of Iona, had been travelling through the land of the Picts preaching of his conversion to Roman teaching and the dating of Easter. His decision to accept Roman rule had isolated him from his own community and he spent the rest of his life trying to convert his fellow Celts to abandon the Celtic Christian traditions. In AD 717 Nechtán, converted to Rome, ordered the expulsion of all those monks in Pictish monasteries who would not accept the Roman teachings. Many of them returned to Iona. It seems that the bishop Ecgberht (d. AD 729) of Northumbria was now instrumental in helping the Picts change to Roman practices. In AD 712 he went to Iona to preach and may also have gone to 'Mayo of the Saxons', which converted and became a centre of Roman orthodoxy in Ireland. There is irony here as the foundation had been set up by Colmán and his Northumbrian monks because they had refused to accept Roman ritual. Bede asserts that Iona was persuaded to adopt the Roman Easter and celebrated it for the first time in AD 716. Ecgberht lived an astonishingly (for the age) long time and finally died in his nineties on Iona.

Nechtán himself retired to a monastery in AD 724 but his abdication as king of the Picts was marked by a dynastic conflict and anarchy. Nechtán came out of the monastery two years later to challenge his successor, Drest, who took him captive. Four rivals fought for the kingship until Oengus (Angus) Mac Fergus emerged as the successful claimant and Nechtán was able once more to retire to a monastery, where he died in AD 732.

Oengus I, son of Fergus, became king of the Picts in AD 729 and ruled until AD 761. He was the most successful and strongest of the Pictish rulers. Having sorted out the dissenters within the land of the Picts, he turned against the Dál Riadans and, in AD 736, stormed Dunadd, one of the major fortresses, capturing Dúngal, son of Selbach, the king of Dál Riada, as well as his younger brother. Oengus's own brother, Talorgen, in the same year, defeated a cousin of Dúngal, at the battle of Cnoc Coirpre in Calathros. Oengus now claimed not only the Pictish kingship but the overlordship of the Dál Riada. It was not until Aed Find (the Fair) became king of Dál Riada in AD 748 that Pictish domination began to ebb. First the Strathclyde Britons defeated the Picts and Talorgen was slain. Then Aed Find emerged as a powerful force in Dál Riada. When Oengus I died in AD 761, Aed Find fought a victorious battle in Fortriu against his successor, Ciniod. Aed Find had a reputation as a law-giver and for rule by the tribal assemblies – his nickname became Airechtech, 'of the assemblies'.

While these developments were taking place, the Northumbrians, under Eadberht (AD 737–58), seized the opportunity to move northwards once again. Eadberht was earning a reputation as a 'hard man'. When Offa, another son of Aldfrith, made a bid for the Northumbrian kingship and failed, he sought sanctuary in Lindisfarne but Eadberht had his men drag the royal claimant out of the church. Offa was slain. Eadberht even went so far as to imprison the bishop.

Sir Frank Stenton correctly describes Eadberht as 'the last Northumbrian king to lead effective expeditions beyond the northern border'. According to the Jarrow chronicler, Eadberht had started a war with the Picts in AD 740. But Aethelbald of Mercia seized this opportunity to lead an army into Northumbria and sack York. Symeon of Durham claims that the Strathclyde Britons, Dál Riadans and Picts 'were happy in showing him marks of deference'. That is rather an exaggeration for the Irish annals show the wars were long and protracted. Eadberht seems to have conquered what is now Ayrshire in AD 750 and established a line of Northumbrian bishops at the great monastery founded by Ninian at Whithorn. The last mention of a Northumbrian bishop there is in AD 803. But a few years after the Northumbrians were claiming victories, Eadberht had withdrawn to Northumbria and abdicated in favour of his son, Oswulf, seeking to retire to a monastic life in York.

A new enemy was threatening the Celtic kingdoms of the north now – the Vikings, raiders from Scandinavia. The first raid on the Scottish islands is recorded in AD 794. The year before, Vikings had raided Lindisfarne. Within a few years, Vikings had made devastating raids throughout the islands and Iona was burnt in AD 802. The *Book of Kells*, being written on Iona, was transferred with members of the community to Ireland. In AD 806 Vikings slaughtered sixty-eight monks on Iona; the Holy Island, from where missionaries had brought the teachings of Christ to most of the English kingdoms, was abandoned for a century.

Significantly, we now find Constantine, son of Fergus, acclaimed as king of both Dál Riadans and Picts, building a new ecclesiastical foundation at Dunkeld, and his brother Oengus building another at St Andrews. Dunkeld was to become the centre of the northern church for a while and then was succeeded in the role by St Andrews as the primacy of Scotland. Constantine was one of three kings of the Cenél Gabhráin, the descendants of Gabhrán, who held the kingship of both Dál Riadans (Scots) and Picts before Cináech Mac Alpín, who, in popular tradition, is acclaimed as the king who first united both kingdoms. Constantine, however, came to power in AD 789 and appears to have ruled the Picts first, before succeeding to the Dál Riada kingship in AD 811. His reign over both kingdoms is an important stage in the unification of the country which was to become Scotland.

His brother Oengus II succeeded him in AD 820 and ruled for ten years. During this time the Vikings continued to raid along the west coast and form settlements; they would gradually claim all the Hebridean Islands as well as the Orkneys as their fiefdom. Blathmac mac Flainn, a monk on Iona, is recorded as meeting a violent death there in the *Annals of Ulster* in AD 825. It is implied that he was acting as abbot on Iona after the main body of monks had departed and was tortured and killed by the Vikings for refusing to show them the shrine of Colmcille.

In AD 839 Eóganán, the son of Oengus, was slain in a disastrous battle with the Vikings or Norsemen. His brother, Bran, was also slain with many of the Pictish chieftains. It was mainly as a result of this battle that Cináech Mac Alpín was able to establish his dynasty as rulers over both the Scots of Dál Riada and the Picts. It would seem from the evidence that Cináech was actually in alliance with the Norse in order to further his own political ambitions. He later gave his daughter in marriage to Olafr the White, who had made himself king of the settlement of Vikings at Dublin and who also claimed authority over the settlements throughout the western isles. After the Norse had slain Eoganán and Fergus, Cináech made his moves. He established his base in Dál Riada and then fought off a series of Pictish claimants during a five-year period. The last of these was Drust son of Ferat, who was slain in AD 848. Cináech was now undisputed king of both kingdoms, diplomatically dividing Colmcille's relics, with one portion being taken by the abbot of Iona back to Ireland, while the other portion was taken to Dunkeld, which he made his capital. The two kingdoms were jointly called Alba, 'the mountainous country'.

It was in AD 858 that Domnall I of Alba had the laws of the country proclaimed at both Forteviot and Fortriu, indicating that Dál Riadan and Pict would henceforth live under the same laws. As it is clear that this law system was a Dál Riadan one, it is obvious that the laws would closely approximate to the Brehon system of Ireland. The new kingdom was divided into seven provinces, each with its petty king or Mormaer (high steward), owing allegiance to the High King. The first mention of the office of *mór-mhaor* occurs in AD 918.

It was under Constantine II MacBeth (AD 900–43) that the period of the crucial consolidation and development of Alba began. During his reign the Strathclyde kings and the kings of the southern remnant of Rheged, called Cumbria, acknowledged the overlordship of the High Kings of Alba who now ruled from Sgàin (Scone). Until the late medieval period, the term 'Scot' applied to an Irishman and to the Dál Riadans. Thus medieval writers with the appellation 'Scotos', such as Sedulius Scotos, Johannes Scotos Eriugena and Clemens Scotos, were Irishmen. Only in the late medieval period, with another language change under way in Alba, the change from Gaelic to English, did the terms 'Scot' and 'Scotland' begin to be applied in their modern sense. This caused some confusion, demonstrated by the example of the famous Würzburg Schottenklöster, which was an Irish Benedictine foundation until 1497. With the change in terminology, the 'Scots' asked the Pope to expel the 'Irish' on the grounds that it was their foundation. The Pope, Alexander VI, did so and Würzburg remained a 'Scottish' foundation until 1803. In the Scottish Gaelic language, the country has always remained Alba and a Scotsman, an Albannach.

[13]

The Vikings

No more dreadful deed has been done in this land since the
Norse came and destroyed our peace.

Anglo-Saxon Chronicle

I N the ninth century a Irish monk, working on copying a manuscript which we now call St Gall's *Priscian Grammar*, raised his
head one night to listen to the howling storm outside the monastery walls. He thought a while and then wrote in the margin of his
work:

> *Is acher in gaíth innocht,*
> *Fu-fuasna fairrgae findfolt;*
> *Ní ágor réimm mora mind*
> *Dond laechraid lainn ó Lochlaind.*

> Bitter and wild the wind this night,
> Tossing the white combed ocean.
> I need not dread fierce Norsemen,
> Crossing the quiet seas.

In AD 793 ships containing raiders anchored off the island of Lindisfarne, then sacked and burned the monastery and settlement there.
In the following year, similar raiders appeared in their longships off
the Holy Isle of Iona and attacked the monastic centre. The year
afterwards, identical marauders were raiding the coast of Ireland.
The *Anglo-Saxon Chronicle* refers to them as *wicing* or pirates. The
Icelandic sagas mention *víking* as being a raiding expedition and
vikingr as a warrior or pirate. The age of the Viking had come to
Europe.

The Irish annalists referred to these first raiders as *finn-gaill*, 'white
foreigners', and later as Lochlannaigh for they came from Norway,

'the land of the loch' or lakes. It is not until fifty years later that *dubh-gaill*, 'black foreigners', occur in the annals; these are identified as Danes who, initially, fought the first Norse raiders. Both peoples, however, were referred to as Northmen or Norsemen and both were called Vikings by those they raided. It was not only Britain and Ireland that were to suffer their ravages. During the ninth and tenth centuries, they raided and settled on the coasts of north-west Germany, the Low Countries, France and Spain, even appearing in Sicily and reaching as far as Constantinople (Istanbul).

What had caused these raids and expansion? The tradition has been that the Norsemen were fleeing from the tyrannical growth of royal power in Norway. The country was also suffering a population growth; massive forests were being cleared for land but the area was becoming unable to sustain the people. Prior to the expansion the land had been held by the tribe; now the strongest person was exerting individual power and creating private property. Large estates were emerging. It has been suggested that the rune stone monuments were more inheritance claims than memorials to the dead. As the areas were united under absolute rulers, such as Gorm and his son Haraldr, the people needed to expand – the age-old cry for 'living space' was taken up.

Following the raiders came the settlers. Farmsteads in western Norway were abandoned and entire families set sail with their dependants, bringing farm tools, household goods and even farm stock.

Culturally the Norse were part of the Germanic family and it is not impossible that some of them had heard of the land, wealth and prestige to be had for any ruthless war bands in Britain and Ireland. After all, their cousins, the Angles and Saxons, had achieved tremendous successes having first raided and then settled Britain three centuries before. The Vikings were merely repeating the experience.

The expansion of the Norse had lasting impact in northern France where their raids, starting in AD 850, disrupted the Frankish kingdom and the neighbouring Breton kingdom. The abbey at Redon, founded by the Breton king Nominoë in AD 833, was devastated in AD 868. However, the Bretons under Alan I (the Great) managed to keep the Norse at bay, defeating them decisively at Questembert in AD 888. But on Alan's death in AD 907 the Norse raids began again. The Norse managed to establish themselves at Nantes, causing many

Bretons to migrate, especially the *religieux* who carried away Breton manuscripts, which found their way to Angers, Boulogne, Douai and Lille. However, Alan II, known as Barbertorte, who had curiously sought shelter for a time at the court of the West Saxon king Athelstan, returned to Brittany in AD 936 and commenced a series of military victories over the Norse starting at St Brieuc, then at Nantes (AD 937) and Trans (AD 939), thus driving the Norse out of Brittany.

In the mean time, the Franks had decided to come to terms with the fierce raiders; the area which was to be named after them, Normandy, was ceded to them in AD 911. Rollo, the Viking chieftain, was recognized as the first duke of Normandy. Rollo was supposed to recognize the suzerainty of the Frankish kings but the Norsemen, or Normans as they had become, were only nominally 'vassals'. They did accept Christianity, and also Frankish law and speech. Rollo's descendant, William, was to lead the conquest of England in 1066, becoming king there. Normandy was still regarded as the 'home land' by the Normans in England until the end of the Hundred Years War in 1450, when it was finally officially given back to the French kings. In fact, Normandy had been captured by the French as early as 1204. The 'loss' of Normandy caused an alteration in attitudes in England. This was the time when 'English' re-emerged as the language of the state for, between 1066 and 1450, Norman French was the official language of the ruling and middle classes. Dr Pei writes of Old English: 'The speech of the conquered was banned from all polite society and official usage, it was despised as the jargon of peasants and practically ceased to be a written language.'

Indeed, a flourishing French literature was produced in England following the Norman Conquest. Henry III encouraged scholars from Poitou into England to bolster the French literature and learning. From the Celtic perception of today, now that English has displaced the Celtic languages, the struggle of the English during the fourteenth century to gain status for their language is grimly ironic. The author of the *Cursor Mundi*, writing in 1300, pleading for status for English, argued: 'If we allow everyone their own language, it seems to me we are doing them no injury.' But as Robert of Gloucester reported, in the same year: 'Unless a man knows French, he is thought little of.' The modern Celt must experience a feeling of *déjà vu* when confronted with the comments of the English chronicler, Ranulph Higden, writing in 1364:

This impairing of the native tongue [English] is because of two things. One is that children in schools, contrary to the usage and customs of all other nations, are compelled to drop their own language and to construe their lessons and their other things in French, and have done so since the Normans first came to England. Also gentlemen's children are taught to speak French from the time that they are rocked in their cradle and can talk and play with a child's trinket; and up country men want to liken themselves to gentlemen and try with great effort to speak French so as to be thought the more of.

Perhaps the biggest historical 'bad joke' for the Celts is that in the fourteenth century an 'English Language Rights Movement' was started at Oxford by Celts and, moreover, Celtic-speakers. John Trevisa, of St Mellion, Cornwall (d. 1402), who wrote an encyclopaedia, refers to the fact that John of Cornwall and Richard Pencrych, both Cornish-speaking clerics who went to Oxford to teach grammar, were the first to start urging the use of English as against French. They had been so successful, says Trevisa, that 'in all the grammar schools of England, children are now dropping French and construing and learning in English'. In 1345, the chronicles of London were still being written in French.

However it was the Hundred Years War with France, with its bitter animosities, which gave the death blow to Norman French as the language of the ruling class and merchants in England. The Normans realized that to galvanize the Anglo-Saxon peasantry into fighting against France they would have to dissociate themselves, in the eyes of the peasantry, from the French enemy. In 1349 English was formally recognized as a language of academic instruction. In 1362 Edward III directed that all pleas to the courts could be made in English and not, as before, in Latin or French. 'Law French' was not entirely ousted, though, until an Act of Parliament as late as 1731. Also, in 1362, the Parliament was opened in English and discussions among its members were allowed to be conducted in that language. Most importantly, English was allowed to be used as a language of the royal court from 1403; by 1413, under Henry V, it was the official language of the court. English now had status for the first time since the Norman Conquest and the introduction of English in religious services, in 1547, was the final 'official recognition'.

The switch from French to English in the latter half of the four-teenth century was the most important development for English nationhood. But, of course, the language which emerged after three centuries of suppression by Norman French was not simply the Old English, or Anglo-Saxon. Its vocabulary had accepted much from Norman French. John Wyclif's first translation of the Bible into English, in 1380, dropped many Old English compounds in favour of French, while Geoffrey Chaucer (1340–1400), in his *Canterbury Tales*, merges the two languages into the compound form in which we recognize modern English. There were some who were not happy about this state of affairs and tried to revive 'pure' English, such as Bishop Richard Peacock, who attempted to cleanse the language of Norman influence, and Thomas Cheke, who produced a New Testament in 1561 in 'pure' English. But the compound language had won.

It has to be remarked that the linguistic struggle seems to have left no great understanding in English cultural consciousness about the value of language and culture. What the Norman French-speakers had attempted to do to English, summarized by the charge against the French kings of 1295 of wanting to wipe out the English lan-guage, the English now enthusiastically began to do to their Celtic-speaking neighbours with varying degrees of success.

Before we continue to examine the impact of the Norse invasions and settlements on the island of Britain, we must first turn our atten-tion to Ireland, for the Norse kingdom of Dublin was to be the base from which many raids on Britain were conducted. The Norse had first appeared in Ireland in AD 795, raiding the island of 'Rechra' (Rathlin) on the north-eastern point. Rathlin was the site of a sub-house of the Iona community. The annals clearly identify these raiders as Norwegians or 'white foreigners'. They not only raided but, after some years, established settlements on the coast of Ireland, most notably at Dublin, Wexford and Waterford and even on the west coast at Limerick. The Dublin settlement had been established by one Thorgil, who built a fort there which had developed into a fortified Norse township by AD 841. Thorgil was the founder of Norse power in Ireland and his policy was made plain by the saga writers: he wished to conquer the land and destroy Christianity. Many churches were converted into pagan shrines to the Norse gods.

Proof of Dublin's perceived strategic position was given in AD 849 when the king of Norway sent warriors to attack it and bring the settlers under his rule. By AD 851, Olafr the White, a kinsman of the king, became the ruler of Dublin, recognizing the Norwegian king as his suzerain. He continued in power for the next twenty years while his brothers Ivarr and Sigtrygg ruled at Limerick and Waterford. Olafr exerted his influence throughout the western isles of northern Britain and married the daughter of Cináech Mac Alpín.

A few years later the Danes, 'black foreigners', were raiding and attacking the original Norse settlers. By this time, a new breed of people called the 'Gall-Ghaedhil', the Norse-Irish, were emerging. They were the offspring of Norse and Irish intermarriages. The Norse had become bilingual and would eventually be totally absorbed into the Irish nation.

While the Irish were content to ignore the adventures of the Norse-Irish in Britain, any attempt by them to exert dominance over lands in Ireland other than their coastal townships was met with firm rebuke. One High King, Aed Finnliath mac Néill (AD 862–879) drove the Norse out of the north of Ireland with a campaign in AD 866. No further Norse settlements were made in the area.

In AD 857, however, the king of Norway had sent Ivarr the Boneless, a son of Ragnarr Lothbrook, to take Dublin and establish himself there. Ivarr also campaigned in Britain with his brother Halfdan. They devastated Sheppey, in East Anglia, and southern Northumbria (Deira) before Ivarr returned to Dublin where he died in AD 873, regarded as 'king of all the Norse of Ireland and Britain'. Therefore Aed Finnliath, the Irish High King, decided to form an alliance with the Norse-Irish rather than continue to fight them. He died peacefully in the monastery of Dromisken, Co. Louth.

Another High King, Niall Glúndubh Mac Aeda (AD 916–919), decided to make an attempt to control the Norse power-bases in Ireland. In AD 917 he marched against the Norse of Waterford, named Vadrefiord by the Norse, and Port Lairge by the Irish. At a site outside the city, called Cenn Fuait, the Norse defeated the Irish High King. Undeterred, Niall marched his army on to Dublin in the following year. At Cell-mo-Shámhóg, on the north bank of the Liffey (identified as Islandbridge), Niall was slain and his army defeated.

The check to Norse power in Ireland, a check which had

repercussions throughout Britain, was not made until the victory of the Irish High King, Brían Bóramha Mac Cennétig (1002–1014), at Clontarf. The situation had arisen, as in a classical tragedy, with the anger of a woman. Gormlaith, daughter of Murchadh, a petty king of Munster, had been wife to Olafr, a Norse king of Dublin, then to Mael Sechnaill Mac Domnaill, the former High King who resigned in 1022, and was now wife to Brían. She was obviously a lady who liked power. There was a quarrel between Gormlaith and Brían, after which she decided to plot his overthrow. She enticed her brother, Maelmore of Leinster, and her son, Sigtrygg Silkenbeard, by Olafr, to rebel against Brían. Maelmore and Sigtrygg, who was now king of Dublin, realizing that Brían was no easy pushover, called for the Norse warriors from Norway, Denmark, the Isle of Man, the Hebrides and the Orkneys to join forces in a crusade against Brían. It was to be an all-out push to established unquestioned Norse power in the islands.

Cnut, the son of Swein Forkbeard, king of Denmark, after landing in the Humber in 1013, was conducting a fierce war on the Anglo-Saxon kingdoms which would eventually lead to Cnut being acknowledged as supreme king of the Anglo-Saxon kingdoms and establishing a Danish dynasty which lasted until 1042 when Edward the Confessor re-established the Anglo-Saxon line for two decades more. The Norse star was clearly in the ascendant.

Sigtrygg offered the supreme command of the Norse army in Ireland to Sigurd Hlodverson, the fiercesome jarl of the Orkneys.

In turn, Brían, now seventy-two years old, sought assistance from other parts of the Celtic world, and a large contingent of Albannaich (Scots) arrived commanded by Domhnall Mac Eiminn Mac Cainnich, the Mormaer of Cé (Marr and Buchan).

The battle took place at Clontarf on Good Friday, 23 April 1014, and by evening Norse power had been broken. The Norse commander, Sigurd Hlodverson, had been slain and also the rebel king, Maelmore. But the Irish army also suffered. Brían's son, Murrough, his grandson, Turloch, and the Mormaer of the Scottish forces, Domhnall, were dead. More devastating was the fact that Brían himself had been killed. He had been slain by a Manx-Norse chieftain, Brodr, while standing at the door of his tent awaiting the final reports from the battlefield. *Burnt Njal's Saga* relates:

Sword blade rang on Ireland's coast.
Metal yelled as shield it sought.
Spear-points in the well-armed host.
I heard sword-blows, many more;
Sigurd fell in battle's blast,
From his wounds there sprang hot gore.
Brían fell, but won at last.

Indeed, even the Norse annalists paid tribute to Brían and called him 'the best of kings'. Mael Sechnaill, the former High King, who had played a leading role in Brían's campaign, was re-elected as High King and continued to rule until 1022. It was Clontarf that broke Norse power in the islands.

From the beginning of the ninth century the Norse had also managed to establish another independent and strategically placed kingdom from which they could conduct their raids on Britain. They had settled on the Isle of Man (Ellan Vannin) which was then Goidelic Celtic in culture, the change from Brythonic to Goidelic Celtic having started in the fifth century. The Isle of Man was pivotal, half-way between Britain and Ireland, and ideally situated as a base for the raiders. The Norse settled there and began to intermix with the native culture, as they had done in Ireland and also in the Hebrides, first becoming bilingual and then merging indistinguishably into the native Gaelic language and culture.

Olafr the White is recorded as having gained control of the island. Within a few decades the Isle of Man was the centre of a kingdom known as the Sudreyjar, the Sudreys, or Southern Islands, which encompassed the whole of the Hebrides. The name still survives in the title of the Anglican bishop on the island who is known as 'Bishop of Sodor and Man'. The Nordreys were the Orkneys and Faeroes islands. The Faeroes were settled from the Isle of Man by Norse-Gaels led by Grim Camban. The Irish geographer, Dicuil (c.AD 775–c.850), mentions that a hundred years before this Irish monks lived on the Faeroes and settlements had been formed there.

The kingdom of Man and the Isles, ruled by Gaelicized Norse kings, remained fairly independent until Magnus III, on his death, ceded his kingdom to Alexander III of Scotland in 1265. Until that time, representatives from the Hebrides would journey to the parliament, the Thing-völlr (Tynwald), on the island. The Manx

Parliament is the oldest recorded continuous parliament in the world. The Norwegian kings, who had long claimed to be suzerain lords of the kingdom, formally gave up their claims to the Isle of Man and the Hebrides when Magnus the Law Reformer of Norway accepted the Treaty of Perth in 1266.

As the Norse moved westward they had established settlements in the Shetlands, the Faeroes, the Orkneys and through the Hebrides. They also established settlements on northern Britain itself, annexing territory in the northern lands of the Picts in Caithness and Sutherland. The Celtic people of northern Britain, the Dál Riadans, Picts, Strathclyde Britons and Cumbrians, were feeling the full force of their raids. In AD 839 came the major disaster when the king of the 'Scots and Picts', Eoganán, was slain in battle and Cináech Mac Alpín made an apparent alliance with Olafr the White of Dublin to become king in his stead. Cináech seemed to recognize the Norse right to settle and rule the territories they had won.

A few years later came a series of attacks through the Western Isles as the Danes raided the earlier Norse settlements.

It was around AD 850 that Sigurd the Powerful (c.AD 850–870), a brother of Rognvaldur of Moer, in western Norway, and father of Rollo, the first duke of Normandy, established the jarldom of the Orkneys. This jarldom, or earldom, included not only the Orkney group but also the Hebrides, with claims over the Isle of Man and Dublin. The Orkneys, some ninety islands and islets, were to remain in Norse possession until they were ceded back to Scotland in 1472. From his base Sigurd, in alliance with Thorstein the Red, son of Olafr the White of Dublin, mounted a campaign against the people of the now united kingdom of Alba. It was Sigurd who annexed Caithness and Sutherland to his jarldom. Near Dornock Firth, Sutherland, he slew Máelbrigte, the local ruler, and cut off his head, hanging it from his saddle. The teeth of the severed head grazed the Norse jarl and the wound turned septic and fatal. The *Heimskringla* seems to imply a poetic justice. He was buried in Sutherland and his son Guthorm succeeded him.

To the south the Saxon kingdoms had been coming under increasing threats from the Norse since the first sack of Lindisfarne in AD 793. In AD 835 there came Halfdan's major attack on the Isle of Sheppey, Kent. The following year Ecgberht (AD 802–39) of Wessex faced a Norse army which landed from thirty-five longships and marched on Carhampton, Somerset. Ecgberht, who was regarded as Bretwalda, was routed. Seizing their chance, the Celts of Cornwall had decided to make common cause with the Norse, or Danes as these newcomers clearly were. A joint Cornish-Danish army fought Ecgberht at Hingston Down but Ecgberht had recovered and they were defeated.

When Ecgberht died in 839 his son Aethelwulf became king of Wessex. He immediately sought to consolidate his power, driving out Baldred, the last independent king of Kent, and uniting the entire south under his control. In AD 851 he faced a new Danish threat. The Saxons 'inflicted the greatest slaughter on a heathen army that we have ever heard of until this day', quoted the *Anglo-Saxon Chronicle*. Athelstan, Aethelwulf's eldest son, who had been made sub-king of Kent after the defeat of Baldred, is said to have fought the first naval battle in recorded English history. With his *ealdorman*, Ealhhere, in AD 851, he took a Saxon fleet off Sandwich and defeated the Danes in a major victory. Ealhhere was killed later with Huda, another *ealdorman*, when he tried to repulse the Danes at the Isle of Thanet.

Aethelwulf found himself able to hold back the Danish threat. In AD 855 he was so secure that he decided to go on a pilgrimage to Rome, leaving Wessex under the control of his two sons. Aethelbald was to rule in the west and Aethelberht controlled in the east. When he returned, Aethelbald refused to give up his portion and Aethelwulf was forced to retire, unable to retrieve his kingdom. He died a few years later.

There was a short respite from the Norse attack until AD 864 when Ivarr the Boneless and Halfdan arrived with a 'great army' among the Saxon kingdoms. For the first time a Norse army wintered in the Saxon lands, destroying Sheppey in AD 865 and overrunning East Anglia where the last king, Edmund, was killed in AD 869. Edmund, now accorded sainthood, fell at a battle at Hoxne and was first buried at Hellesdon in Norfolk, before being taken to Bury St Edmunds where a cult quickly developed, based on the story of his death as related by his armour bearer to Athelstan and St Dunstan. During this time the Saxons imposed a tax to raise money in an attempt to buy off the raiders. It was called Danegeld and it was first imposed in AD 868. It was to become a regular tax until the thirteenth century, long after the Danes had ceased to pose any threat. The English kings simply saw it as a convenient method of raising money for themselves.

The ravaging Danish army moved north again to southern Northumbria, formerly Deira, where they killed Osberht of Northumbria and the usurper Aelle in an assault on York. In later Scandinavian legend it is recorded that Ragnarr Lothbrok, the father of Ivarr and Halfdan, had been captured by Aelle and thrown into a snake pit. The assault upon Northumbria was said to be in revenge for their father's death. There is nothing to substantiate this tale. However, the result of this attack was that Ivarr returned to Dublin while Halfdan made himself king of York. Here the Danes built a settlement and 'began to plough and support themselves'.

There now appeared another Norse leader, Guthrum, who had joined Ivarr and Halfdan in AD 871 and began to ravage Wessex. Alfred, the youngest son of Aethelwulf, had succeeded as king, and was struggling grimly to keep the Danes at bay. When they attacked his royal residence at Chippenham, Alfred barely escaped with his life and went into hiding into the marshes of Somerset.

In the north of Britain, Olafr the White and Ivarr were raiding in Pictland. In 871 they turned south and sacked the Strathclyde capital of Alcluyd (Dumbarton). It was about this time that a group of Gall-Ghaedhils began their famous settlement of Iceland. Norse settlers from the Hebrides and Caithness, under the leadership of Aud the Deep-Minded (c.AD 855–65), a daughter of Ketil Flatnose, a local Hebridean Norse chieftain, and mother of Thorstein the Red, led the exodus. On the death of her son she organized a mass migration of Norse to Iceland and founded a settlement in Laxárdal. Her traditions show that she belonged to the Gall-Ghaedhil, or Norse-Irish culture. Irish settlers and religious groups were well established in Iceland at this time. In c.AD 795, the Irish scholar, Diciul, reported a number of Irish monks making the journey to Iceland. It is perhaps significant that, among the Norse sagas about the settlement of Iceland, such as the *Islendingabok* (Book of the Icelanders) and *Lannámabók* (Book of Land-Taking), compiled in the twelfth century, is the saga of Burnt Njal. Njal is the Irish name, Niul, in later form Niall or Néill. The Burnt Njal saga is one of the best-known of Icelandic tales.

In AD 874 Halfdan, who had extended his rule over most of the former Northumbrian kingdom, was leading his Danes to attack the

Strathclyde Britons and Scots (we shall use the modern name for the people of Alba) and in AD 877, Constantine I was slain by the Danes. In 903 the Danes plundered the ecclesiastical centre of Dunkeld but the next year they were checked when Ivarr, the grandson of Ivarr the Boneless, was killed in a battle in Strathearn.

In 877, Halfdan decided to return to Dublin in an attempt to claim the kingship when his brother was killed. He left behind him a new, strong Danish kingdom in Britain – that of Danish York, dominating what had once been Northumbria.

The Celtic kingdoms in what is now Wales were also under the Norse threat. A witness of the initial Norse raids was the historian Nennius whose *Historia Brittonum* provides us with another essential source from the British Celtic viewpoint. Nennius, alive during this crucial period, describes himself as a disciple of Elfoddw (d. AD 809), a bishop of Gwynedd who had been responsible for persuading the British Celts to accept the Roman dating of Easter in AD 768. Little else is known of Nennius. One intriguing glimpse is given in a manuscript dated AD 817 in the Bodleian Library, Oxford, which records that Nennius was once attacked by a Saxon churchman who sneered that the Celts had no native alphabet but had to use Latin characters. How soon had the Saxons forgotten that it was the Celts who had taught them literacy only two centuries before and that the Celts had taught the very Latin alphabet which the English were using. The Irish Ogham alphabet had been discarded around that time. The manuscript reports that Nennius had, however, risen to the ignorant attack, and invented a 'Celtic alphabet' to confound his critic. Alas, we have no record of it. Did Nennius truly 'invent' an alphabet or did he merely show his antagonist the Ogham alphabet which had been used by the Irish settlers and monks in Wales?

Nennius's history is concerned with the origin legends of the British Celts and then moves to the coming of the Saxons and their conflict with the Celts. What is clear, as Cecile O'Rahilly demonstrates, is that Nennius had access to Irish works of the pre-Danish period. Heinrich Zimmer also shows that he made use of at least three Irish documents in the pre-Danish form, especially texts concerning Patrick, now preserved in the *Book of Armagh*, the *Leabhar Gabhála* (or Book of Invasions) and a tract *De sex aetatibus mundi* now preserved in the *Book of Ballymote*. The *Historia Brittonum*, which has also been preserved in five surviving Irish manuscripts, was added to and edited a number of times in the subsequent two centuries. One of the editions was compiled by a pupil of Beulan, an Irishman. Although there is no record of the year Nennius died, it was probably around AD 840, so the monk of Gwynedd would have lived through many of the early attacks of the Vikings.

At this time Gwynedd and the other British Celtic kingdoms were undergoing fundamental changes of attitude and moving towards the unity of what we can recognize today as Wales. The process started with Merfyn Frych, 'the Freckled', ap Gwriad (AD 825–855) who became king of Gwynedd and married Esyllt, the sister of Cyngen ap Cadell, the last king of the old line of Powys. It was Cyngen who set up the famous Eliseg Pillar at Llantysilion-Ial near Llangollen to honour his grandfather's military exploits against the Saxons. Merfyn twice went on pilgrimages and died in Rome. From a manuscript preserved in Vamburg, Bavaria, based on a ninth-century original, we have a letter from Merfyn to Cyngen regarded as the earliest 'Welsh' letter in existence. Merfyn was well respected and his court was a cultural centre. The *Annales Cambriae* in their present form were drawn up during his reign and Nennius was writing his *Historia Brittonum*. What we now call 'Welsh' literature and scholarship was flourishing.

The son of Merfyn Frych, Rhodri ap Merfyn, according to the Irish annals, had become king of Gwynedd by AD 856. Through his mother's connections he was elected as king of Powys and by marrying Angharad, sister of Gwgon of Ceredigion, he was recognized as ruler of the southern kingdom of Seissyllwg, which had been formed by the union of Ceredigion and Ystrad Tywi. It was not until the time of his grandson that Dyfed, on the Pembroke peninsula, came under the rule of his dynasty. Under Rhodri Mawr, however, the greater part of what we know as Wales was united under one ruler.

Rhodri was, however, still vulnerable to the continued attacks from the Saxons as well as the new threat of Norse raiders along the Welsh coast. Even while the Saxons were fighting Danish incursions they still had not lost sight of their designs on Wales. In AD 822 the *Annales Cambriae* note an incursion by the Saxons into Powys and the *Anglo-Saxon Chronicle* says that Ecgberht of Wessex, having conquered his neighbouring Saxons in Mercia in AD 828, attempted to invade Wales. Even in AD 853, at a crucial point of the Danish raids into the Saxon kingdoms, Bugred of Mercia sought the help of Aethelwulf in an attempt to conquer Powys.

In AD 856, scarcely a few weeks in power, Rhodri had to face a strong Norse challenge to the security of his kingdom. The *Annals of Ulster* record that he met a Norse fleet off Anglesey and slew the leader Gormr. The news of this victory was received with joy at the court of Liège of Charles the Bald, king of the Franks, who was also suffering from Norse raids. At Liège, the Irish scholar Siadhal (AD 820–880), better known by his Latin name, Sedulius Scotos, wrote an ode on the victory. Siadhal was a highly respected confidant of both the emperors Lothar and Charles. His poems were said to have been sewn in tapestry by Lothar's empress Ermingarde. From the evidence, both Merfyn Frych and Rhodri were known and respected at the Frankish court. Nora K. Chadwick claims Rhodri as 'the greatest of all Welsh kings'.

After Rhodri had reigned for twenty prosperous years, in AD 877, Ceolwulf II (AD 874–9), the last independent king of Mercia, whose hatred of the Celts was matched by his hatred of Alfred and the power of Wessex, struck up an alliance with the Danes against Alfred. The *Anglo-Saxon Chronicle* is naturally hostile to him. He allowed the Danes to occupy Repton in Derbyshire. It was undoubtedly the Mercian-Danish alliance launched against Gwynedd in AD 877 that forced Rhodri Mawr to seek temporary asylum in Ireland, according to the *Annales Cambriae*, following a 'Sunday battle' in Anglesey. Rhodri returned the next year, only to be slain in battle with the Saxons. These, undoubtedly, were Ceolwulf's Mercians.

For the next forty years, Rhodri's son, Anarwad ap Rhodri, was supreme ruler over the Welsh kingdoms, with local kingships being divided between Rhodri's five other sons. The Danes seemed too involved in establishing their power among the Saxon kingdoms to bother any more about attempting to establish a foothold among the Celts of Wales.

Meanwhile, following his initial defeat by the Danes, between AD 877 and 879, Alfred of Wessex was waging a guerrilla war from a base on the island of Athelney. The campaign was successful in that he had been able to gain time to raise a Saxon army and bring it into the field at Edington. His victory and later siege of what had been his former residence and fortress at Chippenham, but which was now the stronghold of the Danish leader Guthrum, forced the surrender of the Danes. A peace was agreed at Aller, near Athelney, and in the

Treaty of Wedmore (AD 879) Guthrum accepted Christianity and took the baptismal name of Athelstan, with Alfred standing as his godfather. Guthrum's Danish settlement of East Anglia was recognized. The Danelaw, the area in which Danish law and custom were recognized by the Anglo-Saxons, was agreed. Danish rule more or less ran north of a line from Chester to London. There were more Norse raids into Wessex towards the end of Alfred's reign in AD 892–5 but he was able to contain them.

The Danes, however, were consolidating their power from their bases in the former northern Anglo-Saxon kingdoms. Ragnall, a grandson of Ivarr the Boneless, expelled from Dublin in AD 902, harried the Celts in Cumbria, Strathclyde and Alba until he heard of the defeat of the Danish kingdom of York by Edward the Elder of Wessex in AD 910. Edward was the eldest son of Alfred, and he had made it his ambition to drive the Danes out of the Saxon kingdoms. He conquered the Danish settlements in East Anglia and those in Mercia, incorporating them in his kingdom of Wessex. Having dealt with an unsuccessful revolt by his cousin, Aethelwold, he launched an assault on the Danish settlements of York and defeated the Danes at Tettenhall. Building fortresses as he went, he presided over the political incorporation of the former kingdom of Mercia into Wessex.

Ragnall, however, arrived in York and rallied the Danes. He attacked Ealdred, lord of Bamburgh, who fled to Alba and enlisted the help of Constantine II. The Scots, to give them recognizable form to English readers, were defeated in Corbridge in AD 914 and again in AD 918. But it seems the Scots did reinstate Ealdred and his brother Uhtred into part of the former Northumbrian kingdom. Ragnall moved back to Ireland, in order to support his brother Sigtrygg of Dublin, and during his absence, Edward's sister, Aethelflaed, organized a coalition of Mercians, Scots and Strathclyde Britons against the Danes. Ragnall returned, overcame the opposition but died in York in AD 920. He was succeeded by his brother Sigtrygg Caech, who made terms with Athelstan, the new king of Wessex, and converted to Christianity, marrying Aethelstan's sister, Eadgyth. When he died in AD 927 Athelstan was able to seize control of York which then led to the great confederation of Celt and Norseman which we will deal with in 'The Prophecy of Great Britain'.

When Eadred (AD 946–955) became ruler of the English kingdoms, the antagonism between the Saxon and Danish areas had considerably lessened and the Danelaw submitted to Anglo-Saxon rule in AD 954. The submission of Eirikr Bloodaxe marked the creation of 'England' in more or less its modern form. Eirikr was the son of Harald Finehair of Norway. He was jarl of the Orkneys and had been invited by the Danes of York to become their king in AD 947. His rule was opposed not only by Eadred but by Olafr Sigtryggson of Dublin, who claimed the York kingdom. Eirikr was therefore hunted by the Saxons and also opposed by some of the Danes loyal to Olafr. He was killed in an ambush. Eadred made his son, Osulf, earl of Northumbria. The former kingdom of Northumbria now became an earldom and an integral part of the English kingdom. The Danes, Christianized, eventually merged into the Anglo-Saxon kingdoms, though their language and culture left a distinctive heritage especially in those areas where the Danelaw ran.

The Danes and Saxons, living as uneasy neighbours, now realized that their languages had the same Germanic roots and the language frontier was almost non-existent. There was a tendency to merge the languages, and Norse words such as *they, get, till, both* began to be commonly used. Professor Thomas Alan Shippey, of the University of Leeds, has demonstrated how close the two languages actually were and how easily Saxon could communicate with Dane. If the Saxon wanted to say, 'I'll sell you the horse that pulls my wagon,' he would say, '*Ic selle the that hors the draegeth minne waegn.*' The Dane would have phrased the statement thus: '*Ek mun selja ther hrossit er dregr vagn mine.*' The grammatical structure might be slightly unsynchronized but the words are basically the same and communicable. One contribution made by the Danes to the creation of modern English was the simplification of word-endings to convey meanings for which prepositions (such as 'to', 'with' and 'from') are now used. However, the exact impact on the vocabulary of Old English by the Norse influence is hard to evaluate because of the similarities of the two languages.

The submission of the Danelaw in AD 954 was not, of course, the last that the Saxons saw of Danish attempts to take over the Anglo-Saxon kingdoms. Swein Forkbeard, king of Denmark (*c.*AD 986–1014), started to raid England and with his third campaign in 1013 he brought his son Cnut (Knútr) with him. The victories over the English were immediate and Aethelred II was forced to flee to Normandy. Swein was recognized as king of England but died within a few days. Aethelred tried to return but Cnut led his army against him and then against his successor Edmund Ironside. Five battles resulted in Cnut founding the Danish dynasty of kings of England. Cnut was also acknowledged king of Denmark in 1018 when his brother King Haraldr died. The two kingdoms seemed on the verge of total unification but when Cnut died, in 1035, Magnus of Norway began an invasion of Denmark. The union of England and Denmark dissolved with the Danish kings losing Denmark and only managing to keep hold of their English possession.

The last major attempt to establish Norse control of the Anglo-Saxon kingdoms came in September 1066, when Haraldr ('The Hard') Sigurdsson, the king of Norway (1042–1066), landed in the Humber estuary with an army of 18,000 warriors. He claimed to be the heir of Cnut. He was supported in this by Tostig, the earl of Northumbria, and by Maol Callum a' chinn mhor, the Scottish king. The Anglo-Saxon king, Harold Godwineson, himself married to a Danish wife, hurried north and inflicted a devastating defeat on Haraldr at Stamford Bridge, near York. Haraldr was slain. Harold Godwineson was just celebrating his victory at York when he heard that another branch of the Norse people, William and his Normans (the Norsemen who had settled in northern France in AD 911), had landed at Pevensey. Harold hurried south to Hastings and defeat. Once again, the face of the Anglo-Saxon kingdoms was to be changed, but now for the last time.

In 793 AD, at Lindisfarne, there occurred the first 'Viking' raid recorded in the British Isles. They came in ships like the 'Edda'. This is a full-scale replica, made in 1988, of the Oseburg ship which was excavated in 1904.

Did the Irish religious leader, Brendan the Voyager (c. 486–578 AD), land on the American continent as the popular tale 'Brendan's Voyage' seems to indicate? Tim Severin and his companions demonstrated it could be done.

Eliseg's Pillar, a 9th Century tribute by Cyngen (d. 854 AD) to his famous great-grandfather Elise, king of Powys, the contemporary and chief opponent of the Anglo-Saxon king, Offa of Mercia.

The Hunterston Brooch, National Museum of Scotland, regarded as 7th Century, one of the earliest of the Celtic richly decorated penannular brooches, demonstrates that the Celts had developed metalwork techniques of their own.

The Ardagh Chalice, made in Ireland in the 8th Century, and generally regarded as one of the greatest works of Celtic ecclesiastical art. It is now in the National Museum of Ireland.

A folio from the Book of Kells, Trinity College, Dublin, once called 'the most beautiful book in the world'. It contains the Four Gospels and was said to have originated among the monks of Iona to commemorate the bicentenary of the death of Colmcille.

Iona, I-Shona, the Holy Island of Colmcille. Colmcille, exiled from Ireland, arrived with his companions in Dál Riada (Argyll) and established a monastic settlement on Iona in 563 AD. This became a cradle of Celtic Christianity.

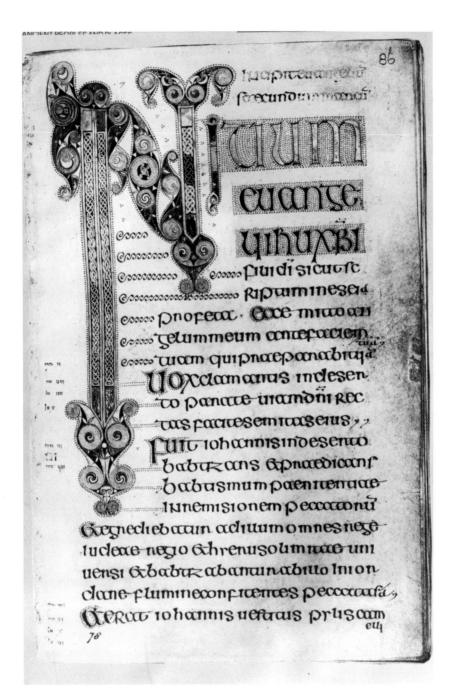

The Book of Durrow, Royal Irish Academy, has attracted a wide spectrum of datings, some putting it as early as early 7th Century while others favour an early 8th Century date.

Glamis Manse (Angus) Pictish Stone dated to the 8th Century, with its intricate Celtic knotwork, showing a Christian cross decorated with some typical Pictish symbols.

The Monymusk Reliquary, now in the National Museum of Scotland, was said to have contained a relic of St Colmcille (Columba) when it was carried into battle at Bannockburn, when the Scots defeated the English invaders in 1314, and secured four more centuries of independence.

Statue of Nominoë, king of Brittany, who secured six centuries of Breton independence when he vanquished the Frankish army of Charles the Bald at Ballon, near Redon, on November 22, 845 AD. The statue stands on the battlefield.

The Norrie's Law hoard of Pictish silver, now in the Royal Museum of Scotland, dated to the 6th Century by the association of a coin found with it. Usually, the Picts used silver looted from the Romans and remelted it to their use.

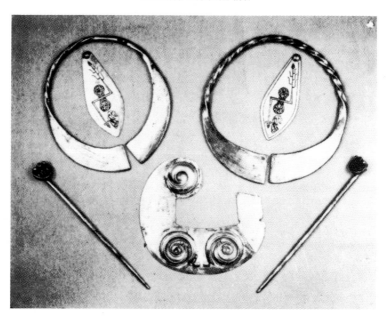

Celtic ecclesiastical art reached breath-taking artistic and technical brilliance in the Cross of Cong, made by Maelisu from Cong, in Co. Mayo, 1123–1136 AD.

[14]

Asser the Celt: Adviser to Alfred

'... my countrymen, who were dependent upon me, perceived their greater security, were I to accept the position of
counsellor to the King of the Saxons.'

Asser,
Life of King Alfred, c. AD 893/4

DURING the late ninth century one of the most fascinating
Celtic scholars and churchmen of his day made his appearance. His work had tremendous influence on English law and
literacy but, perhaps for the obvious reasons, it was hardly credited
by subsequent historians. Around AD 885, a Welshman, Asser, had
achieved a reputation for his scholarship. He was a kinsman of Nobis
(AD 840–873/4) who had been bishop of St David's on Mynyw in
Dyfed. This was the great Celtic religious centre founded in the sixth
century by Dewi Sant, son of Non and descendant of Ceredig whose
name had been given to the kingdom of Ceredigion. St David's was
so important in the Celtic religious world that two pilgrimages to it
were considered equal to a pilgrimage to Rome. St David's was, of
course, a major scholastic centre and home of the original chronicles
which acted as sources to many of the extant Welsh annals.

It would appear that Asser was of a prominent Dyfed family. He
was also learned in several languages, including Saxon. But little is
known of Asser's life before he received what was, on the surface, a
curious invitation from the king of Wessex – Alfred. Alfred's star
was in the ascendant and, following the Treaty of Wedmore, in which
he had dealt with the Danish threat, albeit as a short-term policy, he
had been busy building a series of fortresses to protect his borders,
making an alliance with Mercia through marriage, with his sister,
Aethelswith, being married off to Burgred of Mercia, while he had
married a Mercian lady named Ealhswith. The Mercians, with the

old antagonist Ceolwulf dead, had accepted Wessex overlordship. In AD 886, following Alfred's capture of London, all the English king-doms submitted to Wessex except those areas which were under Danish rule.

In AD 885, Alfred sent an invitation to Asser at St David's. He asked the scholar to meet him to discuss an important proposition. Asser had to travel over 'great expanses of land' and finally met up with the Saxon king in Sussex, at either East or West Dean. Alfred's proposition was that the Celtic scholar should go to work for him. The terms agreed were generous. Asser was to spend only six months in any year in his service. He would have to read aloud to the Saxon king when requested to do so, translate works from Latin and Greek into Saxon, and help devise a law system for the Anglo-Saxons. It was also Asser's task to teach the Saxon king to read and understand Latin, which was indispensable to the 'educated'. Indeed, Alfred had only learnt to read and write Anglo-Saxon after his twelfth birthday. So the Celtic monk was to come as teacher to the Saxon king. And to this proposition Asser agreed, after some thought, although he seems apologetic about deserting his own countrymen, explaining that he felt he could serve the British Celts better at the court of the Saxon king than he could among his own people. It was an excuse that many Celts, in later years, were to use in order to justify a decision to 'go where their bread was buttered' and take jobs with the conquerors.

Very likely there were also political concerns behind the offer. Alfred, in his search to complete the Saxon conquest of Britain, wanted to bring the Welsh kingdoms under his control, especially as they were now more or less united, first by Merfyn Frych and then by Rhodri Mawr. With Asser at the Saxon court, Alfred could secure first-hand information and advice as to what diplomatic manoeuvres were possible to secure his recognition as overlord among the Welsh. Indeed, Asser seems to have entered the profession of diplomacy quite well for we find that, between AD 885 and 893, three petty kings of South Wales acknowledged Alfred's power. One of them was Hyfraidd ap Bleddri, king of Dyfed, and therefore Asser's own king. These southern kings sought Alfred's assistance against the successor to Rhodri Mawr, his son Anarawd ap Rhodri (AD 878–916). Rather ingenuously, Asser assures us, in his *Life of Alfred*, that the Welsh kings were not siding with Alfred for any other reason than for his successful stand against the Norse, who were intent on destroying Christianity among the Celts as well as the Saxons. But Asser also points out that the king of Dyfed, Hyfraidd, had several times sacked St David's and implies that his kinsman, Nobis, and he had had to flee on those occasion. Hyfraidd's concerns about saving Christianity therefore have a hollow ring. The real reason is, quite obviously, that the southern Welsh rulers resented the rising power of Anarawd.

It is interesting that Asser may have been a third choice for teacher and adviser to Alfred. Fulco, archbishop of Rheims, had sent Alfred a Frankish scholar named Grimbald from the monastery of St Bertin, at St Omer. And a Continental Saxon monk named John had also arrived, but he was so austere that his fellow monks at Athelney, where Alfred had placed him, nearly killed him. Neither Grimbald nor John had any apparent influence on Alfred's later educational programme. As a footnote to the reference to Grimbald, a dubious source has it that it was Eriugena (Johannes Scotos) who went to England from the court of Charles the Bald at Alfred's invitation in about AD 877, and was killed by his enraged students at Malmesbury. However, this is clearly a confusion of the story of Grimbald and there is no evidence to support the contention that Eriugena was ever in England.

Asser's diplomatic role in persuading the kings of southern Wales to accept Alfred's overlordship rather than the overlordship of their fellow Celt, Anarawd, seems curious from this point in time and with the hindsight of the Saxon conquest of Wales. Anarawd's response to Alfred's military interference in his affairs was to turn to Guthfrith, the Danish king of York, and conclude an alliance. Guthfrith (AD 883–895), a convert to Christianity, was not a good ally, and in AD 893, the year when Asser was completing what was to be his famous Life of Alfred, Anarawd decided that the best policy would be to acknowledge Alfred as overlord. But Anarawd received the worst of both worlds. Alfred's terms were harsh and there was a curious clause which demanded that Anarawd accept Alfred as his godfather. This was the usual formula when a pagan king submitted to a Christian king but not when a fellow Christian submitted. Guthfrith's Danes then ravaged Anarawd's kingdom during the following year, presumably in retaliation because they felt that their ally had 'sold out'.

Anarawd, having formed an alliance with Alfred, marched into the southern kingdom of Seissyllwg and forced it to reaffirm the union made by Rhodri Mawr. The Wessex support for the southern Welsh kingdoms appears to have ended once Anarawd had acknowledged Alfred as suzerain.

Nevertheless, Asser was rewarded for his services by the grateful Alfred. He was made bishop of Sherborne around the mid-AD 890s, a position which he held until his death in AD 908/9. Alfred had, with Asser's help, established a school at his court in which his own children were taught.

According to Messrs McCrum, Cran and MacNeil, in *The Story of English*, Alfred appeared at 'the moment at which it became suddenly possible that English might be wiped out altogether. With no English-speaking kingdoms left, the country would gradually speak Norse.' They see the Treaty of Wedmore as the point by which Alfred not only saved the Anglo-Saxons but, through his education programme, began 'appealing to a shared sense of Englishness, conveyed by the language. Alfred quite consciously used the English language as a means of creating a sense of national identity.' It was his inspiration to use English rather than Latin through which to educate his *ealdormen* and thanes. In a preface to a translation of Bede's *Historia Ecclesiastica gentis Anglorum*, Alfred writes:

> Therefore it seems better to me . . . that we should also translate certain books which are most necessary for all men to know, into the language we can all understand, and also arrange it . . . so that the youth of free men now among the English people . . . are able to read English writing as well.

Asser obviously set into motion many projects, including the compilation of the *Anglo-Saxon Chronicle* and the gathering of the works for rendering into Saxon under Plegmund, archbishop of Canterbury (AD 890–923), and Waerferth, bishop of Worcester (AD 872–914/5) who, according to Asser, translated the *Dialogues of Pope Gregory*. Under Asser's tuition, Alfred improved his Latin so that he was able to translate Gregory's *Cura Pastoralis*, 'Pastoral Care', himself. Other works, such as Bede's *Historia Ecclesiastica*, Augustine's Soliloquies and Boethius's *De Consolatione Philosophiae*, 'Consolations of Philosphy', were also produced.

The most important of all the major works produced under the influence of Asser and patronage of Alfred was the first law code to apply to all the Saxon kingdoms. It is a landmark in English legal history. The work was issued just before the end of Alfred's reign and in a brief preface, Alfred states that the laws had been collected from the law codes of Ine of Wessex, Offa of Mercia and Aethelberht of Kent. Alfred, it is stated, had gone through them, rejecting some and retaining those which he had thought just.

However, Sir Frank Stenton states that 'there are important features in his laws which are not derived from any known source and may well be original. They include provisions protecting the weaker members of society against oppression, limiting the ancient customs of the blood feud, and emphasizing the duty of a man to his lord.'

Sir Frank Stenton overlooks the obvious. What influence did Asser have on the compilation of the law code, shaped, as he was, by the Celtic legal system of his own culture? So far as our records show, there was no known codification of the Welsh laws at that time. A few years later, in the time of Hywel Dda (AD 910–950), a codification was made so that the system was called 'The Laws of Hywel Dda'. But we know that the laws existed before this date and that Asser would have been well acquainted with them. All Hywel did was order the setting down of laws already known. Hywel's chief adviser on this matter was Blegywryd ab Einon, archdeacon of Llandaf, a man acknowledged as being of great learning and experience in the native law. J. Goronwy Edwards, however, believes that there is no satisfactory evidence that Blegywryd existed because all the references to him occur in prefaces to the surviving manuscript books of law, of which there are seventy, the majority dating from between 1200 and 1500. This is a curious argument: if Edwards is saying that we cannot accept Blegywyrd's existence because there is no contemporary evidence for it, then one shudders to think how many other historical personalities there are whose existence we must question on the same basis.

The prefatory remarks to most of the law books agree in one essential: that Hywel Dda, having asked Blegywryd to collect the laws, summoned an assembly consisting of the bishops and scholars, with six men from each of the local sub-divisions of the country, presumably elected civic leaders. The assembly examined and discussed the laws for a period of forty days and made recommendations. The laws, thus revised, were set down in writing and embodied in a single code which applied to the entire territory of what was to be Hywel's kingdom.

There is other evidence for a Celtic law system before this date. Geoffrey of Monmouth mentions a Celtic law system in Cornwall, the Molmutine law. The basis of the Molmutine law was, significantly, the protection of the weak against oppression. However, while we cannot take Geoffrey's word as creditable on the early Celtic law system, we are reminded that just before Alfred's reign, Domnuil I of Alba had the ancient laws of Dál Riada promulgated at Forteviot and Fortriu, demonstrating their existence. Later, when the kingdom of Alba incorporated the Strathclyde Britons and the Cumbrians, it was important that a legal code be drawn up to reconcile any discrepancy between the law systems of the Goidelic and British Celts. A document, the *Leges inter Bretonnes et Scotos*, dates from the eleventh century and includes terms which have connections with the Laws of Hywel Dda. According to Professor Kenneth Jackson: 'This may imply the existence of a common Brittonic legal tradition of considerable antiquity.' More importantly, as evidence of the Celtic law tradition, we have an entire corpus of ancient law known as the Brehon laws, which, so tradition has it, Patrick first ordered to be set down in writing. The *Annals of Ulster* state under the year AD 438: '*Senchus Mór do scribenn.*' The *Senchus Mór* deals with civil law while the *Book of Acaill* dealt with criminal law. The Irish law tracts are probably the most important documents of their kind in the whole of western Europe by reason of their extent, their antiquity and the tradition they preserve. Their roots are in ancient Indo-European custom and not in Roman law, and they cover both civil and criminal law. One of the earliest and most complete manuscript survivals of the laws occurs in the *Leabhar na hUidri*, compiled at Clonmacnoise *c.* 1100 and also known as 'The Book of the Dun Cow'. It was stolen and disappeared during the Cromwellian invasion but, miraculously, found its way into the hands of a Dublin bookseller in 1837.

In spite of English attempts to destroy the native Irish law system, following their various conquests, it persisted for centuries with many English colonists turning to it for judgements rather than to English law. The Brehon laws were finally suppressed during the period of the eighteenth century English Penal Law system in Ireland.

Importantly, the Celtic commonality can be seen by a comparison of the Brehon laws of Ireland with the Laws of Hywel Dda. It becomes obvious that there was a lengthy and ancient tradition among the Celtic people of a sophisticated law system, and that such law codes were passed from one generation to another in oral fashion. Caesar commented that it took the Celtic druids, who were also the living repositories of the law system, twenty years to qualify, having to learn the laws by memory.

Bearing in mind the Celtic legal tradition, we come back to Sir Frank Stenton's observation that there are certain things in Alfred's laws which surprise him as an Anglo-Saxon scholar. Sir Frank puts his finger on the matter when he says that concern for the weakest in society against oppression does not occur in previous Anglo-Saxon thinking. Yet it is a basic tenet of Celtic law. The rights of all members of society are clearly defined. Similarly there is no room in Celtic society for the violent continuation of blood feuds. Homicide, intentional or unintentional, can only result in clearly defined compensation. Ritual fasting, not violence, was the method of asserting one's rights against someone who had transgressed. Everyone had recourse to the law and judges. Was this the contribution made by Asser the Celt to his Saxon master's 'great work'?

Asser served the Saxon king well and was duly rewarded. Asser paints a picture of Christmas Eve at the king's royal residence at Winchester. Alfred calls Asser in to see him and gives him two pieces of paper. They contain lists of the contents of two monasteries – one at Congresbury and the other at Banwell, both in Somerset. The monasteries, and their contents, are his, a reward from the grateful king. There is thought behind the gift, for both foundations had once been Celtic, belonging to Dumnonia. Congresbury was a monastery founded by Congar, whose life was written at Wells in the early Middle Ages. He appears to have been a contemporary of the sixth-century Cadoc and Petroc and is remembered at Lanivet, near Bodmin, in Cornwall. At Congresbury, the remains of Congar were buried. At Wint Hill, at Banwell, was another Celtic foundation.

Alfred grew more expansive, giving Asser a foundation at Plymton and then making him suffragan bishop of Sherborne. As suffragan bishop, Asser was given 'Exeter with all the *paruchia* belonging to it in Devon and Cornwall'. By this, Asser means that he was given the abbey church in the city of Exeter, which still had a strong Celtic population at this time, living side by side with the Saxon conquerors.

Indeed, an early tenth-century church has been discovered in the Cathedral Close. Perhaps this was the very church in which Asser administered. Regarding the '*paruchia* of Devon *and Cornwall*', it has been pointed out that the Cornish kings had probably attempted to 'buy off' the inevitable Saxon conquest by gifts of some lands to the church in Wessex.

Eventually, Asser was to become bishop of Sherborne, whose bishop Aldhelm, 200 years previously, had been so vehemently against the Celtic Church practices.

King Alfred died in October 899. It is true that Alfred's reign marked the beginning of a 'national kingship' and the idea of a single Anglo-Saxon state. But Alfred was not quite the scholar and innovator that the title 'Great', bestowed on him in the sixteenth century, implies. We could better argue that he was a good organizer who, seeing the necessity for literacy and learning in the kingdom, managed to seek out an excellent scholar in the person of the Celt, Asser. Indeed, could he have become 'Great' without the Celtic scholar? The fact that Asser was a Celt tends to be glossed over in many histories. It is Asser's *Life* which has given us an intimate portrait of Alfred. Yet even Asser's authorship was once denied by V. H. Galbraith in a polemical essay, 'Who wrote Asser's Life of Alfred?' (*An Introduction to the Study of History*, London, 1964). This idea has been firmly demonstrated to be a fallacy by Sir Frank Stenton and other Anglo-Saxon scholars.

In terms of our historical perspective, we can learn one very important fact from Asser's biography of Alfred. Even at this period, the British Celts still regarded themselves as *British* and their land, restricted as it was to the northern and western parts of the island, was still *Britain*. There is no mention of the new descriptive terms which were to replace 'British' and 'Britain' fifty years later – the term 'compatriots', or the Cymry.

[15]

The Prophecy of Great Britain

When they come to the battle
they will not deny themselves;
they will ask the Saxons what they seek,
what claim have they to the land
they hold in subjection.

Armes Prydein Vawr, Anon, tenth-century Welsh

THROUGHOUT the ninth century, the Cornish had been fighting a losing war with the West Saxons, who had emerged victorious from several battles fought in Cornish territory. Cornwall had been devastated by the invasions of Ecgberht of Wessex (AD 802–39) but the Saxon victory was not as permanent as was claimed by their historians. Cornwall had not become part of Wessex in AD 814 when Ecgberht was reported to 'have laid waste the land from east to west' and accepted the homage of the Cornish ruler. Wessex, in fact, was soon fighting for its own existence when Mercia invaded it in AD 825. The Cornish seized the opportunity to send its army into Wessex during the same year. But Wessex had managed to turn back the Mercians and was able to check the Cornish. The Cornish king then made a treaty with the Danes and a joint army of Cornish and Danes fought a battle at Hingston Down in AD 838. The West Saxon victory is the last recorded event of Ecgberht's life. Sir Frank Stenton (who argues that the *Anglo-Saxon Chronicle* is three years out on recording these events and that the battle was actually fought in AD 835) comments: 'It is probably this victory which made Cornwall finally a part of England, for there is no evidence for any later movements for Cornish independence.'

Even if Stenton is correct and Cornwall was ruled by Wessex from this time, it did not make Cornwall 'part of England' for through the late Middle Ages, until the time of the Tudors, legal documents enacted legislation '*in Anglia et Cornubia*'. Thus Cornwall was still recognized as a separate entity from England. But did Ecgbehrt's victory over the Cornish and Danes secure Wessex domination? Ecgberht was dead within a year after his battle, and I believe that Wessex was unable to follow up its advantage.

Indeed, independent Cornish kings still emerge into record. In AD 875 the *Annales Cambriae* record that Dumgarth, king of the Cornish, was drowned, presumably in a swimming accident. Charles Woolf, correcting the date to AD 878, identifies Dumgarth as Doniert, of Saxon record, and points to a ninth-century stone which stands in the parish of St Cleer, north of Liskeard, which reads: '*Doniert Rogavit pro Anima*' (Doniert ordered [this to be set up] for [the good of] his soul'. Dumgarth/Doniert has also been claimed as the last of the Cornish kings. But we find references to even later kings with which we will deal shortly.

It may well be that the Cornish were not entirely independent and, in all probability, were paying tribute to the West Saxons, for we find Alfred, in his will, dispensing some Cornish lands (the future Hundreds of Trigg, Lesneweth and Stratton) on the Cornish border to his heir, Edward.

By AD 931, however, Athelstan, the new ruler of Wessex and almost undisputed Bretwalda, appears to be taking aggressive action against the south-western Celts. Athelstan, the eldest son of Edward the Elder and grandson of Alfred, was crowned in September 925, at the age of thirty. He was to be one of the most dynamic kings of the Saxons, although, from this point in time, he is obscured by the reign of his grandfather Alfred. Within two years he had expelled Olafr Sigtryggson from York, eliminated a rival, forced a treaty with Constantine of Scotland and with the rulers of the Welsh kingdoms. Then he turned on Cornwall. Perhaps we should be specific, and say Cornwall and the remnant of Dumnonia. For there is evidence that there were still British Celts, the hardy remnant of the Dumnonian kingdom, clinging to lands between the River Tamar and Exeter, even at this period, 200 years after the Saxons had captured the Dumnonian city of Exeter (Isca in British Celtic and cognate with the Old Irish *easc*, water, for Exeter was standing on the River Exe). It has been argued, from William of Malmesbury's evidence, that the city still had a prominent British Celtic quarter in it, just as Jerusalem today still has a Palestinian quarter a quarter of a century after the

Israelis captured it. So, in Exeter, the Celts lived side by side with Saxons.

Throughout this area, according to R. A. S. MacAlister's *Corpus Inscriptionum Insularum Celticarum* (Dublin, 1940), there occurred a number of inscribed stones showing native Celtic names. One stone at the south door of the Lustleigh parish church, near Moreton-hampstead, to the east of Dartmoor, commemorates Dettuidoc son of Conhinoc, and is said to date to a period nearly 200 years after the capture of Exeter.

William of Malmesbury reports that in AD 927 Athelstan and his Saxons 'attacked them [the south-western Celts] with great energy, compelling them to withdraw from Exeter, which until that time they had inhabited on a footing of legal equality with the English. He [Athelstan] then fixed the left bank of the Tamar as the boundary, just as he had made the Wye the boundary for the North Britons. [A mistake meaning the Welsh.] Having cleansed the city of its defilement by wiping out that filthy race, he fortified it with towers and surrounded it with square-hewn stone.'

William, having access to lost sources, is quite clear what happened. What we are witnessing is the overrunning of the last remnant of what had been the Dumnonian kingdom, a sizeable area west of Exeter stretching to the Tamar. There is a silence as to how the Celtic population of Exeter and the country to the west was driven across the Tamar so that the border could be 'fixed', and how it was 'policed' thereafter. It is significant that William of Malmesbury uses the ominous word 'cleansed'. He defines a policy of 'ethnic cleansing'. There is certainly no reason to suppose that the Saxons would flinch from the previous harsh measures by which they had driven the Celts from other territories. In order to restrict them west of the Tamar, as they had restricted the Welsh west of Offa's Dyke, or as Cromwell's administration would constrict the Irish west of the Shannon in the seventeenth century, they quite possibly threatened punishments of death or mutilation for any Celt found on the eastern bank. The situation becomes understandable if seen in the same context as the modern Serbian philosophy of 'ethnic cleansing' in the former Yugoslavia.

The popular idea that this action represented a military conquest of Cornwall is clearly untenable. It is more likely that, after the driving of the remaining Dumnonian Celts across the Tamar or their slaughter, together with a century of victories over the Cornish by the West Saxons, the Cornish ruler decided to attempt a peace treaty with Athelstan. There is no reference to Athelstan conducting any military campaigns in Cornwall but he certainly asserted his suzerain authority there.

The *Anglo-Saxon Chronicle* refers to Athelstan receiving a deputation of British Celtic rulers at Eamont Bridge, near Carlisle, at which Howell, king of 'the West Welsh', was present and formally accepted Athelstan's authority. Most commentators are inclined to believe that the *Chronicle* was mistaken about which of the *welisc* submitted to him and believe that this Howell should be identified as Hywel Dda of Wales. But even if the *Chronicle* had confused the name, I believe, from the circumstances, that it was correct as to the identity of the ruler – that he was, indeed, a king of 'the West Welsh' (Cornwall). And why should the name be incorrect? Certainly Hywel ap Cadell ruled in Wales at this time. But 'Hoel' also occurs as a king's name in Cornwall. A strategic submission to Athelstan, in the wake of the 'ethnic cleansing' of west Devon, would have prevented the West Saxons continuing their campaign west of the Tamar and thus allowed Cornwall to survive as an identifiable Celtic country to modern times while Devon became firmly part of England.

We know the names of other tenth-century kings of Cornwall as well as Hoel. We hear of Cynan from Welsh sources, at the time of the battle of Brunanburh, and at Penlee House, near Penzance, there now stands a tenth-century memorial to '*Regis Ricati Crux*', 'the cross of King Ricatus', which name could mean 'king of battles', who must have ruled about this time or soon afterwards. My contention is that Athelstan had no need of military conquest in Cornwall in AD 931; the mere displacement of the Celts from Exeter to the Tamar border had persuaded the Cornish rulers that they should acknowledge Saxon overlordship to prevent further attack.

Athelstan initially set up a series of Saxon earls to be reeves of Cornwall, as Alfred had appointed Wulfheard as reeve, chief magistrate or steward, of the Welsh kingdoms. Those filling the Cornish office were Ordgar, Eadulf, Ethelmar and Algar. Whether the office actually meant a significant Saxon role in Cornwall, or whether it expressed merely an aspiration, as did the office of reeve of Wales, is in contention. This action might imply that Cynan, at the time of Brunanburh, after his predecessor Hoel had submitted to Athelstan, had rejected the treaty and joined his fellow Celts in trying to over-throw Athelstan. Further, it might imply that Cynan had been one of the five unnamed kings reported as slain during the battle. In the wake of the Celtic defeat, Athelstan could have sent his magistrates to rule Cornwall directly. Yet I do not think this is so for, at the time of the Norman Conquest, we find a man with a Cornish name, Cador, claiming descent from the native kings, styling himself 'ealdorman' of Cornwall. His son Cadoc (sometimes recorded as Condor II) had a daughter Arvice who married Reginald, illegitimate son of Henry I, who then claimed 'the earldom of Cornwall' by right of inheritance.

Athelstan certainly had enough influence to order the change of Celtic Church structures and practices in Cornwall. While in AD 864, Centsec, then bishop of the Cornish, had written a letter to Ceolnoth (AD 833–70), archbishop of Canterbury, and promised to bring his church in line with Rome, the Cornish clergy remained independent and clung to their Celtic monasticism. Athelstan ordered the introduc-tion of a parochial system and introduced a diocese of Cornwall under a native Cornish bishop called Conan. The Celtic Cornish centres of scholarship were dissolved and Celtic forms of service forbidden.

Our first evidence of the Cornish language, as distinct from its British Celtic parent, shared with Welsh, Bretons, Cumbrians and Strathclyde British, emerges in the form of glosses during this time, particularly in *St Petroc's Gospels*, dated to the ninth or tenth cen-turies, which were housed in Petroc's Monastery (Padstow) until its sack in AD 981. They were taken to the monastery at Bodmin and became known as the *Bodmin Gospels*. Details of the state of Cor-nish at this time are revealed in a twelfth-century Latin/Cornish Vocabulary – *Vocabularium Cornicum*, now in the British Museum. It was not until the Tudor period and, particularly, when the Reformation hit Cornwall that the Cornish language and its culture began to be seriously affected.

However, by the mid-tenth century, Cornwall was firmly under Saxon political control. Edmund (AD 940–946) declares himself 'King of England, and this British province (of Cornwewalas)'–although, as we have seen, laws were enacted '*in Anglia et Cornubia*', demonstrating that Cornwall was regarded as a separate adminis-trative and national unit to England.

The Celtic dream of finally being able to turn back the Anglo-

Saxon invasion of Britain, and reassert Celtic influence and authority over the island once again, finally ended in AD 937 with the battle of Brunanburh. Sir Frank Stenton says that 'the battle has a distinctive place among the events which made for the ultimate unity of England'. The *Anglo-Saxon Chronicle* and William of Malmesbury hailed Athelstan's victory there as 'the greatest feat of arms since the coming of the English to Britain'.

A dispute had arisen between Athelstan and the Danes which the Celtic rulers thought they could exploit. Athelstan was now the dominant force in the island, loftily styling himself '*basileus*' (the Byzantine title meaning 'emperor') 'of all Britain'. He also, in his charters, called himself king 'of the English and of all the nations round about'. While his enemies were divided, no one could really challenge that grandiose aspiration. But then an alliance was formed among the Celts.

The flashpoint was the Danish succession at York. Sigtrygg Caech (squint-eyed) had been king of Dublin but had abdicated when he had been elected king of the Danes of York in AD 920. In AD 926 he had made a peace treaty with Athelstan at Tamworth, married Athelstan's sister, Eadgyth, and become a Christian. Within the year he had renounced both his new faith and his bride. Athelstan, enraged, marched an army on York and defeated him. Sigtrygg was slain. This caused a backlash within the Danish world. Gothfrith, Sigtrygg's brother, who had succeeded him in Dublin, led an invasion of Northumbria but was repulsed by Athelstan.

In AD 934 Gothfrith died and was succeeded as king of Dublin by his son Olafr. Olafr Gothfrithson was determined to make Athelstan pay for the defeat of his uncle and father and claimed the Northumbrian kingdom for his own. He began to set up an alliance. The leading member of this alliance was the elderly Constantine II of Scotland, who had ruled since AD 900. Constantine's daughter was married to Olafr but Constantine had been forced to sign a treaty with Athelstan agreeing that he would not support the claims of Gothfrith. Constantine might have had a literal turn of mind and read the treaty as excluding Gothfrith's son Olafr. He now made an alliance with Olafr. Athelstan retaliated to this news by invading Scotland, laying waste the country as far as Dunnottar or even Edinburgh. Clearly other allies were needed and a plan of concerted action had to be made if Athelstan was to be checked.

A *realpolitik* had been creeping into British Celtic perception. The fact that the Anglo-Saxons had occupied their settlements in Britain for five centuries, and that the Norse or Danes had also carved themselves settlements, now seemed irreversible. Instead of calling themselves Britons, the British Celts were beginning to see themselves as members of the successor states to Britain. They began to call themselves 'Cymry' – fellow countrymen or comrades. It is not until the ninth century that we find evidence for this change in British perception, although there is a remarkable passage in the earliest known version of the Laws of Hywel Dda (*c.*AD 910–950) which states that the king's bard should sing 'Vnbeinyaeth Prydein' before the army on the day of a battle. This 'Vnbeinyaeth Prydein' – 'the monarchy of Britain' – seems a very early 'national anthem'. The fact that the song talks about the monarchy *of Britain*, rather than of the successor states, is significant. The concept of Celtic Britain as a single unit is still there. Moreover, Nennius says that the title of this song is inscribed on the Pillar of Eliseg in Powys. Vandalism in the English Civil War plus a thousand years of weather had caused the stone to suffer by the time the scholar Edward Lhuyd, in 1696, made a careful transcription of it. The title indicates the continuance of the idea of British Celtic unity but during the tenth century that notion was changing. However, it was not to change without one final and dramatic kick.

From the tenth century survives a poem of 199 lines which is contained in the *Book of Taliesin*, a fourteenth-century compilation. The poet is anonymous and the title is *Armes Prydein Vawr* – the Prophecy of Great Britain. The poem is written with great vigour. It calls on the Celts of Wales, of Cornwall, of Brittany, of Strathclyde and of Scotland to unite with the Irish and Danes of Dublin and the Isle of Man: this vast confederacy would rout the Saxon foe and drive him out of Britain (*a mal balaon Saesson syrthyn*)! The poet knows well his history for he mentions how the Anglo-Saxons, led by Hengist and Horsa, had driven the Celts out of their lost territories which had now become England. If the British Celts would rise as one man, the poet assures them, they would be led by the re-embodiment of the great Cynan ap Brochfael and the almost legendary Cadwaladr ap Cadwallon of Gwynedd, of whom it had been prophesied that he would one day return and deliver his people from the thrall of the English. Dewi Sant would pray for them from on high.

The poem is stirring. Raising the holy banner of David, the British would lead the Irish and Danes of Dublin against the Saxon warriors. And their own warriors would not deny their courage when they came to battle. They would call on the Saxons and ask them what right had they to hold the lands of the Celts in subjection.

Curiously, while Cecile O'Rahilly, who examines the poem carefully, correctly identifies it as from the period 'in which a Cymric poet would be most likely to have dreamt of such an alliance of Welsh, Irish, Norse-Irish, Cornish and North British against the Saxon', she fails to make the connection. 'It was, unfortunately, but a poet's dream, and no such powerful confederation ever opposed the Saxon in Wales.' No, not *in Wales*, but elsewhere – for such a confederation arose of the very people mentioned in the poem, centred around the struggle between Olafr Gothfrithson of Danish Dublin and Athelstan.

Unfortunately, we can only be sure of the involvement of some of the leaders of the confederation against the Saxons. The nominal leader of the alliance was, of course, Olafr of Dublin. Constantine II of Scotland was an important figure. Owain Mac Domhnuil, king of Strathclyde and Cumbria, had declared for Olafr with Constantine in AD 934. We know that Owain Mac Domhnuil of Strathclyde participated in the battle and that there is no evidence to suggest he was alive after it. It seems likely that he was one of the five unnamed kings who fell.

As Olafr exerted his authority over the Isle of Man and the Isles, a Manx contingent would have undoubtedly taken part in the alliance. Aralt was then king of Man and the Isles. We hear from the *Anglo-Saxon Chronicle* and the *Annála Rioghachta Éireann* that Olafr, following his defeat by Athelstan, returned to Dublin by way of the Isle of Man and found a rebellion being organized there by a chieftain called Mac Ragnall. Had Aralt been killed at Brunanburh, one of the five unnamed kings, and was Mac Ragnall seizing the opportunity to take power? Olafr was successful in suppressing this rebellion and we find him exercising suzerain power over the Isle of Man in AD 940, using it as a base of operations.

Now *Armes Prydein Vawr* mentions the Cornish and the Cymry of Wales. Cynan is mentioned as a member of the alliance in some later sources but there is no mention of the involvement of Hywel ap Cadell, which is why Cecile O'Rahilly overlooked Brunanburh in her discussion of *Armes Prydein*. Hywel had succeeded in binding together the Welsh kingdoms. An astute politician, in AD 927 he had seen the military and political wisdom of meeting with Athelstan on the banks of the Wye and acknowledging him as his overlord. The Wye was then fixed as the border between the Saxon kingdoms and the Welsh. This political manoeuvre allowed him to go on a pilgrimage to Rome in AD 928/929 earning himself the epithet Dda, the Good. But in AD 934, Hywel was humbled by Athelstan when he was forced, with Idwal the Bald, petty king of Gwynedd, and Morgan ab Owain, petty king of Gwent and Glywysing, to accompany the Saxon king in his campaign against Constantine in Scotland. This humiliation must have created some resentment. The fact that *Armes Prydein Vawr* was composed in Hywel's own territory becomes significant. Curiously, no references survive which describe the role of the Welsh in the confederation; while this could indicate that Hywel did not play a part in the alliance, the writing of *Armes Prydein Vawr* in Dyfed, and the politics of the time, suggest that the Welsh must have been involved.

Armes Prydein Vawr also mentions the native Irish as well as the Danes of Dublin. The High King at this time was Donnchad Donn mac Flainn (AD 919–944). Again, we do not have conclusive proof that he responded to the alliance. There were plenty of internal problems in Ireland at this time and the relationship with the Danes of Dublin was not an entirely amicable one.

However, the peoples named by the anonymous poet as being part of this confederation were surely named for a purpose. We are assured of the involvement of some of them, of the Norse-Irish, of the Manx, of the Scots and of the Strathclyde British, and there is a later reference to Cornish involvement. Accepting this, why not accept the involvement of the Irish and Welsh who are also mentioned by the poet? Perhaps only token forces were sent to join Olafr's army from these two groups, small contingents which were not thought worthy of mention by the chroniclers? Or mention of which did not survive?

The chronicles say that Olafr arrived from Dublin with a great fleet from which he disembarked his army which was then joined by the armies of the kings of Scotland and Strathclyde. Athelstan marched to meet them and the two armies met at Brunanburh. The site of Brunanburh has been the cause of some debate, many suggesting that it was in Northumbria and that Olafr's fleet landed on the Northumbrian coast. Professor H. P. R. Finberg has more recently suggested that the site is at Bromborough, on the Mersey shore of the Wirral in Cheshire. Indeed, no other place has a name which fits the name provided. Bromborough, in its earliest form, is given as Brumburh – the burgh where the broom grew – for which Brunanburh could easily be a corruptive spelling. The site also makes sense of Olafr's army landing directly from Dublin.

The battle was one of the bloodiest fought in Britain. According to the *Anglo-Saxon Chronicle*: 'Never yet in this island before this, by what books tell us and our ancient sages, was a greater slaughter of a host made by edge of the sword, since the Angles and Saxons came hither from the east, invading Britain over the broad seas, and the proud assailants, warriors eager for glory, overcame the Britons and won a country.' The battle was fought over a two-day period. Among the alliance, it left dead upon the field five kings, seven earls, and the son of Constantine of Scotland, as well as countless others.

It was a clear victory for Athelstan and his men; the one single event which secured him in power and united the petty kingdoms under his suzerain rule as England. The *Anglo-Saxon Chronicle* records:

> The field grew dark with the blood of men, from the time when the sun, that glorious light, the bright candle of God, of the Lord Eternal, moved over the earth in the hours of the morning, until that nimble creation sank at its setting. That day many a man was destroyed by the spears, many a man was shot over his shield, and likewise lay weary, sated in battle.

Professor A. J. Church has described it as 'one of the most famous battles of English history'. Yet Brunanburh is now hardly mentioned in any English history even though it inspired one of the great Anglo-Saxon saga poems, written shortly after the battle. Additionally references in the Icelandic sagas, *Annals of Tigernach*, *Brut y Tywysogion* (Chronicle of the Welsh Princes) and William of Malmesbury supply us with details of the battle.

We find Athelstan and his brother Edmund at the head of an army of men from Wessex and Mercia. There were also a few hundred Anglo-Danish serving in the Saxon army. An account of the battle occurs in the Icelandic *Saga of Eigil Skallagrimsson*, who fought for Athelstan. It repeats the *Anglo-Saxon Chronicle*'s estimation: 'Greater carnage had not been in this island ever yet, of men slain by the edge of the sword, as the books of old writers tell us, since the Angles and Saxons came to land here from the East, and sought Britain over the broad seas.'

On the evening before the battle, according to William of Malmesbury, quoting a source now lost, Olafr himself, disguised as a minstrel, went through the Saxon encampment, pretending he was one of the Anglo-Danish warriors. He made his way to Athelstan's tent and sang for him and his nobles as they feasted. He was seen and recognized by one of the Anglo-Danish warriors who then informed Athelstan – but not until Olafr was safely out of the encampment. The man explained to the enraged Saxon king: 'The same oath that I have sworn to you, I once swore to Olafr; had I betrayed him, you might well expect that I should betray you. But now, if you will condescend to listen to my advice, change the place of your tent.'

Athelstan saw the wisdom of this. When night came, Olafr's men launched an attack, making their way to the king's tent. A Saxon bishop had unwittingly pitched his tent in the spot vacated by the king, and so he and his attendants were slain. One wonders why no one warned this pious gentleman? Whether Olafr had, indeed, gone in person to the Saxon encampment, or whether he had simply sent a spy, with the chroniclers claiming the glory for Olafr, it seems like a good military tactic. But the attack did cause alarm among the Saxons and held up the battle for a few days more until Athelstan gave the order. According to the *Anglo-Saxon Chronicle* there then followed 'the fiercest and bloodiest fight that had been fought since the Saxon people first came to the island of Britain'.

> . . . the field streamed with warriors' blood
> When rose at morning tide the glorious star
> The sun, God's shining candle, until sank
> The noble creature to its setting.
>
> As fled the Scots, weary and sick of war,
> Forth followed the West Saxons, in war bands
> Tracking the hostile folk the livelong day.

> ... There lay five kings
> Whom on the battlefield, swords put to sleep
> And they were young, and seven of Olafr's earls
> With Scots and mariners, an untold host.

But the casualties were not as one-sided as the saga poem would claim. Two members of Athelstan's own family were killed: his cousins, sons of Aethelweard, the youngest son of Alfred, were removed from the field and taken to Malmesbury for burial. These were Alfric and Athelwin. Also there is the reference to the Saxon bishop, who had pitched his tent in the place where Athelstan's had stood and so had been killed by mistake.

But Olafr's alliance army fell apart. The Scots began retreating while the Norse, led by Olafr, realizing the battle was lost, took to their longships.

> Through the deep water,
> Dublin once again,
> Ireland to seek, abased.

While Athelstan and his brother returned home to savour their victory.

> ... Fame bearing went,
> Meanwhile, to their own land, West Saxon land,
> The brothers, King and Atheling. They left
> The carcasses behind them to be shared
> By livid kite, swarthy raven, horny beaked,
> And the white eagle, of the goodly plumes,
> The greedy war-hawk, and grey forest wolf,
> Who ate the carrion.

Aelfric, the abbot at Cerne Abbas (1005–c.1010), acclaimed as 'the greatest prose stylist of the Old English period', significantly acclaimed Athelstan as one of the three greatest English kings for his victory at Brunanburh. Certainly, after Brunanburh, Danish power, as a serious rival to the Anglo-Saxons, collapsed and did not re-emerge for another hundred years. When Eadred became ruler of the English kingdoms (AD 946–955), the antagonism between the Danes and Anglo-Saxons had lessened. The Danelaw submitted and England – Angle-land – had become a politically united kingdom.

More significantly, the aspiration of the British Celts to turn back the Anglo-Saxon invasion was now no more than a dream. They began to fortify themselves in the areas into which they had been confined and the map of Britain began to take on its modern lines.

The Britons or *welisc* of the western peninsula would start calling themselves Cymry, compatriots, and their land Cymru, with Hywel Dda exercising supreme kingship. To the English this would become 'the land of the foreigners' or Weahlas (Wales) just as 'the land of the Kern foreigners', confined west of the Tamar, would be Kern-weahlas or Cornwall.

The country of Alba, a confederacy of the older kingdoms, now including Strathclyde and, for over a century, Cumbria, would keep its borders and become better known as Scotland. The Cymry of Cumbria (as the English pronounced the name of their country – Cymru) would face an almost immediate invasion from Athelstan's brother Edmund (AD 940–946). The Cumbrians sought aid from their northern neighbour, the all-powerful Maol Callum I (AD 943–954) who had succeeded his brother Constantine when he abdicated and retired to a monastery. Maol Callum marched to the aid of his fellow Celts and in AD 945 Edmund was forced to accept that Cumbria was now a province of Scotland continuing with its own petty kings. It was not until 1092 that William Rufus led an English army into Cumbria, defeated Dumnail (Domhnuil), the last Celtic king of Cumbria, and annexed it to England. Anglo-Saxon settlers were encouraged to swamp Cumbria and the natives were driven to the hills or northwards into Strathclyde. Some of the intelligentsia also seem to have taken refuge in Wales. Celtic place-names remain a strong feature of Cumbria, particularly in the hilly regions, while Anglo-Saxon names are to be found in the fertile valleys. While the British Celtic language is noted as surviving, especially in the Eden valley, until the fourteenth century, it is a curious fact that Cumberland shepherds counted their sheep in a distorted but recognizable form of British Celtic numerals until the turn of this century.

The jarldom of Orkney, the Shetlands, the kingdom of Man and the Isles, and Ireland would not feel their independence threatened for some time to come.

But the threat was there. Brunanburh had seen to that. For England had emerged, united, and the most aggressive and dominant kingdom on the island of Britain.

The impetus for conquest still remained with the Anglo-Saxons and continued to be part of their make-up after the Norman Conquest. Danes and Normans (Norsemen) were part of the same Germanic culture as the Anglo-Saxons, in spite of the Normans' intermingling with the Germanic Franks and Gaulish culture. The mix of these people into the Anglo-Saxon scheme of things merely reinforced England's military impulse. The initial urge to establish their dominance over the entire island, and subsequently, over the neighbouring island of Ireland, was unquenchable. That stimulus was the driving force behind the eventual world-wide empire, but that empire had to begin with a conquest of the peoples in Britain and Ireland. It was a conquest never completely achieved. It resulted in a further thousand years of conflict and uneasy relations between Celt and Saxon. The subsequent empire which emerged was, therefore, an English empire.

[16]

Do 'The British' Really Exist?

Life has conquered: the wind has blown away
Alexander, Caesar, and all their power and sway:
Tara is grass, and behold how Troy lies low—
Maybe the English, too, will have their day.

Anon, eighteenth-century Irish

AN understanding of what took place during the 500 years
following the Anglo-Saxon invasions, and the conquest of
those parts of Britain which became England, is essential for
understanding the dynamic which saw the Saxons, reinforced by
Danish and Norman settlement, move on to create the largest empire
the world has seen, an empire covering one quarter of the world's
lands and people. Today, largely because of the success of that
empire, it is estimated that 750 million people speak English in some
form or another around the world while 350 million speak it as a
mother tongue. As the Roman Empire left behind Latin as a *lingua
franca* between its former subject peoples during the Middle Ages,
so the English Empire has left the English language in its wake – but,
of course, English is more widely spoken and written than Latin ever
was or, indeed, any other language in history.

The Saxon compulsion for conquest, plunder and control of land
and people, the dynamic which caused their original settlement in
Britain, was only reluctantly abandoned during the second half of
this century. In recent times England has started an attempt to come
to terms with itself and its history, having finally been constrained
in its imperial ambitions. In doing so, England now flounders in a
perplexity of self-justifying myths about empire. It seeks to persuade
itself that its empire was, by and large, a good thing for the world,
and that it brought 'civilization' to its colonial subjects instead of
devastation and instability, whose ramifications are still felt in the

wake of England's withdrawal as a colonial power. It seeks to persuade itself that its retreat as a colonial power was accomplished
voluntarily and peacefully, that the empire was given up without
bloodshed, hiding its eyes from the countless bloody colonial wars by
calling them simply 'police actions' against 'extremists' or 'terrorists'.

For Colin Cross, in *The Fall of the British Empire* (London, 1968),
the empire was merely 'an historical accident'. Careful to avoid
defining too specifically 'British', Cross, in passing, refers to the idea
that 'the particular mixture of English with Scots, Welsh and Irish
had produced a "race" peculiarly suitable for administering the
affairs of other, less fortunate, peoples'. But the language, law, social
structures and dynamic of the empire were clearly *English*. In an
attempt to explain this, quite ignoring the positions of the languages
and cultures of the Celts within 'Britain', Cross maintains that
'regional differences were relatively slight'. This is a curious observation, for the languages and cultures of Celt and Saxon are as different
as those of Russia and England. And, as Victor E. Durkacz has
observed, in *The Decline of the Celtic Languages* (Edinburgh, 1983):
'One of the most consistent trends in modern British history has been
the cultural and linguistic conflict between Anglo-Saxon and Celtic
Britain. It is a conflict which the Celts have consistently lost.' At the
end of his study, Colin Cross maintains: 'Taking the story as a whole,
and admitting many faults, the British can be proud that they once
had an empire.' That exhortation would surely indicate that Cross
had learnt nothing from his study; he merely adds to the mythology
of empire.

The more discerning historian, Christopher Hill, the Master of
Balliol, Oxford, in his thought-provoking study, *History and the
Present* (London, 1987), comments: 'There have been many worse
institutions than the British Empire; but it is time we faced up to the
fact that it was not an unqualified source of blessings for humanity.'
I would also add that it is high time we faced up to the fact that the
empire was not an Irish one, nor a Welsh one, nor a Scottish one –
it emanated solely from England.

Naturally, it would take a lengthier study to consider the internal
dynamics and contradictions within the English nation which created
the conditions of empire. It is acknowledged that the empire only
benefited a small class, or section, of the English people. At the height
of the empire, in the nineteenth century, the social conditions of

the working class in that empire's capital city were as appalling as anywhere within the colonial possessions. A. L. Morton's *A People's History of England* (London, 1938) still remains an excellent overview of the social and economic considerations of England's empire. And E. P. Thompson's *magnum opus, The Making of the English Working Class* (London, 1963), deals with such contradictions. In his work, Thompson followed the polemic of Ridley and realized that the Irish, Scots and Welsh had entirely different histories and social perceptions from the English. That, in fact, there was no such thing as a 'British working class'. He writes: 'I have neglected these histories, not out of chauvinism, but out of respect. It is because class is a cultural as much as an economic formation that I have been cautious as to generalizing beyond English experience.'

Nevertheless, popular misconceptions die hard and general works, especially for the young, were produced which taught historical delusions. In 1948, the last year of the empire's zenith, a popular children's encyclopaedia, *The Wonder World Encylopedia*, edited by John R. Crossland and J. M. Parrish (Virtue & Co., London) could summarize the 500 years of bloody struggle, with which this book has been dealing, in the following manner:

> When the Roman Empire fell into decay, Britain, as an outlying part of it, was one of the first portions to go, and the poor Britons, thus left unarmed and helpless, fell an easy prey to the wild northern tribes. In despair, they turned to a race of sea-rovers, the English, of whom they had for long been greatly afraid, but whom they now begged to save them from the dreadful Caledonians. The English were quite willing to come and help them, and did so.
>
> But having driven out the rude Caledonians, they looked upon the land and saw it was very fair. Instead of going back to their own home, they settled in the best portions of the land and pushed the Britons farther and farther into the barren and hilly regions of the north and west. Then, in their turn, the English settled down to be a peaceful, hard-working and civilized race

Indeed, nowhere is the myth-making about the empire so intense as in dealing with the relationship between England and her first colonial acquisitions. But in this new post-imperialist era, percipient observers are looking beyond appearances to reality. Some historians are now recognizing that the shape of history and culture in the British Isles has been moulded by the continuing struggle between Celt and Saxon. Moreover, the friction between them, the Saxon struggle for conquest over the original inhabitants, helps us to understand the ruthless attitudes apparent in the rise of the later world-encompassing empire.

Dr Durkacz believes that the cultural struggle between Celtic and Saxon only sprang from the Reformation during the sixteenth and seventeenth centuries.

In fact, linguistic repression sprang from the Reformation which presented exactly the same challenges to the indigenous cultures of Ireland, Wales and Scotland. The religious and political conflicts following in the wake of reform manifested themselves also in the form of a cultural clash between Saxon and Celtic Britain. Since language was a natural vehicle for the cultural and political aspirations of the Celtic peoples, this cultural clash naturally escalated into a linguistic confrontation. Thus it was that the indigenous cultures and mother tongues of the Celtic periphery found themselves under attack from the early sixteenth century – an attack which persisted until the present century, albeit in a variety of guises and generally in less harsh a manner than that adopted by the English government in the sixteenth and seventeenth centuries.

While it is true, as Dr Durkacz argues, that the languages of the Celts were 'brutally repressed by central government', following the Reformation, the conflict, as this book demonstrates, was already there and the Reformation was simply a new engine for shaping English imperialism.

To return full circle to the contention I put forward in my introduction: the English socialist historian and sociologist Frank A. Ridley first pointed out in the 1950s that: 'The British Empire is a misnomer. What has existed was an English Empire, the first colonies of which were Ireland, Wales and Scotland in that order.' So how did the 'British' myth come about? The advent of a united England, secure within its borders, with the original native population dispersed to the western and northern extremities of Britain, or simply annihilated, did not halt the English ambition to conquer the whole island of Britain and then, as a logical consequence, its neighbour Ireland. Frank A. Ridley argued that:

> ... the non-English Celtic fringe of what was later to be denominated as 'Great Britain', represented the first colonial empire of the rising English imperialism at the dawn of the modern epoch. Cornwall, Ireland, Wales and Scotland were conquered by England between the first Anglo-Saxon invasions and the final Cromwellian conquest of 'Great Britain', which went to form England's initial English empire.

The process of attempting to assimilate or destroy the Celtic peoples, as this book has attempted to demonstrate, has been going on since the Saxons first arrived. In Elizabethan times that impulse found its first degree of success and this, of course, was the period in which historians recognize the rise of 'the first English empire', when England began to expand its influence in the world, both in trade and in military conquest. This does not discount Dr Durkacz's argument for the importance of the role of the Reformation, but the Reformation was only part of the new dynamic. Strangely enough, few historians dealing with this period have made any attempt to examine that Tudor dynamic for conquest nor to explain the impulse for English expansion into the lands of their Celtic neighbours.

The historian of the Tudor period, A. L. Rowse, who has made much of his Celtic Cornish roots, simply dismisses the process briefly: 'Expansion is the natural and instinctive impulse of any healthy society.' In *The Expansion of Elizabethan England* (London, 1955) he argued: 'What more natural and indeed inevitable – for here we may for once use the word legitimately of an historical process – than that so thrusting a society as Elizabethan England should push outwards in the margin of Celtic societies, yielding, or resentful or resistant?'

Rowse sees England in terms of bringing 'civilization' to 'backward' Celtic society, an excuse for empire since time began. He sees England expanding

> ... outwards into the backward areas of the borderlands – the Scottish borders, Wales and Cornwall, Ireland; then overseas to the opening up of the new English world in North America; finally,

in the realm of the spirit, in literature, the wonderful outburst of the drama, the arts; in science and knowledge, where Bacon, William Gilbert and Camden were spirits as representative as Spenser and Marlowe, Drake and Ralegh.

He curiously fails to acknowledge that, during the enforcement of English culture on these populations, there could be anything worthwhile in the native civilization to defend. The point is that the Celts, too, had their great writers, philosophers, artists, scientists. Rowse only writes with the hindsight of the victor and makes no reference to the native equivalents of the people he eulogizes. In Ireland, for example, in Tudor times, there existed poets such as Tadhg Dall Ó hUiginn (d. 1591) and Aonghus Fionn Ó Dálaigh (d. 1570), philosophers such as Muiris Ó Fihely (d. 1513) and Archbishop Aodh MacCathmhaoil (1571–1626), and the soldier historian Philip Ó Súilleabháin Béara; while in Wales there were poets like Gutun Owen, William Llyn, Salbri Powel or Siôn Gruffudd, scholars such as Griffith Robert, Morris Clynnog, William Morgan and John Davies of Mallwyd. Why are these people not seen in the same cultural terms as Spenser, Marlowe, Drake or Ralegh? Simply, they were on the losing side and the languages they wrote in were all but destroyed before the burgeoning of the language of the conquerors. Rowse slavishly follows the general tendency of English empire apologists to marginalize, denigrate or ignore the native literatures and learning or, at best, to discuss them as quaint provincial or folkloric survivals.

Ridley argues that it was Oliver Cromwell who was 'the first effective conqueror of "Great Britain"', followed by the consolidating conquests of William of Orange. Only when England had finally dominated the nations within the British Isles could the real spread of an empire begin through the world. The corollary of this is that the empire must end where it began – in Britain and Ireland. Ridley felt that this 'represents a logical nemesis in the realm of historical dialectic'.

To understand this, we must briefly examine what happened to the Celtic realms after the emergence of a politically united England.

Cornwall

Of the Celtic kingdoms which survived the initial Saxon settlement in the tenth century, Cumbria was to be permanently annexed in the eleventh century, settled and absorbed by the fourteenth. While Cornwall had been forced to accept English monarchal overlordship in the tenth century, it was not simply annexed and settled at this time. A charter of Edmund in AD 944 styled him as 'King of England and this British province'. Laws were still enacted '*in Anglia et Cornubia*' demonstrating, as I have previously argued, that Cornwall was regarded as a colonial possession and not a part of England. On 17 March 1337, Cornwall was created a duchy in recognition of its constitutional position, and only the heir apparent to the reigning monarch of England could inherit the dukedom.

Cornwall retained another unique institution which marked it as a different administrative entity to the rest of England. It had a Stannary Parliament, an ancient parliament originally of tin-workers. Royal Charters, the earliest dated 1198, confirmed ancient rights and customs which had existed in Cornwall for centuries. Tin-workers and their families, a category which included most of the inhabitants of that time, were exempt from English taxes and laws, could appoint their own magistrates, raise their own taxes and issue their own coinage. In 1508 the Stannary Parliament was granted a power of veto over the Westminster Parliament by Henry VII. After 1337 Stannary laws were confirmed by ducal assent and if there was no incumbent duke they were confirmed by the Crown.

In spite of the theoretical protection afforded it by the Stannary Parliament, Cornwall felt the intense centralization and Anglicizing policies of the Tudor monarchy. Henry VII had overthrown Richard III by using the 'Celtic card', encouraging Welsh, Cornish and Bretons to fight for him at Bosworth by making great play on his Tudor ancestry. But Henry Tudor, Earl of Richmond, was a second-generation Englishman, whose grandfather had claimed descent from an ancient native Welsh ruling house. Apart from rewarding individual Welsh and Cornish followers, and calling his first son Arthur as a token gesture to their feelings, Henry had little sympathy with the Celts. The myth of the Tudors being a 'Welsh' monarchy has, again, been one of the great English propaganda exercises to keep the Celts in order.

Because of Tudor centralization and taxation, in 1497 came the remarkable Cornish uprising led by a blacksmith from St Keverne, Myghal Josef An Gof, who marched his insurrectionist army from Cornwall across to Blackheath in Kent, menacing London itself and nearly toppling Henry VII, having already defeated an army led by his most senior general and Lord Chamberlain, Lord Daubeney, near Guildford. Another Cornish rising took place within six months in an attempt to put the pretender Perkin Warbeck, who also had support from the Scots and Irish, on the throne. The third and last Cornish uprising was in 1546 when the English language was officially imposed on Cornwall in matters of religious worship as part of the Reformation. One of the reasons given by the insurrectionists for this uprising stated: 'We, the Cornishmen, whereof certain of us understand no English, utterly refuse this new English!' The defeat of the Cornish insurgents was followed by the Earl of Bedford's army entering the country and indulging in mass hangings, burnings of villages and wholesale pillage. Sir Anthony Kingston, appointed as Provost Marshal, achieved an extremely unsavoury reputation for his 'pacification' of Cornwall.

The Anglicization proceeded with efficiency but it was not until the late eighteenth century that Cornish, as a community language, finally died. Some native knowledge was retained and these embers finally became the sparks for the start of a Cornish language revival movement at the start of the twentieth century.

Administratively, and with some surprise in the wake of three risings in Tudor times, the Stannary Parliament continued and its right of veto was last reaffirmed in 1753. But, now in the hands of Anglicized gentry, it fell into disuse. It was never legally dissolved, nor were its laws, right and privileges revoked. In 1888 the English County Councils Act was made law, in which elected councils were formed in the counties. A Cornwall County Council, whereby Cornwall was designated a county of England for the first time, did not come into being until a year after the English county councils because of the extra considerations which had to be faced due to the unique constitutional position of Cornwall. Even so, some constitutional lawyers believe that the designation of Cornwall as an English county in 1889 was not in accordance with constitutional law. Indeed, in May 1974, Cornish people, representing a cross-section of the community, after legal advice, reconstituted the Stannary Parliament in defiance of central government and even of the Duke of Cornwall, both of whom have steadfastly refused to recognize the parliament.

The Cornish language revival also brought political independence groups in its wake. Tyr ha Tavas (Land and Language) existed in the 1930s. Then Mebyon Kernow (Sons of Cornwall) was formed in 1951, winning its first election with a seat on Redruth Council in December 1953, and gaining its first seat on Cornwall County Council in 1967. In June 1969, a splinter group of Mebyon Kernow formed a Cornish National Party which was reconstituted in 1975 as the Cornish Nationalist Party. The fortunes of these parties have waxed and waned, especially against the increasingly used argument that Cornwall has, in the body of the Stannary, with its history and laws, an existing parliamentary body.

So even in Cornwall, first conquered by Athelstan in AD 931, the conflicts between Celt and Saxon have not been resolved.

Wales

After the tenth century, the Saxons continued to attempt to expand their western borders into 'the land of the foreigners' – Wales. In 1282 the Welsh ruler Llywellyn ap Gruffudd ap Llywellyn was defeated and killed. His brother, Dafydd, only reigned for six months before he was captured, brought before an English court, 'tried' and executed. In 1301, the son of Edward I of England was named as 'Prince of Wales'. Subsequently, the custom has been that the heir apparent to the English throne has assumed the title 'Prince of Wales'. The hundred years following the death of the last native ruler of Wales were marked by numerous uprisings against English rule. In 1400 Owain Glyn Dwr reasserted Welsh independence, re-establishing a parliament at Machynlleth and setting up embassies abroad. However, by 1409 the English had reconquered Wales.

The coming to the English throne of Henry Tudor spelt disaster for the Welsh nation, who had been misled into supporting him on the grounds that he was a 'Welsh king'. As soon as it became clear that Henry Tudor was just as eager for the absorption of Wales by England, unrest started. In 1533 Sir Edward Croft, Henry's Vice Chamberlain, was complaining that the Welsh were refusing to abide by English law. Rowland Lee was appointed to subdue Wales in 1534 and within a year he had executed 5000 Welshmen.

In 1536 Henry's administrators passed what is now known as the Act of Union, which annexed and incorporated Wales fully into England, abolishing its laws and declaring that the Welsh were to 'enjoy' the same rights as the people of England. The injustice of this was obvious. An important clause, among the thirty-nine sections of the Act, was one which declared that the Welsh language was to be 'utterly extirpe' as well as 'all and singular the sinister usages and customs differing from the laws of this Realm'. No person who spoke Welsh could hold any office in Wales unless they also spoke English. In other words, Wales was no longer to exist; she was to be left with no national institutions, no native administration and no language with its attendant culture. A second Act was passed in 1542 which clarified the administration and created another myth which lasted 400 years. In the 1536 Act it was clear that the county of Monmouth was part of Wales. The 1542 Act was so worded as to cause confusion regarding the position of Monmouth. But Monmouth had already been defined in the previous Act. Until the 1960s and 1970s, when new local government legislation was enacted, many claimed that Monmouth was not part of Wales.

These Acts of 1536 and 1542 attempted to annex and incorporate Wales politically and culturally into England. This position remained until 1948 when the Labour Government set up an advisory Council of Wales, thereby granting some recognition to its existence as distinct from England. In 1951 the Conservative Government established the post of Minister for Wales, subsequently Secretary of State for Wales. In 1968 a Welsh Language Act was passed after years of civil disobedience by Welsh people, organized by Cymdeithas yr Iaith Gymraeg (Welsh Language Society). This granted the Welsh language, for the first time since the annexation, some degree of official status within the state. It fell far short of the recommendation by a Royal Commission which, at the time, suggested that Welsh should be granted equality of status with English within Wales. However, Anglicization had proceeded to the point where, by 1981, only 18 per cent of the population of Wales (503,549) spoke Welsh. Various bodies continue to press not only for better status for the language but for its restoration to its former position in Welsh cultural and political life. From the nineteenth century a movement to establish

Welsh 'Home Rule' has grown into a movement for political independence from England.

Ellan Vannin: The Isle of Man

In 1265 Magnus III (1252–65), king of Man and the Isles, died without a direct heir but ceded his kingdom to Alexander III of Scotland. Norway released its claims on the Hebrides and the islands became part of Scotland. As for the Isle of Man itself, England immediately attempted to annex it and for the next century Scotland and England struggled militarily over the island. Even as late as 1456 David II of Scotland dispatched an army to retake the island but was unsuccessful. In 1405 Henry IV allowed John Stanley to assume the title King of Man, on condition that he recognize Henry as his suzerain. The heir of the Stanley fifedom, known as 'Lords of Man' after the Cromwellian period, eventually sold his 'lordship' to the Westminster Government in May 1765. George III now became sovereign of the island. The Manx Parliament was allowed to continue to meet and in 1866, after some electoral reforms, it was fully recognized by Westminster as a 'home rule' parliament. A Royal Commission on the Manx Constitution in 1959 recognized that the Isle of Man was a 'Crown Dependency outside of the United Kingdom'.

One sad aspect of Manx independence has been the destruction of the Manx language and culture. At the beginning of the nineteenth century the great majority of the Manx population were Manx-speaking but an English ruling class had been introduced, which drew into itself an Anglicized Manx element. No provision was subsequently made for the teaching of the language and by the beginning of the twentieth century only 8.1 per cent of the island's population spoke Manx, with just sixty people who could speak no English. The last native speaker, Ned Maddrell, dïed in 1974. A revivalist movement is active and the 1992 census recorded some 643 people as being able to speak the language.

Scotland

Scotland presented the toughest problem to England's ambition to dominate the island of Britain. Scotland itself had grown from a loose confederation of Goidelic and Brythonic Celtic kingdoms under High Kings into a more centralized kingdom under the heirs of Maol Callum a' chinn mhòir (Malcolm Canmore). The Brythonic Celts of Strathclyde, like the Brythonic Celts of the Pictish kingdoms, had eventually merged culturally with the Goidelic Celtic Dál Riadans. The northern tip of Northumbria, the old kingdom of Bernicia, had extended beyond the Tweed to the Lammermuir Hills. In 1018 Maol Callum II, with the help of the petty king of Strathclyde, Owain Mac Domhnuil or Owain the Bald, won a decisive victory over the Saxons led by Eadulf of Northumbria at Carham on Tweed. This victory confirmed the border of Scotland as being on the Tweed. This was merely a confirmation of the recognition given by Edgar at Chester, in AD 973, to Cináech, or Coinnech II (AD 971–995), acknowledging his overlordship of Strathclyde, Cumbria and Lothian. Professor W. J. Watson, in his inaugural address at Edinburgh University in 1914, entitled 'The Position of Gaelic in Scotland', confirmed that 'Gaelic attained its greatest extent when, at the time of Carham, in 1018, it ran from Tweed and Solway to Pentland Firth.' Professor Kenneth Jackson, in the light of modern research, confirmed, in his essay 'The Celtic Aftermath in the Islands', that 'in consequence of this [Carham] the whole of Scotland became for a time Gaelic in speech.'

From the eleventh century, therefore, England was facing a united Gaelic-speaking Celtic country across its northern border. Their ambition to conquer this northern neighbour spurred the Saxons to continue their aggressive warfare against the Celts. One weakness discovered by the English was the Celtic electoral kingship system: this gave them an opportunity to support deposed or unsuccessful monarchal candidates using the excuse of 'hereditary right'. Time and again, English armies made attempts to put their own 'sponsored candidates' on the throne. In 1291 Edward I of England claimed suzerainty over Scotland and tried to set up puppet rulers. William Wallace conducted an insurrectionary warfare against the English from 1297 until his capture and execution in 1305. By then Robert Bruce had emerged and defeated Edward I and his successor Edward II in several battles, notably at Bannockburn. Finally, England reluctantly recognized Scottish independence by the Treaty of Northampton in 1328, though within a few years England was again attempting to conquer the kingdom. Almost every few years, English monarchs, ambitious to succeed where their ancestors had failed, marched their armies northward and failed.

However, an important change was taking place in Scotland at this time. In the twelfth century the language of the Scottish court had changed from Goidelic Celtic to Norman French and, in turn, a change was subsequently made to English. By the fourteenth century the Celtic language of Scotland began to recede. Hector Boece, writing in about 1527, said that the Scots living along the English border had forsaken their mother tongue (Gaelic) and learned English, being driven thereto by wars and commerce. John Major in *The History of Greater Britain*, 1521, said that the majority of Scots a short time before he was writing had spoken Gaelic. The linguistic change had taken place because of the wars against England, particularly during the fifteenth century. By this time the ruling and merchant classes had changed to 'Inglis' but to admit that they were speaking the language of their enemy would not do. So that they could retain their Scottishness without becoming Scottish in speech, they merely changed the labels.

John of Fordun (d. 1384) had made it clear that 'Scottish' in his time was Gaelic, while the English spoken by the ruling and merchant classes was patently 'Inglis'. Now 'Inglis' was designated as 'Scots' and later as 'Lowlands' (Lallans) while 'Scottish', the Goidelic form of Celtic, was dismissed as Irish, or, in the spelling and pronunciation of the day, Yrisch, Ersch or Erse. Gavin Douglas (1475–1522) was the first writer to call 'Inglis', as spoken in Scotland, 'Scots'. Thus a major cultural wedge was driven between the rulers of Scotland, and those who would ape them, and the people. The Scots themselves became instruments of the English policy of cultural conquest.

Scottish Gaelic became one of the most persecuted languages in Europe and it was pushed to the western reaches of the country with particular rapidity during the nineteenth and early twentieth centuries. By 1981 only 1.6 per cent of the Scottish population (79,309 people), mainly confined to the western islands, spoke the language. But the Anglicization of Scotland did not necessarily mean that Scotland was becoming Anglophile. It still retained its independence as fiercely as ever against the pretension of England.

As well as the acquisition of the Kingdom of Man and the Isles, Scotland made other acquisitions of territory. To the north of Scotland, the Orkneys, originally part of the Pictish kingdoms, then claimed by Dál Riada and then by the united kingdom of Alba, had been conquered and settled in the ninth century by Vikings, who ruled them as the jarldom of the Orkneys. These islands were finally passed back to Scotland in 1472. At the same time, another group of islands further north – the Shetlands, also conquered by the Vikings in the ninth century – were formally handed over to the Scottish Crown. The Norse had introduced their language into the islands with their settlement and this language began to diverge from Norwegian, Icelandic and Faeroese around the eleventh century. Norn survived on the Orkneys and Shetlands until comparatively recently.

The end to Scottish independence began when the Stuart monarch, James VI, was invited to succeed Elizabeth I of England, as James I. 'Jamie Baggy-breeks' accepted the Union of Crowns in 1603 and became a keen promoter of a political union between the two countries. For a short while, James was styled as 'King of Great Britain', the old Celtic name being revived as a sop to Celtic sensibilities.

A proposal to unite the parliaments was, however, surprisingly rejected by the English in 1607 as not being financially advantageous. But, by the end of the seventeenth century, Scotland was seen as becoming a trading rival of England and it now became politic for England to exert some control. The idea of the Union of 1707 was that both England and Scotland should merge as co-equal partners in a state called 'Great Britain'. From 1 May 1707, according to Article 1 of the Treaty of Union and its subsequent Act of Ratification, passed on 16 January 1707, England and Scotland would no longer exist. The United Kingdom of Great Britain would come into existence with the Act providing a written constitution for the state. The long-cherished belief that the United Kingdom has no written constitution is yet another of those historic myths. The expert on the Scottish judicial system, Professor T. B. Smith (*A Short Commentary on the Law of Scotland*, Edinburgh, 1962), has clearly pointed out that 'the Union Agreement took effect as a skeletal but none the less fundamental written constitution for the new kingdom of Great Britain when it came into being'. This written constitution was added to by the Act of Union between Great Britain and Ireland of 1 January 1801. It should, of course, be pointed out that the English-controlled Parliament has continuously ignored the provisions of these treaties and thus the state has continued *de facto* without a written constitution while it exists *de jure*. Therefore, the body that sits in Westminster remains an English parliament in which a small group of representatives from the Celtic periphery, impotent to act on the will of that assembly, and unable to address it in their native languages, are allowed to sit.

The only tangible survival of the provisions of the Treaty of Union is in the fact that Scotland still retains its separate and distinct judiciary. Scottish advocates cannot practise at the English Bar, unless qualified to do so, and vice versa. However, when expediency demands, this law system is overturned by Westminster. For example, the eighty-eight trials for High Treason which occurred in the wake of the 1820 insurrection in Scotland were conducted under the English High Treason laws and not under Scottish law.

The English Parliament's failure to abide by the clauses of the Union of 1707 was almost immediate. One should, perhaps, now refer to the 'British' Parliament as England and Scotland were supposed to have 'disappeared'. The reality was that the Treaty resulted in only forty-five Scottish members being allowed to sit in the House of Commons in an assembly of 500 members. English members still controlled the assembly and the Scots had a limited ability to promote and protect Scottish interests. The subtlety of the point that there were now no Scots or English but only 'British', thus making any decision by the majority at Westminster a 'democratic' one, was lost in Scotland. It was little wonder that the first attempt at insurrection was in 1708, the year after the Union.

'If ever a nation gained by being conquered it was here,' enthused Daniel Defoe with disarming candour. He had been the leading English agent in bringing about the Union and was well aware of the reality of England's political coup. Defoe had managed to overturn a Scottish majority against Union within a few years by the judicious dispersal of monetary bribes and offers of titles and positions. In 1714 the Scots, realizing they had been duped, proposed the first Self-Government Bill in Westminster. It was dismissed by the Lord Treasurer who demanded: 'Have we not bought the Scots and the right to tax them?'

There followed a series of unsuccessful uprisings to reassert Scotland's independence, both Jacobite and Jacobin in complexion. The exiled Stuarts persuaded the Scots to support their cause by promising a dissolution of the Union but when the Scots realized that the

Stuarts only saw Scotland as a stepping stone to England, they turned to the new political creed of the 'Rights of Man' and republicanism, born out of the American War of Independence and the French Revolution. The last major Scottish insurrection was in 1820 when Scots combined social revolution with an attempt to establish a Scottish state.

The modern Scottish 'constitutional' self-government movement came into being in 1889 and since then twenty-five Self-Government for Scotland Bills have been proposed in Westminster. In those which have been allowed to come to a vote, the majority of Scottish Members of Parliament have always voted in favour, only to be outvoted by the majority of English Members of Parliament.

Ireland

In 1169 the Saxons, or to be more accurate the Anglo-Normans, began to expand into Ireland and in 1172 Henry II, of the Angevin Empire, took an army to Ireland, following hot on the heels of the Earl of Pembroke who had seen the conquest of Ireland as a private enterprise. In fact, Henry saw the very real threat of the earl, Strongbow, grabbing the High Kingship and setting himself up as a rival. Henry II defeated the Irish High King, Ruairí Ó Conchobhar. On 6 October 1175, the Treaty of Windsor was agreed whereby Ruairi recognized Henry II as his suzerain while Henry recognized Ruairi as 'king under him'. In 1184, in accordance with Celtic tradition, Ruairi resigned his kingship and entered the monastery at Cong, where he died in 1199. But there were no more High Kings of Ireland after him. England had established a 'legal' foothold in the country by its Treaty.

However, Ireland had an amazing ability to subsume its conquerors, assimilating them into the Irish nation, so that by the seventeenth century, in spite of centuries of conquest and colonization programmes, the Irish nation remained fairly culturally intact. The seventeenth century saw the most ruthless system of colonization, in which the English administration attempted nothing less than the annihilation of the native Irish by removing them on pain of death west of the River Shannon, forcibly transporting thousands of men, women and children to Barbados and other colonies, and dividing the land between new English settlers. The Irish survived even this genocidal plan. A new conquest began at the end of that century, resulting in the introduction of Penal Laws which allowed civil rights only for members of the Established Church of England. No Catholics nor Dissenting Protestants were to enjoy any rights whatsoever.

The eighteenth century colonial parliament in Ireland began to come into conflict with the English Parliament on trading matters. The same solution as had been applied to quench Scottish trading rivalry was now applied to the Irish colonial parliament – union. The attempt by Protestants and Catholics, joining in an organization called the United Irishmen, to establish an Irish republic in 1798 was met with ruthless suppression. Between 30,000 and 70,000 people, the number is varyingly recorded, were killed or executed in its wake. Then on 1 January 1801, the Act of Union was passed. The English Government were under no illusions about what they had achieved. As Under Secretary of State of the Civil Department, Edward Cooke wrote to William Pitt in 1799: 'By giving the Irish a hundred members in an Assembly of six hundred and fifty, they will be impotent to operate upon that Assembly, but it will be invested with Irish assent to its authority.'

Uprisings followed during the nineteenth century. Immediate moves were made to give civil rights to Dissenting Protestants, particularly the Presbyterians of Ulster, who had first imported the creed of republicanism into Ireland having played a prominent role in the American War of Independence. It was the Presbyterians who played a major part in the formation of the Irish republican movement. By the middle of the century, the English Government had bribed and propagandized most of the Presbyterian community into supporting the union.

But the Penal Laws also had to be relaxed against Catholics. In 1829 came a Catholic Emancipation Act allowing property-owning Catholics to vote for the first time. However, uprisings continued against English rule. Following the suppression of the 1802, 1848 and 1867 uprisings, a 'Home Rule' movement was launched in 1870. An Irish Party was established to secure self-government and this party held four-fifths of all the Irish seats within the London Parliament over the next forty years. In spite of this, as Under Secretary Cooke had foreseen, the Irish Members of Parliament were impotent to secure legislation for independence against the majority English vote. No fewer than twenty-eight Self-Government Bills were defeated in the first few years of the Irish Party being in Westminster.

In the general election of 1910, the Irish Party, having won another majority of eighty-four seats out of the 105 representing Ireland, found itself holding a balance of power between the major English parties. It seemed inevitable that the Irish would achieve a measure of self-government. But the proposals were delayed by every political device available, including the rejection of the House of Lords, and finally they were shelved when the United Kingdom entered the Great War in August 1914.

On 24 April 1916, the Irish rose in arms once again. The suppression of the rising, and the protracted executions of its leaders, led a swing of support to Sinn Féin. Founded in 1905, Sinn Féin was actually a dual-monarchist party, seeking a separate Irish parliament but under the English monarch on the same lines as Hungary had separated from Austria to form the dual-monarchy of the Austro-Hungarian Empire in 1867. The English media, not having troubled to get their facts right, had called 1916 the 'Sinn Féin Rebellion'. In 1917 the Irish took advantage of the publicity given to Sinn Féin to reconstitute it as a republican party pledged to Irish separation. In the December 1918 general election, Sinn Féin won seventy-three seats, the Irish Party's representation fell to six, and the Unionists increased their representation from eighteen to twenty-six, mainly on the split voting between Sinn Féin and the Irish Party. Sinn Féin's manifesto declared its intention of reaffirming the republic declared in 1916 and establishing a parliament in Dublin without attending the London Parliament. This led to an attempt by the English authorities to arrest all Irish Republican Members of Parliament and to suppress the Dublin Parliament. In the words of one of the Irish Members of Parliament, the English Government had declared the entire Irish nation as 'an illegal assembly'. A War of Independence followed. In 1921 the English Government finally entered into negotiations and succeeded in coercing Irish delegates, under threat of a continuation of 'an immediate and terrible war', into accepting the Partition of the country with the majority area being recognized as a Free State, being a Dominion within the British Commonwealth.

Faced with a *fait accompli* by their delegates, the Irish Parliament split among themselves when asked to ratify the Treaty. A bitter civil war broke out lasting from 1922 to 1923. The Pro-Treaty forces won with military aid from the London Government. The Free State came into being on 6 December 1922, and the following day the place of the six Partitioned counties within the United Kingdom was affirmed.

Of the northern nine county provinces of Ulster, militant Unionists had won majorities in only four. The militant Unionism was the result of a century of 'divide and rule', the encouragement of Irish Dissenters to forget their radical republican roots and the careful development of sectarian antagonisms. However, as four counties did not constitute a viable economic unit, two nationalist/republican counties were arbitrarily seized to create a statelet called Northern Ireland, separated from the three other Ulster counties and the rest of Ireland.

A Unionist majority was guaranteed in perpetuity but further reinforced by the systematic disenfranchisement of groups of Catholic/nationalist voters; segregation in all walks of life, especially in local and provincial government, was enforced. The Partition and enforcement of an apartheid system were undemocratically established by any standard. The Partitioned area was created out of bloodshed, violence and coercion and not through the will of the Irish people. Injustice was a necessary tool by which control could be asserted and the area kept within the confines of the United Kingdom. This has ensured that bloodshed and violence continue as a factor in the colonial history of Ireland until such time as the democratic will of the Irish nation is respected by the Westminster Parliament.

For fifty years London attempted to ignore the fact that there was a lack of civil rights in an area which it claimed was an integral part of the state – the United Kingdom of Great Britain *and* Northern Ireland.

On 18 April 1949, the twenty-six Counties of Ireland which had formed the Free State declared themselves a Republic. They were then deemed to have left the British Commonwealth and the reaction by London was to pass a new Government of Ireland Act guaranteeing the Unionists their position in the United Kingdom. But violence has erupted time and again. During the 1960s Catholics tried to claim civil rights by the formation of a Northern Ireland Civil Rights Association. Marches and demonstrations were attacked by the agents of the Six County Government to such an extent that in 1969 London felt obliged to send troops to stop a massacre of Catholics in front of the eyes of the world's press. The part played by these troops changed when the Conservatives came to power in 1970 and they were used in their traditional role as the enforcers of Unionist policies. Once more, England found itself with a colonial war on its hands but one in which they have stubbornly refused to move from a position of aggressive intransigence.

Over two decades have gone by with only the increasing toll of dead and injured to mark the passing of the years. The British Army in Ireland has established a record of dishonourable conduct matched by few other comparable forces in Europe. In terms of economic costs, borne by the taxpayer, the war has been an incredible burden. The collapse of the economy of the area, the spread of the worst social conditions in Western Europe and the frightening erosion of civil liberties have made the establishment of a just and lasting peace there the most pressing issue facing the people of these islands. One thing was clear from the start, the deployment of the British Army in Ireland was not part of any solution to the situation; it was an integral part of the problem. The intransigence of Westminster politicians in pursuing this colonial war might be understood in the continuing sad history of relations between Celt and Saxon.

So far as its Celtic cultural identity is concerned, Ireland, naturally, suffered the same ruthless attempts to extinguish its language and culture as the other Celtic peoples. Yet only in the nineteenth century did Irish cease to be the language of the majority of people in Ireland. The tremendous shock of the artificially created famine, 'The Great Hunger', in the middle of the century, which saw a decrease in the Irish population in real terms within four years of 2.5 million, was a severe blow. Most of the decrease in population was to be found among Irish-speakers. By 1911 only 14 per cent (553,717 people) of the population spoke the language. It became the first official language of the newly emergent Irish state but attempts to revive it have been half-hearted. Nevertheless, the 1981 census showed 31.6 per cent of the Irish Republic (1,018,312) returning themselves as Irish-speaking. Between 1911 and 1991 no figures were issued for Irish-speakers in the Partitioned area of Ireland but it was estimated that they numbered about 60,000 (around 4 per cent). Attempts to speak or use Irish in the Partitioned area caused severe difficulties to be placed in the way of speakers by the mechanism of the state.

This is the result of the last thousand years of the conflict between Celt and Saxon.

There'll always be a 'Britain' . . . ?

The image of 'Great Britain' which has been, and still is, presented to the world – and, indeed, which is presented to the internal population – is that of a homogeneous nation state. So successful has the propagation of this concept been, that it is now popularly believed that there exists an entity called 'the British nation' and that the empire once governed from London was a 'British Empire'. The reality is that there does not exist a British state, let alone a British nation.

The state, as we have seen, has changed its name several times within the last 200 years but, from 7 December 1922, it has been the United Kingdom of Great Britain and Northern Ireland. Contrary to popular belief, this state excludes the Channel Islands and the Isle of Man, which have their own governments and which constitute Crown dependencies outside the United Kingdom. The United Kingdom, through the Crown and Privy Council, can legislate on matters of international defence but has little other administrative or legislative authority within these islands.

Outside the United Kingdom it is widely assumed that the term 'British' is merely a synonym for 'English'. Indeed, when George Santayana wrote his famous essay on 'The British Character' (1922) he was referring only to the English. An example of the concept that 'British' is merely an interchangeable term with 'English' is clearly demonstrated in *The International Thesaurus of Quotations*, compiled by Rhoda Thomas Tripp (first published by Cromwell Inc., in the USA, in 1970, and since 1973 a standard Penguin reference work). One would look in vain for a section on 'Britain and the British' but, under 'England and the English', among those quotations specifically referring to 'England' there are several which actually refer to 'Britain and the British'. Clearly, then, the compiler believes 'British' and 'English' to be one and the same.

Ask anyone to imagine a 'typically British' person and the image would come back in English form. No monoglot Welsh-speaker, of whom there are several thousands, nor monoglot Scottish-Gaelic speaker, of whom there are several hundreds, would be deemed 'British' in foreign eyes.

But one cannot blame outside observers for this confusion; the casual interchange of 'British' and 'English' has emanated from England itself. In November 1985, for example, a Conservative Party political broadcast by the party education spokesman referred to the comparative standards of education between English and German children. A few seconds later the spokesman was referring to *British* figures which he apparently believed were the same as the English figures. On 15 June 1992, the then Conservative Environment Secretary, David Mellor, was rebuked by a Scots Member of Parliament in the House of Commons for having referred, in the media, to 'British soccer hooligans' rampaging in Sweden. It was pointed out that the hooligans in question had been English and that Scottish supporters had been extremely well behaved at their respective games in Sweden. On the same day the BBC (Ceefax service) confused matters more by referring to 'United Kingdom soccer hooligans'. As neither Wales nor Northern Ireland, the other constituent parts of the United Kingdom, were even playing, the definition became even more misrepresentative.

As we have seen, the ancient Celtic name 'Britain' was first revived as a sop to Celtic sensibilities in 1604 when James VI of Scotland eagerly accepted the invitation by the English Privy Council to succeed the childless Elizabeth I as James I of England. The idea may well have been brought to the English court by James himself for it was the Scots historian, John Major, in 1521, who wrote his history of 'Great Britain'. But Major's 'Great Britain', unlike the 'Great Britain' of tenth-century Celtic perception, was one which now fully accepted the presence of the English kingdom. Neither did Major envisage a 'Great Britain state' but only used the term as a convenient geographical label for the entire island. James must have been well acquainted with Major's work for Major had been the tutor of James's own tutor, George Buchanan (1506–1586). However, only for a short time was James hailed as 'King of Great Britain'. The title was soon dropped.

William of Orange was acclaimed as William III but he was only William I in Scotland. Even after 1707 the administration made no attempt to number the monarchs either from the Union of Crowns or from the Union of the two countries. The monarchs of the United Kingdom are still numbered on the English succession. Thus, today, Elizabeth II is not the second of her name to reign in Scotland but only the first; likewise she is the first of her name to be Queen of the United Kingdom. Nowhere is the fact that Scotland is not seen as an equal partner in the 'United Kingdom of Great Britain' more clearly demonstrated than here. When Elizabeth was crowned as Elizabeth II in 1953, some Scots objected and, for a while, there was a campaign of destroying the new 'Elizabeth II R' mail boxes in Scotland as a protest. The matter was also raised in the Courts of Scotland, in *MacCormick* v. *Lord Advocate*, commonly called the 'E II R case'. In trying to form a constitutional judgement Lord Cooper, the Lord President, whose powers came from Elizabeth II, felt a little out of his depth. He hazarded that 'an advisory opinion of the International Court of Justice might be competent' but he clearly did not want to bite the hand that fed him. No such opinion could be made binding on Westminster or the monarchy. While some books are now more sensitive in their titles, such as Eric R. Delderfield's *Kings and Queens of England and Great Britain* (David & Charles, 1992), nevertheless the numerical designation of monarchs follows the English succession instead of dating from the Union of Crowns.

Scottish children are still expected to know the dates of the English monarchs before the Union of Crowns, rather than those of their own rulers prior to that date, while English children would not know a Scottish monarch from a Russian tsar. When Scots complain about such matters it is blandly accepted that it is they who are being nationalist.

It was, of course, not until the Union of 1707 that the term 'British' came into use as a popular but occasional term whereby it was hoped to incorporate the Celtic nationalities which shared the island with the dominant English nation and so defuse any other national identity among them. But because the term is a political one, a synthetic term in the modern scheme of things, some hilarious problems arise with its usage.

On one memorable occasion the then Prime Minister, Margaret Thatcher, praising the work of pop star Bob Geldorf for his Ethiopian famine relief activities, vehemently declared, in the presence of the Dublin-born and -raised citizen of the Irish Republic, that he made her 'proud of British youth'. It could have been argued that Margaret

Thatcher was simply making a comparative judgement and was thus denigrating Irish youth. But that was not the case. She was simply unaware of what she was saying.

What becomes clear to the observer is the fascinating use of terminology demonstrated in the media. The rule of thumb tends to be that when the Welsh, Scots or Irish do something laudable in international eyes then they are described as 'British'. If something displeasing is done, then they become Welsh, Scots or Irish. Conversely, if an English person achieves fame then they are English but if they do something wrong, they are British. In the London media coverage of the 1991 Tokyo athletics, in which the United Kingdom was competing, ITV news commentators on 29 August could not make up their minds whether 'England' or 'Britain' or the 'United Kingdom' was competing. The rule of thumb that emerged was that when a white English person won the medal they were described as English, but if they were black, Welsh, Scots or Irish then they were British. Needless to say, this is a general observation and there are doubtless honest exceptions, but the conscious or unconscious juxtapositions of the terms are revealing.

The English media have been overfond of claiming members of the Irish nation as 'British', even as 'English'. A standard reference work, for example, claims that Bram Stoker, author of the classic novel *Dracula* (1897), is 'English'. Yet Stoker was born in Clontarf, Ireland, of a well-known Irish family and educated in Dublin. The press went a little too far in trying to claim the playwright Samuel Beckett as 'of British origin' when he won the Nobel Prize for Literature in 1969. Beckett was then a naturalized French citizen but he had been born and educated in Dublin and settled in France in 1928 without doing anything more than pass through the isle of Britain.

Often we get flashes of honesty from the English themselves and the pretence of a British nation and empire is dropped. Cecil John Rhodes (1853–1902), financier, politician and leading Victorian empire-builder, was not concerned with 'Britain' as he made clear in his Ruskin Inaugural Address at Oxford in 1870. He talked of '*England's* inescapable duty'

to found colonies as fast and as far as she is able, formed of her most energetic and worthiest men; seizing every piece of fruitful waste ground she can set her foot on, and there teaching these her colonists that their chief virtue is to be fidelity to their country, and that their first aim is to be to advance the power of England by land and sea; and that, though they live on a distant plot of ground, they are no more to consider themselves therefore disfranchised from their native land than the sailors of her fleets do, because they float on distant waves . . .

When Prime Minister William Ewart Gladstone (1809–1898) spoke of empire he did not see it as something born of Wales, Scotland or Ireland, but only of England. In *The Nineteenth Century*, September 1878, Gladstone wrote of 'England's Mission' and declared that the empire was 'part of our patrimony, born with our birth, dying only with our death'. George, Lord Curzon of Kedleston (1859–1925), when Viceroy of India in 1898–1905, often spoke of the justification not of a 'British Empire' in India but of an 'English Empire'. He spoke of Englishmen creating in India 'a sense of manliness or moral dignity, a spring of patriotism, a dawn of intellectual enlightenment or a stirring of duty' and declared that 'that is the Englishman's justification in India'. The Royal Colonial Institute, whose *Proceedings* in 1875/6 report a debate on the development of the empire in Africa, had no illusion about who owned the empire when one of its leading members declared: 'Now this country of Africa . . . is a country which I hope some day will belong to England.'

Anthony Eden, a more modern example, in October 1955, was nothing loath to talk about 'the greatness of England and its empire . . . England is the metropolitan country of the Commonwealth . . . It is England which links the group of nations, old and new, that now form the Commonwealth with America and Europe.'

That England exists as the dominant country in political reality and in the perception of most English people, and not the eighteenth-century creation of 'Britain', is made clear from countless studies. Kenneth Mackensie's study of the United Kingdom Parliament was, in fact, entitled *The English Parliament*, while M. A. Thomson wrote *A Constitutional History of England*. The Treaty of Union of 1707 which abolished England and Scotland and created 'Great Britain' is best forgotten when fervent English patriots sing, 'There'll always be an England . . .'

The use of political labels to disguise, or fudge, English dominance in the United Kingdom has confused many people. The labels are often accepted without question. One of the most curious was the introduction in 1980 of the term 'mainland Britain' in an attempt to reinforce the political will that the Partitioned Six Counties of Ireland would remain an integral part of the United Kingdom. While the *New Statesman* (21 November 1987) once attempted a more correct label with 'mainland United Kingdom', the more popular, but incorrect, label of 'mainland Britain' has stuck. As we have seen, the name of the state is the 'United Kingdom of Great Britain and Northern Ireland' – Ireland is not, and never has been, part of Great Britain. But the term was so eagerly seized upon in its political context that one enthusiastic BBC presenter managed to refer to the Isle of Lewis, in the Outer Hebrides, as part of the 'British mainland'. Political leaders from the sovereign independent Republic of Ireland are told that they are journeying to the 'mainland' when they visit their counterparts in London. The insult to Ireland seems lost on the British media.

As another example of the bolstering of English political attitudes toward Ireland by inaccurate labels, we find that many people refer to the twenty-six-county Republic as 'Southern Ireland', ignoring the fact that the county which stretches to the most northerly point of the island of Ireland (Donegal) is part of the Republic. Then there is the use of the term 'Ulster' for the Partitioned Six Counties of Ireland; but what of the three Ulster counties of Donegal, Cavan and Monaghan which are in the Irish Republic and presumably should no longer, after 2000 years, consider themselves part of Ulster? Another attempt to form a political label is the use of the Irish name for Ireland when speaking of the Irish Republic, calling it Éire (usually mispronounced 'Air'). Éire is of course the name, in Irish, for the entire island and its use by English-speakers is curious: they do not refer to Germany as Deutschland or Austria as Oesterreich or Greece as Hellas when speaking in English. Why then speak of Ireland as Éire except through ignorance or as a means of making a political statement?

What becomes obvious is that people in the United Kingdom have become totally bewildered by the use of political labels.

The Leeds Permanent Building Society organized a promotion for new accounts in 1985, offering a holiday in the Barbados. Contestants had to answer a simple question: which island in the United Kingdom was nearest in size to Barbados – the Isle of Wight, the Isle of Man or Guernsey? Was this a trick question? No, simply one expressive of the confusion in most people's minds about the country they live in. Only the Isle of Wight is, of course, within the United Kingdom. The other islands are self-governing Crown Dependencies outside the United Kingdom.

It is a *sine qua non* of the attempt to create a homogeneous 'British' nation that the languages and cultures of the Celtic peoples, within the United Kingdom, should be destroyed. The philosophy was best summed up by the poet Edmund Spenser, one of the most enthusiastic of England's colonists in Tudor Ireland. 'It has ever been the use of conquerors to despise the language of the conquered and to force him by all means to learn his . . . the speech being Irish, the heart must needs be Irish.' Indeed, the elimination of the language and culture of the Celts was seen as an essential prerequisite to the creation of England's imperial base within the islands of Britain and Ireland. Sir William Parsons, Master of the Court of Wards, sent to Ireland during the mid-seventeenth-century conquests, summed up the programme: 'We must change their course of government, apparel, manner of holding land, their language and habit of life. It will otherwise be impossible to set up in them obedience to the laws and to the English Empire.' Parsons had no difficulty in describing the realities of an English Empire.

Legislation was enacted in all the Celtic areas to destroy the languages and cultures and supplant them with English. In Wales, where the Tudor Act of Union declared its intention to 'utterly extirpe' Welsh, the policy of linguaecide was carried on with zeal. The policy was described and advocated by a lawyer in the Arches Court of Canterbury in the eighteenth century. Monoglot English clergy had been appointed to livings in Wales as a matter of course. A Dr Bowles had been given the living of Trefdaeth and Llangwyfan where, of 500 parishioners, only five had any knowledge of English. This was in 1768 and the Welsh decided to rebel. They argued that they should have a minister who spoke Welsh. The case took five years to argue. Dr Bowles's counsel was quite clear on the position of Wales:

Wales is a conquered country, it is proper to introduce the English language, and it is the duty of the bishops to endeavour to promote the English, in order to introduce the language . . . It has always been the policy of the legislature to introduce the English language

in Wales. We never heard of an act of parliament in Welsh . . .
The English language is, by act of parliament, to be used in all the
courts of judicature in Wales, and an English Bible to be kept in
all the churches in Wales, that by comparison with the Welsh,
they may the sooner attain to the knowledge of the English.

In 1773 Dr Bowles was confirmed in his position as minister and
remained unable to communicate with all but a few of his flock.

In Scotland, as we have seen, the process of Anglicization had
started under the native rulers and, by the time of the Union of
Crowns, while Gaelic was still spoken in areas such as Galloway, in
south-west Scotland, and in Fife, just across the river from Edinburgh, English was the language of the ruling class, the merchants
and the major towns. More important, it was the language of the
Reformation. In 1609 the 'Statutes of Iona' were drawn up and
ratified by an Act of the Privy Council of James VI of Scotland,
now James I of England, which decreed that the 'English tongue be
universally planted, and the Irish [Scottish Gaelic] language, which
is one of the chief and principal causes of the continuance of barbarity
and incivility . . . may be abolished and removed'. On the evidence,
there is little doubt that Scottish Gaelic has been one of the worst-
persecuted languages in Europe. Indeed, all the Celtic areas have
their histories of nineteenth-and twentieth-century 'beating sticks',
whereby the children were beaten if heard speaking a word of their
languages in school. In one notorious case, in the Isle of Lewis in the
mid-twentieth century, a teacher used to hang a human skull around
the neck of children, aged around five to seven years old, who spoke
their home language in school.

Today, out of the 16 million who inhabit the Celtic countries, only
2.5 million speak a Celtic language. Thus, the rest of the world
generally perceives the Celts as English-speaking or, of course, in
the case of the Bretons, as French-speaking, and is, therefore, more
inclined to accept the 'British equals English' concept without
question.

It is, of course, not simply the non-Celtic populations who are
confused but also the Celtic populations. Suffering the psychological
traumas that inevitably accompany conquest, linguaecide and mar-
ginalization, they have become confused as to their identity. At times,
Celts have attempted to come to grips with their ambivalent place in

the English imperial scheme of things. For many, it is hard to accept that their nation has been conquered and incorporated, their cultural identity disregarded and almost eradicated.

There is a school of thought in Scotland which would ignore the realities of the Union of 1707, the breaking of its provisions by Westminster, the subsequent military suppression of Scotland during the eighteenth century followed by a 'revision' of Scotland's history. These Scots would accept the image of a kilt-swinging, tartan-clad Scots soldier creating a 'British Empire' in which he was master, rather than being merely a mercenary appendage to the real imperial power and culture. Scottish administrators are lauded, while the fact that they administered the colonial peoples as colonials themselves if forgotten. And totally ignored is the legislation that sought to destroy not only the language of the be-kilted 'British' soldier, but also the visible aspects of his material culture; even the kilt, the tartan and the bagpipes were prohibited by law under the Disarming Acts of the late eighteenth century.

This is not to argue that the Scots, or rather a section of them, were not slow to seize the job opportunities provided by the bounds of empire. Nor were members of the other Celtic populations, many of whom were able to exploit successfully, as individuals, the growth of the empire. Take, for example, the extraordinary career of George Thomas (1756–1802) of Roscrea, Co. Tipperary. He began his career in the Royal Navy and wound up in India as a soldier of fortune. He seized power from Appo Rao, the Muhratta ruler of Meerut, made himself rajah of a territory twice as big as his native Ireland and offered to conquer the Punjab for British Raj. While the offer was accepted with alacrity, Rajah George found a fierce resistance from the Sikhs. Yet to use such an example to claim the empire equally for Ireland would be nonsensical.

The empire, being created by individuals, though under the general direction of a government policy, which government was in London, England, can be portrayed as a complicated phenomenon. Indeed, the same argument could be made of the Roman Empire. Many individuals created the Roman Empire who were not necessarily Roman. But the military and cultural dynamic of that empire emanated from a single area on the banks of the Tiber. So, too, with the empire of England. The cultural and military dynamic emanated from the Anglo-Saxon ethos. The role of individual Celts in exploiting the empire, or in seeking jobs within it when they were denied lands and security in their own exploited countries, does not give any foundation to a claim that the empire was equally a Celtic one. The migrations of Celtic populations to the far corners of the English Empire was not an imperialist dynamic but simply an effect of imperialism within their own countries; they wanted to escape penury, dispossession of lands, suppression of their languages and cultures and religious intolerance. Their subsequent role in other colonial territories was a side-effect of the imperial dynamic and not its mainspring.

For example, a large section of the population of India was encouraged by the dynamics of the empire to settle in Africa in the nineteenth century. These Indians then formed a 'buffer class' between white colonials and native Africans in such possessions as British East Africa (Kenya and Uganda). The Indian populations created successful businesses, exploiting the situation and individually benefiting commercially from the empire. Indeed, British East Africa was governed by the Indian Penal Code during its early days. We can, of course, argue just how *Indian* was this Indian Penal Code. But the point is, one cannot argue on these facts that the empire was just as much Indian as it was English. So, too, the claim that the empire was equally a Celtic one is fallacious. There is a basic structure to any empire as well as a superstructure. This study has demonstrated that the Celts were never part of the basic structure of the phenomenon known as the 'British Empire' although no one can deny that they, as individuals, played a part, along with other colonial peoples, in its superstructure.

The most fascinating attempt by a Celt to come to terms with his subservient role in the English Empire was put forward by an Irish immigrant, Charles James O'Donnell, from Cardonagh, Co. Donegal, who died in Camberwell, London, in 1935. He was a Member of Parliament for Walworth, 1906–10. In 1929 O'Donnell published a curious book entitled *The Irish Future with the Lordship of the World* (London, 1929) which became something of a bestseller in its day. Chapter XIV of the work contained O'Donnell's main thesis and was entitled 'The Celtic Empire of Great Britain'. In this essay, O'Donnell argued that what existed in the United Kingdom was, in reality, 'a great Celtic Confederacy' and that the English population was not Anglo-Saxon but Celtic. Since 'Celtic' is simply a linguistic/

cultural description it is hard to accept O'Donnell's definition of a Celtic 'race' and the rejection of language as a means of identifying Celts. According to O'Donnell, quoting some of his contemporaries, such as Sir Montagu Sharpe, who put forward the argument in his *Antiquities of Middlesex: Britain in British, Roman and Saxon Times* (London, 1919), and Samuel Rawson Gardiner, an expert on seventeenth-century English history who went 'over the top' in his *Students' History of England* (London, 1890), the Saxons arrived in Britain and intermarried with native Celts. The Saxons only established a ruling class in the country.

O'Donnell enthused:

> The almost instantaneous submission of England to its Norman Conquerors is explicable only on the hypothesis that they were welcomed by the great British (Celtic) serf population. The Saxons continued the struggle for only a very few months and were driven from their homes by the Norman nobility leading British armies . . . the Saxon masters of Britain could not save themselves, except by flight. . . . the Saxon race for the most part disappeared and the Briton, as Celtic as the Scot or Welshman, started out to found the greatest empire in history.

O'Donnell, on his death, made a bequest to establish annual lectures under his name at the Universities of Oxford, Wales and Edinburgh, the National University of Ireland and Trinity College, Dublin, for scholars to investigate 'the British or Celtic element in the existing population of England' and 'the British or Celtic element in the English language and the dialects of the English counties'. With few exceptions, the scholars delivering these lectures have prefaced their remarks by stating their total disagreement with O'Donnell's contention. Professor Kenneth Jackson, delivering one of the lectures, stated immediately that 'the proposition is incapable of proof'. The positive thing, out of O'Donnell's bequest, has been the numerous sound scholastic lectures on aspects of the relationship between Celt and Saxon. D.A. Binchy, referring to O'Donnell's 'somewhat eccentric views', took the opportunity to compare Celt and Saxon kingship but added, 'I can only hope that as a result these venerable walls will not be haunted by Mr O'Donnell's protesting ghost.'

In spite of this, O'Donnell's 'eccentric views' have been picked up again, so that in recent years the origins of England have become a matter of controversy. A group of archaeologists have convinced themselves of O'Donnell's contention that only a small number of well-armed warrior bands arrived in Britain and mounted a series of *coups d'état*, taking over regional Celtic kingdoms and marrying native Celtic women. As Dr Martin Welch, himself a senior archaeologist in the field, has pointed out in *Anglo-Saxon England* (London, 1992): 'There are real problems in accepting such a viewpoint. Firstly it argues that we know much better than contemporary and slightly later commentators who wrote about events in Britain.' Nevertheless, the latest leading proponent of the O'Donnell argument, Nicholas Higham, in *Rome, Britain and the Anglo-Saxons* (London, 1992), believes that the creation of England was achieved by a gradual infiltration of small intermarrying groups.

Apart from the fact that it ignores the evidence of contemporary sources, such as Gildas, the idea of 'gradual intermarriage' is nonsensical. The Anglo-Saxon kingdoms were well established within 150 years. If we accept that a small number of Anglo–Saxons were able to create *coups d'état*, intermarry, and change the language and cultural identity of the natives within a couple of generations as a matter of comparative ease throughout the area now called England, we must ask why it took nearly 1000 years for the British Celtic language to die out in such a relatively small area as Cornwall. Even today the language and cultural identity of Cornwall are not altogether eradicated. As Dr Welch points out: 'If only a few Anglo-Saxon immigrants actually crossed the North Sea, it is difficult to see why English became the dominant language in lowland Britain, replacing the Celtic dialects there.'

In returning to the need for some sections of the Celtic population to find a rationale for their role in a state which is dominated by an unrelated culture, we see some bizarre propositions being put forward. One recent one has been demonstrated by the attempt of the Unionist population in the north of Ireland, claiming to be loyal to the concept of the United Kingdom, and calling themselves 'British' rather than Irish, to find a new identity. In 1974, Dr Ian Adamson published a book called *The Cruthin* (Belfast). He claimed that a people called the Cruthin were the original inhabitants of Ireland, arriving there long before the Goidelic Celts. When the Celts came, the Cruthin were driven to Scotland, but, during the seventeenth-century Plantations of Ulster, the Cruthin returned to take their right-ful place in the Irish scheme of things, displacing the Irish and regaining their lost possessions. At one stroke, the colonial settlers of the seventeenth century were given a new justification for being in Ireland and remaining separate from the natives. Instead of being newcomers, they were the original inhabitants returning to their lands. It was rather like the philosophy of Zionism. They were the 'Chosen People' who had come back to their 'Promised Land'. Dr Adamson attempted to bolster his theory by examples of blood groupings to demonstrate that the Irish comprised two nations – the nationalist Catholics (Gaels) and the unionist Protestants (Cruthin).

Who were these Cruthin? As already shown in this work, they were the British Celts living to the north of Hadrian's Wall, a tribal group whom Roman soldiers, serving on the wall, nicknamed Picti. They called themselves Pretani (the early form of Britoni) but when the Gaelic-speakers arrived, the P-Celtic name was pronounced in the Q-Celtic form. As we know, the most famous change in the two branches of Celtic, which gives them their linguistic appellations of P- and Q-Celtic, is the change in sound value of that particular letter. Thus Mac in Gaelic became Map in Brythonic. Thus did Pretani became Cruthin. Professor Jackson argues that they were 'unques-tionably Celtic, and moreover what is called P-Celtic, that is, sprung from the Continental Celtic milieu from which the rest of the Britons also came and not from the Q-Celtic, which was the source of Irish and Scottish Gaelic'. Now this immediately sends Dr Adamson's theory awry because Q-Celtic is the more archaic, and speakers of this form were the first to reach these islands many centuries before the speakers of P-Celtic. Indeed, the argument is that P-Celtic was an evolution away from Q-Celtic. But in total contradiction to Dr Adamson's 'race theory' is the fact that his Cruthin and Gael were both Celts. Dr Adamson's theories become as nonsensical as O'Donnell's theory that the Anglo-Saxons were wiped out by the Celts.

Such 'race theories' are undoubtedly as dangerous as they are non-sensical and have an insidious influence. In my opinion, they are to be classed with the notorious 'race history', *Die Grundlagen des Neunzehnten Jahrhunderts* (Foundations of the Nineteenth Century), published in 1899 by the Englishman, Houston Stewart Chamber-lain. This account of European history from the viewpoint of a

Germanic race ideology became the basis for Nazi political philosophy in the Third Reich.

In speaking about 'the Celts' it should be made clear that the definition of a Celtic community has always been a linguistic one as far back as the first references to Celts in the writings of the Greeks and Romans. What has differentiated the Celt from other European peoples is language and its attendant culture. When Greeks and Romans attempted to describe a 'typical Celt' they painted varying physical types from tall, blond, gangling Gauls to short, stocky, swarthy Silurians. The linguistic definition has been reiterated by all leading Celtic scholars since Edward Lhuyd's pioneering linguistic work on the Celtic languages – *Archaeologia Britannica* (1707). The definition was put succinctly by Professor Eoin MacNeill in *Phrases of Irish History* (Dublin, 1919): 'The term Celtic is indicative of language, not of race.' A Celtic people, then, are a people who speak, or were known to have spoken within modern historical times, a Celtic language. Once the languages irreversibly disappear then we may argue that the Celtic people have also disappeared and are as dead as the Etruscans. It is a nonsense, therefore, to attempt to apply 'race' definitions in order to identify the Celtic populations.

So among the highly regarded Celtic workers for the furtherance of Celtic culture we can count people like the native Scottish Gaelic-speaking Maxwell brothers, of West Indian origin; Othmar Remy Arthur, the Irish folk-singer, also of West Indian origin; and, indeed, the Irish leader, Pádraig Pearse, whose father was from Devon, in England, and Cathal Ó Sándair, the most prolific novelist in the Irish language (160 novels published), whose father was also English and who was born in London. In Celtic perception, being Celtic is a matter of culture, not of that indefinable and nonsensical thing called 'race'.

It must be pointed out that, during the years of the decline of the English Empire, a new factor has entered the 'British equals English' concept which must be taken into account when discussing definitions. Groups of immigrants from the former colonies started to become a significant factor in the United Kingdom population, particularly those of Asian and Afro-Caribbean origin. Whereas, until the early 1960s, immigrants to the United Kingdom, being predominantly European, were quickly absorbed into the local culture, the new immigrants were still delineated in the perception of the native inhabitants by skin pigmentation. Second-generation Italians, Poles or Spaniards could call themselves English, Scots or Welsh without question. But it was in England that second-generation Asians and Afro-Caribbeans particularly had a problem. They were made to feel it was wrong to claim to be 'English' and so they sought refuge in that indefinable catch-all term 'British'.

While more discerning exceptions to the general rule will insist, and correctly so, that they are Welsh, Scots, Irish or English of Asian or Afro-Caribbean ancestry, the majority use 'British' as a means of solving their crisis of identity; as, indeed, a means of claiming to belong, because they were made to feel that they never could be *English*. It was Enoch Powell, a former Tory minister, and a Privy Councillor, who first spelt out this racist philosophy for immigrant communities in a speech in April 1968, in Birmingham. He put forward an 'England for the English' philosophy which claimed that to be English one had to be white. To make England white, not only was non-white immigration to be banned but those who had already made their homes in England, even those descended from Africans brought here in the seventeenth and eighteenth centuries, were to be 'returned' to their 'own countries'. Powell's extraordinary philosophy was succinctly analysed in *The Enigma of Enoch Powell* by V. S. Anand and F. A. Ridley (London, 1969). The enigma of Enoch Powell, with the support he achieved at the time, caused alarm and confusion among the immigrant community and led the majority of those living in England to claim the label 'British' rather than 'English'. This usage tended to help disguise the reality of the original political label further.

The point we come back to, then, is the contention that there is no British nation nor even a British state. The United Kingdom of Great Britain and Northern Ireland, and its predecessor – the United Kingdom of Great Britain and Ireland – has been a multinational state since its inception. By 'multinational' I mean that the United Kingdom comprises several nations. But it was a state formed by the imperialist ambitions of the dominant nation, England, through military conquest and political power. Therefore, in speaking about the 'British Empire', we can return to Frank A. Ridley's contention that 'the term "British" is a complete misnomer' or, rather, a deliberate political camouflage.

If we accept this and agree that what has existed has been an

English Empire, then we cannot help consider Ridley's argument that the logical historical nemesis would be for the empire of the Saxons to end where it began, among the Celtic peoples, and that that ending would see the reunification of Ireland, and parliaments established for the other Celtic peoples within the United Kingdom state. But even if this happens within the next decade, is it too late for the Celts to survive as a cultural entity? Only 7 per cent of the populations inhabiting the Celtic areas now speak a Celtic language as the result of centuries of official and unofficial state linguaecide. Even if the populations of the geographic areas which were once independent Celtic kingdoms were to regain their own parliaments, would they survive as Celts by the only meaningful definition of the word – the linguistic and cultural one?

Would the Celts and their culture, that bright thread in the tapestry of European civilization, who, indeed, were one of the great founding civilizations of Europe, survive and contribute to the Europe of the future as a Celtic cultural entity or has the process of Anglicization become irreversible? That is something only time will tell.

Meanwhile, it behoves both Celt and Saxon to know and understand their past. I would argue that of the two peoples it is marginally the Saxons who are more in need of the experience of knowledge, especially at this stage of their development. By 1918 the empire, which had first begun when the Saxons landed on the shores of Celtic Britain, had extended over a quarter of the world's land surface, encompassing 450 million people, a quarter of the world population. It was an empire undreamed of by Athelstan as he emerged victorious from Brunanburh, having gained a dominant role for his Saxons on the island of Britain. It was an empire that far exceeded the designs of Persia or Rome, of Genghis Khan or Atilla, of Spain's conquistadors or Napoleon Bonaparte. But within a generation of the zenith of that empire, 'the empire on which the sun never sets', it was crumbling. There is significance as well as irony in the fact that its decay was brought about through the partial success of the Celtic struggle; the Irish War of Independence of 1919–21 pointed the way for the other subject peoples of the empire.

For the people whom the Celts still regard as the Saxons, their tremendous military onslaught through history, their imperial drive and gathering of booty, have finally come to an end and they are generally left perplexed and bewildered by that ending. There is no longer an empire, for the sun has finally sunk *almost* below the horizon in spite of the braggadocio of the early part of this century. I say 'almost' sunk. The one disturbing factor is that, the closer the crumbling empire has receded to home, the more tenacious the Saxon (using the term as a cultural attitude) seems to be in attempting to hold on to central power over the Celtic periphery. The refusal of the London Government to accept the democratic will of the Irish nation in the 1918 general election, not to mention the obstruction of that will during the previous forty years, and the same disregard of the result of the Scottish referendum on self-government in 1979 as well as the 75 per cent majority vote for a Scottish parliament in 1992, are examples which spring immediately to mind.

What, then, does the future hold for the English-dominated United Kingdom? Can Celt and Saxon finally dwell in peace? That should be a fundamental aim of the people of these islands. But to achieve that aim, the basic structures of the state would have to be altered and England would have to give up its dominant centralized role. Where, then, can such aggressive Saxon drives and energies be channelled in the future? Or has that aggressive urge finally been satiated? One thing is certain: without learning from the past, you cannot hope to understand the present and without understanding the present you cannot shape a worthwhile future.

Chronology

In deciding to attempt a chronology in order to help readers find their way through the so-called 'Dark Ages' in Britain and Ireland, I am aware that most of the dates given are approximate due to the character of the annals and chronicles which provide our sources. Indeed, as I have pointed out in my introduction, many of the dates are under 'discussion' by scholars. The following are, however, generally accepted by students in the field.

5th century
AD

400f. Southern Britain constantly raided by Saxons, Irish and Picts. Irish have established two significant kingdoms on British soil (the Dési in Dyfed (Wales) and Dál Riada in Argyll (Scotland)). A third settlement in Gwynedd was destroyed by Cunedda. Irish inscriptions (in Ogham) survive from the 5th and 6th centuries. Of the 369 known inscriptions, the bulk are found in Ireland but with a fair number in southern Wales, a few in the Isle of Man and Cornwall, and some in Scotland plus a small number in what was to become England.

410 Roman Emperor Honorius tells Britain to attend to its own affairs. Britain no longer part of empire and Zosimus reports Roman officials expelled and native government established.

425–450 *Floruit* of High King of Britain '*superbus tyrannus*', identified as Vortigern (overlord).

428 Uí Néill clan in ascendant in Ireland.

429 Germanus, bishop of Auxerre, makes first visit to Britain and commands British in 'Alleluia' victory against Saxon raiders.

430 Palladius sent by Rome as bishop of Irish Christians.

432 British Celt, Patrick, sent as missionary to Ireland. Start of the conversion of the druidic schools of Ireland to monastic schools.

435 Tibatto leads Armorican (Brittany) movement for independence from Roman Gaul.

438   The *Annals of Ulster* record that Ireland's civil law, the *Senchus Mór*, was codified in this year. The Brehon laws of Ireland are now the oldest surviving codified law system in Europe but the surviving complete code dates from the 11/12th century in the *Leabhar na hUidre* (Book of the Dun Cow).

446   British appeal for aid against Saxons to Aetius, commander of the armies of the Western Empire. Vortigern has employed 'Jutish' mercenaries to help against Saxons.

449   Mutiny of 'Jutish' mercenaries employed by Vortigern, led by Hengist and Horsa. Start of Celtic and Jutish war.

c. 450   Cunedda and his sons leave the territory of the Gododdin (Votadini) and eject the Irish settlers from Gwynedd. He establishes the Gwynedd dynasty.

460   Major Celtic victory over Jutes at Richborough. Jutes confined on Isle of Thanet. Ceretic of Strathclyde receives letter from St Patrick. Patrick writes his *Confessio* or autobiography.

462   Death of Patrick.

463   Death of Loeguire Mac Néill, High King of Ireland, during Patrick's period. Succession of Lugaid mac Loeguire.

465   Jutish breakout from Thanet. *Floruit* of Celtic leader Emrys (Ambrosius Aurelianus).

470   Fergus Mor Mac Eirc of the Ulster Dál Riada crosses to Britain and forms a new Dál Riadan kingdom in Kintyre.

473   Hengist and son Aesc secure major victory over Celts.

477   Aelle and sons lead Saxon settlement at Selsey Bill.

488   Aesc becomes king of Jutish Kent.

491   Aelle and his South Saxons, after fourteen years of fighting, reach Pevensey and destroy it.

495   Cerdic and his son Cynric land near Southampton and begin to establish a West Saxon kingdom.

6th century

6th cent.   First extant remains of literature written in insular Celtic languages (Irish and Welsh). Period of *Antiphony of Bangor* (Co. Down), Irish hymns in Latin.

500f.   Start of British Celtic migrations to west of Britain, to Ireland, to Armorica (Brittany) to Galicia and Astrurias and to areas such as Brittenburgh (on the Rhine). *Floruit* of Arthur, commander of the Celts in twelve listed victories over the Saxons. Also *floruit* of Dyfrig (Dubricus), 'chief of the church in Britain' associated with Illtud and Samson.

508	Cerdic and West Saxons defeat Natan-leod, local Celtic ruler in New Forest area.
514	Stuf and Wihtgar reinforce Cerdic.
516/8	Badon. Arthur's most famous victory over the Saxons. Saxon advance halted for a generation.
519	Kingdom of the West Saxons consolidated.
522	Brendan establish Clonfert abbey.
523–550	Angles seize fortress of Din Guoaroy and establish a settlement there called Bebba's Burgh (Bamburgh) which forms centre of a kingdom called Bernicia.
537/9	Camlann. Defeat for Arthur. Arthur and Medraut slain.
546	Colmcille establishes church at Derry.
547/9	Maelgwyn of Gwynedd dies of plague. Ida, king of Bernicia.
552	Celtic defeat by West Saxons at Old Sarum (Salisbury).
554	Comgall founds monastery of Bangor in Ulster.
558	Childebert of the Franks makes war on Armorica (Brittany). Chonoo, king of Armorica, resists. Hostilities continue until 630.
560	Gildas, British Celtic monk writes *De Excidio et Conquestu Britanniae*, only major contemporary source work for the history of period. Death of Cunomoros (King Mark of Cornwall) and Chramm son of Clothair, king of Franks.
563	Arrival of Colmcille, exiled from Ireland, in Dál Riada.
566	Gildas on a visit to Ireland. Swaps Isidore of Seville's encyclopedia for a copy of the *Táin Bó Culaigne*.
568	Athelberht of Kent defeated by West Saxons.
570	Death of Gildas in Brittany. *Floruit* of Cunotigern (Kentigern). Urien rules Rheged and conducts defence against the Angles of Bernicia.
571	West Saxons invade mid-Britain.
574	Colmcille ordains Aedán Mac Gabhráin as king of Dál Riada.
575	Convention of Druim Cett (Co. Derry) attended by Colmcille and Aedán. High King of Ireland recognizes Dál Riadan rights. Dallán Forgaill, chief *ollamh*, or judge, of Ireland, composes *Amra Colmcille* (Eulogy to Colmcille) which survives in 8th-century version.
577	West Saxons win battle of Deorham over Celts. They reach the River Severn, capturing several Celtic cities including Gloucester.
578	British Celtic migration to Brittany transforms Celtic Armorica, now called 'Little Britain'. There emerge small kingdoms of Dumnonia, Cornouaille and Bro Waroc'h.
580	*Floruit* of Rhydderch Hen as king of Strathclyde Britons.

585	Death of Bruide Mac Maelchon, king of Picts.
589	Death of Dewi Sant (St David) in Dyfed.
590	Urien of Rheged besieges Angles in Lindisfarne, slain in battle there.
590/600	Attack of the Gododdin on Catraeth (Catterick) and defeat.
590f.	*Floruit* of the bards Aneirin and Taliesin. Also Llywarch Hen notable war leader in the Strathclyde area.
593	Death of Ceawlin of West Saxons after being deposed.
596	Pope Gregory sends Augustine as missionary to Aethelberht of Kent.
597	Death of Colmcille on Iona.

7th century

600	*Floruit* of the Pictish symbol stones and cross slabs over the next three centuries.
603	Aedán Mac Gabhráin, of Dál Riada, defeated by Aethelfrith at Degastan.
604	Aethelfrith of Bernicia unites Bernicia and Deira into Northumbria.
607	Death of Sinlán moccu Min, abbot of Bangor, first known Irish annalist who incorporated an Irish chronicle in the *Chronicle of Eusebius of Caesarea.*
608	Death of Aedán of Dál Riada.
615	Selyf, king of Powys, slain at battle of Chester. Massacre of 1000 monks from Bangor by the Saxons.
616	Eadbald, king of Kent. Kent reverts to paganism but Laurentius converts him. Saeberht of Essex dies and Essex chases out Christian missionaries. Most of the Saxon areas converted by Augustine revert to pagan worship.
617	Battle of River Idle: Raedwald of East Anglia slays Aethelfrith. Edwin becomes king of Northumbria. Eanfrith, Oswald, Oswiu and Aebbe, three sons and daughter of Aethelfrith, taken for refuge to Iona and are brought up as Christians there. Slaughter of Donnán and fellow monks on Eigg.
625	Ceretic (Caradoc), last Celtic king of Elmet, defeated and driven out. Elmet incorporated into Northumbria and settled by Saxons. Death of Cadfan of Gwynedd. Edwin marries Aethelburgh, sister of Eadbald of Kent, and is converted to Christianity by Paulinus. Foundation of Abernethy by Irish nuns under patronage of Nechtan, king of Picts.

628 Penda of Mercia defeats Wessex at Cirencester. Cadwallon of Gwynedd and Penda of Mercia form alliance against Edwin.

629–642 Domnall Brecc king of Dál Riada.

633 Cadwallon, king of Gwynedd, slays Edwin of Northumbria at Hatfield Chase.

634 Oswald now king of Northumbria. Brought up in exile in Iona he asks for Irish missionaries to convert Northumbria to Christianity. Cadwallon slain by Oswald of Northumbria at Heavenfield. Aidan from Iona establishes monastery at Lindisfarne and becomes bishop of Northumbria.

634f Irish monks flourish in Northumbria, gaining converts and establishing monastic centres.

635 Judicael of Brittany concludes a treaty with Dagobert, king of the Franks, and agrees with him the borders of Brittany.

637 Battle of Magh Rath, Ulster. Domnall Mac Aedo, High King of Ireland, defeats Domnal Brecc of Dál Riada. Dál Riada loses control of its territory on Irish mainland. British Celts are recorded as fighting for Dál Riada. Cenn Faelad, famous Irish scholar and poet, is wounded in battle and is treated by a surgeon for three years.

638 Northumbria attacks Duneidin (Edinburgh) and defeats local Celtic chieftains.

642 Oswald slain by Maserfeld (Oswestry). Oswiu, king of Northumbria, maintains education and Christianizing programme. Domnall Brecc slain by Strathclyde Britons in battle of Strathcarron.

649–662 *Floruit* of Senchán Torpéist, chief bard of Ireland, who visits Isle of Man.

651 Aidan dies, succeeded by Finán. Oswine of Deira killed by Oswiu. Cuthbert enters Maol Ros (Melrose) abbey.

652 Death of Ségéne, abbot of Iona, and friend of Oswald.

653–657 Talorgen, son of Eanfrith, king of Picts.

655 Cadafael of Gwynedd withdraws Celts from alliance with Penda of Mercia on the evening before battle at Winwaed Field. Penda is slain and Mercia is defeated. Mercia ruled by Northumbria for three years. Irish missionaries begin Christianization.

658 Wulfhere, son of Penda, heads Mercia rebellion. Wulfhere becomes king of Mercia.

660 Northumbria attacks kingdom of Rheged.

661 Colmán of Iona succeeds Finán at Lindisfarne. Irish missionaries working in all Saxon kingdoms, including Mercia,

Essex, East Anglia, Sussex and Wessex.

664 Oswiu sets up Synod of Whitby to discuss differences between Roman and Celtic practices. He decides in favour of Rome. Cólman returns to Ireland with his followers. Wilfrid made bishop. Cuthbert prior of Lindisfarne.

668 Wigheard, archbishop of Canterbury elect, dies in Rome. Pope Vitalian consecrates Greek Theodore as archbishop.

669 Chad, upholder of Celtic usage, bishop of Mercia. In conflict with Theodore. Theodore comes up with compromise. Death of abbot Cummène of Iona, author of Miracles of Colmcille (Columba).

670 Death of Cenn Faelad, the chief scholar of Tuaim Drecain (Toomregan) in Brefne, Ireland's premier school of poetry. Known for his Irish grammar and fragmentary remains of poems.

670–85 Ecgfrith king of Northumbria. Adomnán arrives at Iona from Ireland.

672 Major Synod of Saxon church at Hertford. Picts depose Drest from kingship as subservient to Northumbria. But Pictish army is massacred by Ecgfrith. Bruide son of Bili, king of Picts.

673 Maelrubaí founds Applecross.

674 Benedict Biscop founds Monkwearmouth.

675–704 Aethelred king of Mercia

678 Wilfrid expelled from Northumbria.

679 Battle of River Trent, Ecgfrith defeated by Aethelred of Mercia. Adomnán becomes ninth abbot of Iona, succeeding Failbe. Begins work on his book *De Locis Sanctis* (The Holy Places).

680 Bede enters Monkwearmouth.

681 Jarrow founded. Bede enters new monastery.

c. 682 Cadwaladr, king of Gwynedd, dies. Centwine of Wessex claims victory over Dumnonia.

684 Ecgfrith raids Ireland and captures sixty prisoners. Also raids Isle of Man and Anglesey.

685 Cuthbert bishop of Lindisfarne. Ecgfrith invades the Pictish kingdom. Battle of Nechtansmere. Ecgfrith defeated and slain by Bruide son of Bili. Cuthbert sends to Ireland for Aldfrith, son of Oswiu and Fín, a daughter of the O'Neill High Kingship. He is educated in Ireland and a poet in Irish. First remains of 'Old English' (Anglo-Saxon) literature, *Widsmith*, written in Northumbria at this time. The *Beowulf* saga, also written at this time, only survives in 8th-century copies. Similarities with earlier Irish sagas. Wilfrid now bishop of Ripon.

686   Adomnán, former abbot of Iona, visits Northumbria and obtains release of Irish prisoners.

687   Death of Cuthbert on Inner Farne. Succeeded by Ceolfrith of Jarrow.

688–705 Ine, king of Wessex, begins to expand further into Dumnonia. Adomnán's second visit to Northumbria. He writes *Life of Colmcille* (Columba).

689   Death of Benedict Biscop.

690   Death of Theodore. Wilfrid exiled from Northumbria by Aldfrith.

688–692 Adomnán, converted to Roman usages, tries to persuade Picts to adopt them in replacement of Celtic system.

695   Death of Fínsnechta Fledach mac Dúnchado, High King of Ireland. Succeeded by Loingsech mac Oengusso.

697   Synod of Birr in Ireland. Adomnán promulgates his 'Law of the Innocents' designed to protect non-combatants in war (the elderly, women and children as well as clergy). Law enacted and made binding throughout the Celtic world. Ignored by Saxon kingdoms.

698–721 Eadfrith, reputed scribe of the Lindisfarne Gospels, bishop of Lindisfarne.

8th century

700f.   Golden Age of Irish literature and scholarship. Period of composition of *Cín Dromma Snechta* (Book of Drumsnat) known to have survived to late medieval period. A book of heroic tales and thought to be oldest known secular book.

704   Death of Adomnán. Ine of Wessex appropriates two Dumnonian Celtic monasteries at Congressbury and Banwell.

705–716 Osred, king of Northumbria.

706–724 Nechtán, son of Derile, king of Picts.

706   Wilfrid rehabilitated at Synod of River Nidd. Aldhelm, taught by Irish monks, becomes bishop of Sherborne.

708–709 Aldhelm of Sherborne writes letter to Geraint, king of Dumnonia, demanding he instruct the Celtic Church to adopt Roman ways.

709   Death of Wilfrid.

710   Nechtan, king of Picts, sends to Ceolfrith, abbot of Monkwearmouth and Jarrow (Northumbria) for advice on differences between Celtic and Roman usage.

711   Northumbrians defeat Picts near Edinburgh. Ine of Wessex attempts to destroy remnant of Dumnonian kingdom. Geraint, last recorded king of Dumnonia, is slain at Longport. West Saxons capture Exeter.

712   Ecgbert in Iona to persuade Celtic clergy to accept Roman usages.

713   Northumbrian war on Picts ended by peace treaty.

715   Mercia raids Wessex.

716–757 Aethelband, king of Mercia. Wessex raids Mercia. Ceolfrith of Jarrow, Bede's teacher, dies on pilgrimage to Rome.

717   Nechtán of the Picts expels those clergy who follow Celtic practices from Pictland and accepts Roman usage.

722   Battle of Camel. Cornish and Dumnonia remnant defeat Wessex. Boniface in Germany. Seeks to persuade European monarchs, such as Pépin of the Franks, to ignore Celtic influence from Irish missionaries. Twice reports Fearghal (Virgil of Salzburg) to Pope because of dislike for Celtic practices.

723   Ine abdicates in Wessex.

c. 725   Diciul reports Irish in Iceland and Faeroes.

727–761 Oengus I, son of Fergus, king of Picts.

731   Bede completes *Historia Ecclesiastica gentis Anglorum*. Pehthelm, Northumbrian bishop, takes over Ninian's foundation at Whithorn.

733   Death of Kentigerna of Loch Lomond. Mercia subdues Wessex.

734   Death of Bede

740   Eadberht of Northumbria starts new war on Picts.

747   Death of Cú-Chuimne 'the Wise' of Iona, famed as a poet in Latin, also co-author with Munster scribe of *Collectio Canomun Hibernensis*, reference work on church usages.

748   Rumann Mac Colán died at Rathen, near Tullamore, known as 'the Homer and Vergil of Ireland'.

750–752 Teudebur son of Bili, king of Strathclyde, overlord of Picts.

752   Eadberht of Northumbria raids Kyle.

754   Wessex victorious at Burford. Boniface killed by bandits in Holland.

757   Aethelberht of Mercia murdered. Civil war in Mercia.

757–786 Cynewulf, king of Wessex.

757–86 Offa, king of Mercia.

765–792 Jaenberht, archbishop of Canterbury.

766–772 Suibhne, abbot of Iona. Diciul, the geographer, may have been his pupil.

768   Elfoddw, chief bishop of Gwynedd, persuades Welsh kingdoms

	to accept Roman dating of Easter. Charlemagne, king of the Franks.
776	Kent throws off Mercian control at Otford.
778	Offa invades Wales, raiding into Dyfed.
779	Mercia defeats Wessex at Bensington. Offa regarded as 'supreme king' over all Saxon kingdoms.
c. 780–806	*Book of Kells* begun in Iona and completed at Kells in Ireland.
c. 784	Offa builds his famous dyke, fortifications to cut off Wales. *Floruit* of Eliseg of Powys who recaptures territories annexed by Mercia.
781	Alcuin joins Charlemagne's court.
786	Cynewulf of Wessex killed by Cyneheard. Ecgberht flees Wessex and marries Offa's daughter, Eadburh. Papal legation to Saxon kingdoms.
787	Saxon church reorganized at Synod of Chelsea. Lichfield now archbishopric, Canterbury is divided. Ecgfrith king of Mercia.
792	Aethelheard archbishop of Canterbury. Death of Mael Rúain, leader of the Cele Dé (Servants of God), Culdee, reform movement of the Celtic Church at Tallaght.
793	Vikings sack Lindisfarne.
794	Viking raid on Iona.
795	Viking devastation of Iona and of Skye. In August that year Diciul reports Irish monks visiting Iona from Iceland. First Viking raids on Ireland in Rathlinn.
796	Deaths of Offa and Ecgfrith.
796–821	Coenwulf king of Mercia.
797	Death of Donnchadh Midi Mac Domnaill, High King of Ireland. Succeeded by Aed Findliath Mac Néill.

9th century

800f.	*Floruit* of Nennius, author of *Historia Brittonum*, a scholar of Gwynedd and pupil of Elfoddw of Gwynedd. Also of Oengus the Culdee, a pupil of Maelrúin who founded the order – author of many works including the first known Irish martyrology.
800	Charlemagne crowned by Pope Leo III as 'emperor of the Romans'.
802	Vikings burn Iona. Ecgberht king of Wessex.
803	Synod of Clofesho in which Lichfield is demoted as archbishopric.

805–832 Wulfred, archbishop of Canterbury.

806 Vikings raid Iona again and butcher 68 monks.

807 Ferdomnach completes *Canóin Pádraic*, known as the Book of Armagh.

807–814 Abbot Cellach abandons Iona and builds new church at Kells. New ecclesiastic centre for Alba built at Dunkeld.

809 Death of Elfoddw, chief bishop of Gwynedd.

810 *The Stowe Missal* completed which, among other things, contains a treatise in Irish on the celebration of the mass.

811–20 Constantine son of Fergus acknowledged as king of Dál Riada and of the Picts.

814 Death of Charlemagne. Louis the Pious emperor. Brittany seeks to retain its independence under Morvan. Ecgberht of Wessex attempts to conquer Cornwall.

816 Council of Chelsea. Irish missionaries are prohibited from preaching and teaching within the English kingdoms.

816–880 *Floruit* of Eriugena (Johannes Scotus), Irish scholar and philosopher, reckoned as the foremost philosopher between Augustine of Hippo and Thomas Aquinas.

820–834 Oengus II, son of Fergus, king of Dál Riada and of the Picts. Major new ecclesiastical site at St Andrews, site of older church.

820–880 *Floruit* of Siadhal the Irishman (Sedulius Scotos) at Frankish court – renowned scholar and poet.

821–823 Ceolwulf, king of Mercia.

822 Wiomarc'h of Brittany fights Frankish incursions. Mercia invades Powys.

823 Ceolwulf deposed. Beornwulf king of Mercia.

825 Merfyn Frych, king of Gwynedd and suzerain of most of Wales. Torture and murder of Blathmac by Vikings on Iona. Ecgberht of Wessex defeats and kills Beornwulf of Mercia at Ellendun (Wroughton). His son, Aethelwulf, conquers Kent.

825–844 *Annales Cambriae* written in present form during reign of Merfyn at Gwynedd.

829–831 Diarmuid, abbot of Iona, based at Kells, visits Alba and brings relics of Colmcille.

830 Wiglaf, king of Mercia. Louis the Pious subdues Brittany and appoints Nominoë as '*dux in Britannia*'.

835 Vikings attack Sheppey.

836 Ecgberht of Wessex defeated by Vikings at Carhampton.

838 The Celts of Cornwall and remnants of Dumnonia are defeated with Danish allies at Hingston Down by Ecgberht of Wessex.

839 Viking victory over Picts. Eóganán, son of Oengus II, king of

Dál Riada and of the Picts, slain in battle. Athelwulf, king of Wessex.

841	Thorgil establishes Norse kingdom of Dublin.
843	Aethelwulf of Wessex defeated by Vikings at second battle of Carhampton. Frankish empire divided between the sons of Louis the Pious. Charles the Bald becomes king of western Frankia (France).
845	Nominoë of Brittany asserts Breton independence from Frankish empire. Franks are defeated by Nominoë at the battle of Ballon, 22 November.
846	Charles the Bald signs treaty recognizing the independence of the Breton kingdom under Nominoë. Brittany retains its independence until 1488 when the Breton army of Francis II, commanded by Trémoille, were defeated at Saint Aubin du Cormier, leading to the treaty of union of 1532.
847	Cináech Mac Alpín (Kenneth Mac Alpin) recognized as king of Dál Riada and of the Picts.
849	Relics of Colmcille to be divided between Kells in Ireland and Dunkeld in Alba.
c. 850	Danish attacks on Norwegian settlers in the western isles of Scotland. *Floruit* of Ketil Flatnose, ruler of the Hebrides. Norse attacking kingdom of the Franks and Brittany.
851	Aethelwulf defeats Vikings. His son Athelstan wins sea battle against them off Sandwich. Olafr the White, king of Dublin.
852	Bugred king of Mercia.
853	Mercia and Wessex attack Powys.
c. 855	Beginning of Viking jarldom on Orkney under Sigurd the Powerful. Death of Cyngen of Powys in Rome. Aethelwulf pilgrimage to Rome.
856	Rhodri Mawr (the Great), king of Gwynedd and suzerain of most of Wales. Defeats Danes in battle and slays Horm, a Viking leader.
857	Ivarr the Boneless, king of Dublin.
858	Domhnuil I of Alba has the laws of Dál Riada and Pictland promulgated at Forteviot and Fortriu. Aethelwulf returns from Rome, marries daughter of Charles the Bald. Aethelbald, king of Wessex. Refuses to let father return to kingship. Aethelbald displaced by Aethelberht.
865–871	Aethelred I king of Wessex.
865–871	Danish army of Ivarr the Boneless and Halfdan devastates Saxon kingdoms. Aelle of Northumbria killed by Vikings.

866–867   Danes conquer Northumbria while Angles in Bernicia survive only as a satellite of Danish York. Olafr the White of Dublin campaigns against Alba. Finnlaith Mac Néill, High King of Ireland, defeated by Norse near Dublin. Redon monastery in Brittany devastated by Norse.

869   Edmund of East Anglia slain by Vikings.

870   Olafr the White and Ivarr sack Dumbarton. Viking assault on Wessex. Aethelred and Alfred win battle at Ashdown but lose at Basing. Aethelred dies of his wounds. Guthrum and Danish 'summer army' land in the Saxon kingdoms.

870–890   Migration of Norse-Gaels from Hebrides and Caithness to Iceland under the leadership of Aud the Deep-Minded.

871   Alfred, king of Wessex, organizes Saxon defence against the Danes, and is recognized as Bretwalda or 'overlord' of all Saxon kingdoms.

872   Artgal, king of Strathclyde, slain at the instigation of Constantine I of Alba.

874   Vikings settle Repton. Bugred driven from Mercia and goes to Rome. Ceolwulf II, king of Mercia. Halfdan and his Danes settle Northumbrian Danes then attack Alba and Strathclyde.

875   Dumgarth, king of Cornwall, killed in a drowning accident.

877   Constantine I, king of Alba, slain by Danes. Danish attack on Anglesey. Rhodri of Gwynedd seeks refuge in Ireland.

878   Return of Rhodri, his death in battle against Saxons. Guthrum occupies Chippenham. Alfred driven into the marshes of Somerset. He fortifies Athelney. Wins battle of Edington. Guthrum accepts Christianity and establish peace at the Treaty of Wedmore. Guthrum recognized as king of East Anglia.

c. 879   Death of Ceolwulf II of Mercia.

884   Aethelflaed, daughter of Alfred, marries Aethelred of Mercia. Year when Wrmonec, a monk of Landévennec, Brittany, completes his *Life of Pol Aurelian de Léon*. About this time another monk of Landévennec completes life of Winwaloe.

c. 885   Asser, Welsh scholar of St David's, invited to spend six months of each year at Alfred's court, teaching him Latin and helping him in the working of education. Helps Alfred codify the Saxon law system and the *Anglo-Saxon Chronicle* is written at this time.

c. 885–   With Asser's persuasion, petty kings of southern Wales accept
893.   Alfred as suzerain.

886   Alfred captures London from Danes.

888 Alan I (the Great) of Brittany decisively defeats the Norse at Questembert.

889 Giric, king of Alba, and Eochaid, son of Rhun, king of Strathclyde, expelled by Danes.

893 Asser completes his *Life of King Alfred*. Anarawd of Gwynedd accepts Alfred's suzerainty.

892–895 Alfred contains Viking raids on Wessex.

895 *Vita Tripartita Sancti Patritii* (Tripate Life of Patrick) written on parchment in Irish at Cashel.

899 Death of Alfred. Edward the Elder, king of Wessex.

10th century

900f. Period of authorship of *Navigatio Sancti Brendani*, the Voyage of Brendan, which suggests that Brendan might have reached the New World.

900 Constantine II becomes High King of Alba. Alba annexes British Celtic kingdoms of Strathclyde and Cumbria. Codification of the laws of Alba and Strathclyde – *Leges inter Bretonnes et Scotos*. Alan the Great died in Brittany. *Floruit* of Torf Einar, first Viking jarl of the Orkneys. Aethelwold rebels against Edward the Elder of Wessex.

903 Aethelwold killed at battle of Holme.

906 Constantine II and bishop Cellach of St Andrews pledge themselves to maintain the Scottish Church.

907 Norse capture Nantes and threaten rest of Brittany. Many Breton manuscript books are taken out of the country for safe-keeping.

908 Death of Cormac mac Cuileannáin, king and bishop of Cashel, compiler of genealogies and other works. Famous for his *Glossary*, an early work of Irish etymology.

910 Danes of York defeated by Edward the Elder. Ragnall son of Ivarr claims kingship of York.

911 Ragnall captures York. Death of Aethelred of Wessex. King of Franks grants land to the Norse chieftain, Rollo, which becomes Normandy.

913 Vikings devastate Brittany, attacks on the monasteries of Landévennec, Dol and St Gildas.

914 Ragnall victorious over Scots and Bernicians at Corbridge.

916 Death of Anarawd of Gwynedd. Succession of Hywel ap Cadell (Hywel Dda – the Good) who has suzerainty over most of the

kingdoms which constitute Wales. He orders an investigation
of the Celtic law system in his kingdoms, holds a parliament
to discuss them and has them codified.

917   Edward forces submission of Danes of Northampton, East
Anglia and Essex while Aethelflaed, queen of Mercia, takes
Derby and also Leicester.

918   2nd battle at Corbridge. Ragnall loses many men. Death of
Aethelflaed during treaty negotiations with Danes. Norse
defeat Niall Glúndubh Mac Aeda, High King of Ireland, near
Dublin.

919   Edward the Elder annexes Mercia and occupies Manchester.
Donnchad Donn Mac Maelmithig, High King of Ireland.
(d. 944).

920   Treaty between Scotland, Strathclyde Britons, the Bernician
Angles, Ragnall of York and Edward of Wessex. Ragnall
dies.

921   Mac Ragnal ruler in Isle of Man.

924   Deaths of Edward the Elder and son Aelfweard.

924–39   Athelstan king of Wessex.

927   Olafr Gothfrithsson claims York kingship. Athelstan invades
Northumbria and Olafr enters alliance with Constantine of
Scotland and Owain of Strathclyde. Alliance defeated.
Athelstan agrees a Treaty at Penrith. Hywel Dda
acknowledges Athelstan as suzerain at Hereford.

931   Athelstan drives British Celts inhabiting Exeter out of the city
and acknowledges the River Tamar as the border between the
'West Welsh' (Cornwall) and the Wessex kingdom. Cornish
rulers acknowledge him as suzerain and he makes reforms to
Celtic Church there with Conan as bishop.

934   Olafr king of Dublin. Constantine renews alliance with him.
Athelstan invades Scotland as far as Dunnottar.

937   Athelstan gives aid to Alan II of Brittany to drive out the Norse.
Armes Prydein Vawr (Prophecy of Great Britain) composed in
Gwynedd calling up the Celts to drive the Saxons out of Britain
and regain their lost territories. Battle of Brunanburh (near
Chester) where Athelstan defeats a combined army of Olafr's
Dublin Vikings and Celts under Constantine of Scotland,
Owain of Strathclyde, and other Celtic areas. End of Celtic
dream of driving the Saxons out of Britain and regaining their
lost territories. The use of 'Briton' is now dropped by Celts and
term Cymry (Compatriots) emerges. England's borders (with
the exception of Cumbria – derived from the word Cymru,

land of compatriots, – which is annexed from Scotland in 1042) now reach the limits still recognized today. The struggle for the supremacy of Britain is over.

Select Bibliography

In any study of this period there can be no better introduction to source material, from the Anglo-Saxon point of view, than a reading of Sir Frank Stenton's essay on sources in *Anglo-Saxon England* (3rd ed., 1971), pp. 688–730. Perhaps from the Celtic viewpoint, Dillon and Chadwick's *The Celtic Realms* (1967) presents a good introduction to what sources are available during this period. But the most impressive survey of primary source material for the serious student covering the entire period is undoubtedly John Morris's 'works cited in the notes' (pp. 522–546) in his monumental *The Age of Arthur* (1973). The late John Morris was a major scholar of the period and his polemic analysis of the field is still as controversial today as when he first propounded his theses. He was general editor for a series of contemporary texts published by Phillimore, London, from 1978, such as *St Patrick: His Writings and Murchu's Life* and the works of Gildas and Nennius. These remain the most accessible and easy to read of the translations of these prime sources.

I have been very selective in putting together the following bibliography and have divided it into two. Under 'Annals, Chronicles and Laws' I have listed the texts that I worked most with as regards primary sources. Under the 'General' heading, I have listed a representative section of the secondary source material and other translations, consulted in producing this study. There are other studies to which I have referred in my text which are not listed here. I have simply referred to these by place and date of publication within the text.

Annals, Chronicles and Laws

Anglo-Saxon Chronicle, a revised translation, ed. and trs. Dorothy Whitelock, Eyre and Spottiswoode, London, 1961.
Ancient Laws and Institutes of Wales, ed. & trs. Aneurin Owen, English Records Commission, 2 vols, London, 1841.
Ancient Laws of Ireland, Commissioners of Publishing the Ancient Laws

and Institutions of Ireland, 6 vols., Dublin, 1865–1901 (under first editor, John O'Donovan etc.).

Annala Rioghachta Éireann (Annals of the Four Masters), ed. and trs. J. O'Donovan, Dublin, 1851.

Annala Uladh: Annals of Ulster, ed. and trs. William Maunsell Hennessy, Dublin, 1887; and B. MacCarthy, Dublin, 1893–1901.

Annales Cambriae, ed. John Williams ab Ithel (Rerum Britannicorum medii aevi Scriptores; Rolls Series), London, 1858.

Annals of Clonmacnoise, ed. and trs. Denis Murphy, Annuary of the Kilkenny Archaeological Society, Kilkenny, 1893.

Annals of Inisfallen, ed. and trs. Robert I. Best and Eoin MacNeill, Dublin, 1933.

Annals of Inisfallen, ed. and trs. Seán Mac Airt, Stationery Office, Dublin, 1951.

Annals of Loch Cé, ed. and trs. W. A. Hennessy, Dublin, 1871.

Annals of Tigernach, ed. and trs. Whitley Stokes, 1895.

Annals of Ulster, ed. Seán Mac Airt and Gearóid Mac Niocaill, Dublin Institute for Advance Studies, Dublin, 1983.

Anecdota from Irish MSS, ed. and trs., Oscar Bergin, R. I. Best, Kuno Meyer and J. G. O'Keffe, Halle, 1907–13.

Bede: The Historical works of the Venerable Bede, Joseph Steven, Church Historians of England series, Vol 1, London, 1853.

Bede: Venerabilis Bedae Opera Historica, English Historical Society, London, 1841.

Bede: Venerabilis Bedae Opera Historica, 2 vols., C. Plummer, Oxford University Press, Oxford, 1896.

Bede's Ecclesiastical History of the English People, ed. and trs. Bertram Colgrave and R. A. B. Mynors, Clarendon Press, Oxford, 1969.

Book of Ballymote, facsimile ed. R. Atkinson, Dublin, 1887.

Book of Lecan, ed. and trs. Kathleen Mulchrone, Dublin, 1937.

Book of Leinster. ed. and trs. Robert Atkinson, Dublin, 1880.

Book of Leinster, R. I. Best, O. Bergin and M. A. O'Brien, Dublin, 1954.

Book of Llan Dav, The text of: ed. J. Gwenogvryn Evans, Oxford, 1893; reprinted Aberystwyth, 1979.

Brut y Tywysogion (Chronicle of the Princes, 13th Century compilation), ed. John Williams ab Ithel, (Rerum Britannicorum medii aevi Scriptores, Rolls Series) London, 1860.

Brut y Tywysogion. ed. and trs. Aneurin Owen, Archaeologia Cambrenss, 1863. Supplemental volumes, 1864.

Brut y Tywysogion (Peniarth MSS) ed. and trs., Melville Richards, University of Wales Press, Cardiff, 1952.

Chronica Gentis Scotorum, Johannis de Fordun. trs. and ed. William F.

Skene, Historians of Scotland series, vol 1, Edinburgh, 1871, and vol 4, Edinburgh, 1872.

Chronica de Melrose, ed. and trs. Joseph Stevenson, London, 1835.

Chronica de Melrose, ed. and trs. Alan Orr and Marjorie Ogilvie Anderson, Edinburgh, 1936.

Chronicon ex Chronicis (Florence of Worcester), trs. and ed. B. Thorpe, London, 1848/49.

Chronicum Scotum. ed. and trs. William Maunsell Hennessy, Rerum Britannicorum medii aevi Scriptores, Rolls Series, London, 1866.

Cogadh Gaedhel Re Gallaibh (War of the Gael and the Gall) ed. and trs. J. H. Todd, London, 1867.

Florence of Worcester: History of the Kings, ed. and trs. Joseph Stevenson, London, 1853.

Gesta Regum (William of Malmesbury), ed. and trs W. Stubbs, Royal Society, London, 1887–89.

Gildas: De Excidio Britanniae (sic), ed. and trs. Joseph Stevenson, English Historical Society, London, 1838.

Gildas: The Ruin of Britain and Other Works, ed. and trs. Michael Winterbottom, Phillimore, London, 1978.

Irish Liber Hymnorum, ed. and trs. R. Atkinson, London, 1898.

Leabher Na gCeart (Book of Rights), ed. and trs. John O'Donovan, Dublin, 1847.

Lebor Na Cert (Book of Rights), ed. and trs. Myles Dillon, Irish Text Society (Vol 46), London, 1962.

Lebor Na hUidre (Book of the Dun Cow), ed. Robert I. Best and Oscar Bergin, Dublin, 1929.

Marianii Scotii Chronicum (Chronicle of Marianus Scotus), ed. G. Waitz, London, 1844.

Marianus Scotus: The Codex Palatino-Vaticanus, No 830, of the Chronica of Marianus Scotus, B. MacCarthy, Todd Lecture Series No 3, London, 1892.

Metrical Dindshenchas. ed. and trs. Edward J. Gwynn, Hodges Figgis, for Royal Irish Academy, Dublin, 1903–1935 (5 parts).

Nennius' Historia Brittonum, ed. and trs., Joseph Stevenson, English Historical Society, London, 1836.

Nennius (The Historia Brittonum) ed. T. Mommsen, 1894, trs. Arthur Wade Evans (as *Nennius's History of the Britons*) London, 1938.

Orygynale Cronykil of Scotland (Andrew of Wyntoun), ed. David Ley, Edinburgh, 1879.

Orkneyinga Saga, trs. and ed. Alexander Burt Taylor, Oliver & Boyd, Edinburgh, 1938.

Sanas Chormaic (Cormac's Glossary), trs. and ed. John O'Donovan and W. Whitley Stokes, Irish Archaeological Society, Dublin, 1868.

Seneachus Mor: The Oldest Fragment of the Senchus Mor, described and introduced by R. I. Best and R. Thurneysen, Dublin, 1931.

Symeon of Durham, Historia Dunelmensis Ecclesiae, ed. and trs. Joseph Stevenson, London, 1855.

Yellow Book of Lecan, ed. and trs. Robert Atkinson, Dublin, 1896.

General

ALCOCK, L., *Economy, Society and Warfare among the Britons and Saxons*, University of Wales Press, Cardiff, 1987.

ALLCROFT, A. H., *The Circle and the Cross*, 2 vols, Macmillan, London, 1927.

ANDERSON, ALAN ORR and MARJORIE OGILVIE, *Early Sources of Scottish History AD 500–1286*, 2 vols, Oliver and Boyd, Edinburgh, 1922.

ANDERSON, ALAN ORR, *Ninian and the Southern Picts*, Scottish Historical Review reprint, Edinburgh, 1948.

ANDERSON, ALAN ORR and MARJORIE OGILVIE, *Adomnán: Life of Columba*, ed. and trs., London, 1961.

ANDERSON, MARJORIE OGILVIE, *Kings and Kingship in Early Scotland*, Scottish Academic Press, Edinburgh, 1980.

ASHDOWN, MARGARET, *English and Norse Documents relating to the reign of Ethelred the Unready*, Cambridge, 1930.

ASHE, GEOFFREY, ed., *The Quest for Arthur's Britain*, The Pall Mall Press, London, 1968.

ASHE, GEOFFREY, *Mythology of the British Isles*, Methuen, London, 1990.

ATTENBOROUGH, F. L., *The Laws of the Earliest English Kings*, Cambridge University Press, Cambridge, 1922.

BARLEY, MAURICE W. and HANSON, RICHARD P. C., *Christianity in Britain 300–700*, Leicester University Press, Leicester, 1968.

BARTRUM, P. C., *Early Welsh Genealogical Tracts*, University of Wales Press, Cardiff, 1966.

BINCHY, D. A., *Celtic and Anglo-Saxon Kingship* (O'Donnell lectures for 1967/68), Clarendon Press, Oxford, 1970.

BOLTON, W. F., *A History of Anglo-Saxon Literature*. Princeton University Press, Princeton, New Jersey, 1967.

BOWEN, E. G., *The Settlement of Celtic Saints in Wales*, University of Wales Press, Cardiff, 1956.

BOWER, WILFRID., *An Anglo-Saxon and Celtic Bibliography*. 2 vols, Basil Blackwell, Oxford, 1957.

BRANSTON, BRIAN, *The Lost Gods of England*, Thames and Hudson, London, 1957.

BRIGHT, WILLIAM, *Select Anti-Pelagian Treatises of Augustine Bishop of Hippo*, Oxford, 1880.

BROMWICH, RACHEL, *Trioedd Ynys Prydein – The Welsh Triads*, ed. and trs., Wales University Press, Cardiff, 1961.

BROMWICH, RACHEL, *Armes Prydein: The prophecy of Britain*, Dublin Institute for Advanced Studies, Dublin, 1972.

BROOKS, NICHOLAS, *Latin and the Vernacular Languages in Early Medieval Britain*, Studies in Early English History, University Press, Leicester, 1982.

BRYANT, SOPHIE, *Liberty, Order and Law Under Native Irish Rule*, Harding and More, London, 1923.

BYRNE, JOHN FRANCIS, *Irish Kings and High-Kings*, B. T. Batsford, London, 1973.

BYRNE, MARY E., *Táin Bó Fraech*, ed. with notes by Myles Dillon, Dublin, 1933.

CAMPBELL, J. (ed.), *The Anglo-Saxons*, Phaidon, London, 1982.

CARNEY, JAMES, *The Problem of St Patrick*, Dublin Institute for Advanced Studies, Dublin, 1961.

CHADWICK, H. M., *The Origin of the English Nation*, Cambridge University Press, Cambridge, 1907.

CHADWICK, H. M., *Studies in Early British History*, Cambridge University Press, Cambridge, 1954.

CHADWICK, NORA K., *Studies in the Early British Church*, Cambridge University Press, Cambridge, 1958.

CHADWICK, NORA K., *The Age of Saints in the Early Celtic Church*, Oxford University Press, London, 1961.

CHADWICK, NORA K., *Celt and Saxon – Studies in the Early British Border*, Cambridge University Press, Cambridge, 1963.

CHADWICK, NORA K., *The Colonization of Brittany from Celtic Britain* (Sir John Rhys Memorial Lecture) British Academy, London, 1965.

CHARLESWORTH, M. P., *The Lost Province*, University of Wales Press, Cardiff, 1949.

CLEARY, S. E., *The Ending of Roman Britain*, Batsford, London, 1989.

CURWEN, E. CECIL., *The Archaeology of Sussex*, Methuen, London, 1937 (revised ed. 1954).

DEACON, RICHARD, *Madoc and the Discovery of America: Some New Light on an Old Controversy*, Frederick Muller, London, 1967.

DE PAOR, MÁIRE and LIAM, *Early Christian Ireland*, Thames and Hudson, London, 1958.

DILLON, MYLES, *The Cycles of the Kings*, Oxford University Press, Oxford, 1946.

DILLON, MYLES, and CHADWICK, NORA, *The Celtic Realms*, Weidenfeld and Nicolson, London, 1967.

DUKE, JOHN A., *The Columban Church*, Oxford University Press, London, 1932.

EARLE, J. and PLUMMER, C., *Two Saxon Chronicles*, 2 vols, Oxford University Press, Oxford, 1899.

EKWALL, EILERT, *The Concise Oxford Dictionary of English Place-names*, Oxford University Press, 1936 (4th edition, Oxford, 1960).

EVANS, ARTHUR WADE, *Welsh Christian Origins*, Alden Press, Oxford, 1934.

EVANS, ARTHUR WADE, *Vitae Sanctorum Britanniae*, University of Wales Press, Cardiff, 1944.

EVANS, ARTHUR WADE, *The Emergence of England and Wales*, W. Heffer and Sons, Cambridge, 1959.

FAULL, M. L. (ed.), *Studies in Late Anglo-Saxon Settlement*, Oxford University Press, 1984.

FERGUSON, J., *Pelagius*, Cambridge University Press, Cambridge, 1956.

FINBERG, H. P. R., *The Formation of England 550–1042*, Hart-Davis Mac-Gibbon, London, 1974.

FISHER, D. J. V., *The Anglo-Saxon Age c.400–1042*, Longman, 1973.

FOX, C., *Offa's Dyke: a field survey*, British Academy, London, 1955.

FRIELL, J. G. P. and WATSON, W. G. eds., *Pictish Studies – Settlement, Burial and Art in Dark Age Northern Britain* (BAR International series), Oxford, 1984.

GACHER, JAKEZ, *Histoire Chronologique des Pays Celtiques*, Association Keltica International, Guerande, Bretagne, 1990.

GINNELL, LAURENCE, *The Brehon Laws: A Legal Handbook*, London, 1894.

GLOB, PETER VILHELM, *The Bog People: Iron Age Man Preserved*, Faber and Faber, London, 1969.

GOUGARD, DOM LOUIS, *Christianity in Celtic Lands*, trs. Maud Joyce, Sheed and Ward, London, 1932.

GOULD, SABINE (BARING-GOULD) and FISHER, JOHN, *The Lives of the British Saints*, 4 vols, Cymmrodorion Society, London, 1907–12.

GRAHAM, HUGH, *The Early Irish Monastic Schools*, Talbot Press, Dublin, 1923.

HAIGH, DANIEL H, *The Conquest of Britain by the Saxons . . .*, London, 1861.

HASLEHURST, R. S. T., *The Works of Fastidius*, Society of SS Peter & Paul, Westminster, London, 1927.

HAWKES, S. C., *Weapons and Warfare in Anglo-Saxon England*, Oxford University Committee for Archaeology 21, Oxford, 1989.

HENNESSY, WILLIAM MAUNSELL, *The Tripartite Life of Patrick*, trs and ed., Dublin, 1871; 2nd ed., 1874.

HERRON, JAMES, *The Celtic Church in Ireland*, Service and Paton, London, 1898.

HIGHAM, NICHOLAS, *Rome, Britain and the Anglo-Saxons*, Seaby, London, 1992.

HOOKE, D. (ed.), *Anglo-Saxon Settlements*, Basil Blackwell, Oxford, 1988.

HOULDER, CHRISTOPHER, *Wales: An Archaeological Guide*, Faber and Faber, London, 1974.

HUNTER BLAIR, PETER, *An Introduction to the Anglo-Saxon Period*, Cambridge University Press, Cambridge, 1956.

JACKSON, A., *The Symbol Stones of Scotland*, Orkney Press, Kirkwall, 1984.

JACKSON, KENNETH H., *Language and History in Early Britain*, Edinburgh University Press, Edinburgh, 1953.

JARMAN, A. O. H., ed. and trs., *Y Gododdin: Britain's Oldest Heroic Poem*, The Welsh Classic, Dyfed, 1988.

JOHN, CATHERINE RACHEL, *The Saints of Cornwall*, Lodenek/Truran, Padstow/Redruth, Cornwall, 1982.

JOYCE, P. W., *A Social History of Ancient Ireland*, 2 vols, Longman, Green and Co., London, 1903.

KIRBY, D. P., *The Making of Early England*, Batsford, London, 1967.

LAING, LLOYD, *The Archaeology of Late Celtic Britain and Ireland c.400–1200*, Methuen, London, 1975.

LAING, LLOYD, *Celtic Britain*, Routledge Kegan Paul, London, 1979.

LAING, LLOYD and JENNIFER, *Anglo-Saxon England*, Paladin Books, London, 1982.

LAING, LLOYD and JENNIFER, *Celtic Britain and Ireland: The Myth of the Dark Ages*, Irish Academic Press, 1990.

LLOYD, JOHN EDWARD, *The Welsh Chronicles*, British Academy, Oxford University Press, London, 1928.

LOOMIS, ROGER, ed., *Wales and the Arthurian Legends*, University of Wales Press, Cardiff, 1958.

LOOMIS, ROGER, *Arthurian Literature in the Middle Ages*, Oxford University Press, Oxford, 1959.

LOOMIS, ROGER, *The Grail from Celtic Myth to Christian Symbol*, University of Wales Press, Cardiff, 1963. (New ed., Constable, London, 1992.)

LOT, FERDINAND, *Bretons et Anglais aux Ve et VIe Siècles*, British Academy, Oxford University Press, London, 1930.

LOTH, JOSEPH, *L'Émigration Bretonne en Armorique du IVe au VIIe Siècle de Notre Ére*, Paris, 1883.

MACALISTER, R. A. S., *Corpus Inscriptionum Insularum Celticarum*, Stationery Office, Dublin, 1950.

MCCRUM, ROBERT, CRAN, WILLIAM, and MACNEIL, ROBERT, *The Story of English*, Faber and Faber with BBC Books, London, 1986.

MACCULLOCH, J. A., *The Religion of the Ancient Celts*, T.&.T. Clarke, Edinburgh, 1911. (New ed., Constable, London, 1991.)

MCNALLY, ROBERT, ed., *Old Ireland*, M. H. Gill, Dublin, 1965.

MACNAUGHT, JOHN C., *The Celtic Church and the See of St Peter*, Basil Blackwell, Oxford, 1927.

MACNÉILL, EOIN, *Celtic Religion*, Catholic Truth Society, London, 1910.

MARSDEN, JOHN, *Northanhymbre Saga: The History of the Anglo-Saxon Kings of Northumbria*, Kyle Cathie, London, 1992.

MAYR-HARTING, HENRY, *The Coming of Christianity to Anglo-Saxon England*, B. T. Batsford, London, 1972.

MEVILLE, RICHARD, *The Laws of Hywel Dda* (The Book of Blegywyrth), University Press, Liverpool, 1954.

MONTALEMBERT, CHARLES FORBES RENÉ, COMTE DE, *Les Moises d'Occident, depuis St Benôit jusqu'a St Bernard*, 7 vols, Paris, 1860–77. English language ed., Edinburgh, 1861–79. As *The Monks of the West from St Benedict to St Bernard*, J. C. Nimmo, London, 1896.

MOORE, D., ed., *The Land of Dyfed in Early Times*, Cambrian Archaeological Association, Cardiff, 1964.

MOORE, D., ed., *The Irish Sea Province in Archaeology and History*, Cambrian Archaeological Association, Cardiff, 1972.

MORAN, PATRICK F., *Irish Saints in Great Britain*, M. H. Gill, Dublin, 1879.

MORRIS, JOHN, *The Age of Arthur: A History of the British Isles from 350–650*, Weidenfeld and Nicolson, London, 1973.

MORRIS, JOHN, *Nennius: British History and The Welsh Annals*, ed. and trs., Phillimore, London, 1980.

MOULD, D. C., *The Celtic Saints*, Clonmore and Reynolds, Dublin, 1956.

MYRES, J. N. L., *The English Settlements*, Clarendon Press, Oxford, 1985.

NASH, D., *Taliesin or the Bards and Druids of Britain*, J. Russell Smith, London, 1858.

NEWELL, E. J., *A History of the Welsh Church to the Dissolution of the Monasteries*, Elhurst Stock, London, 1895.

O'DONOGHUE, DENIS, *Brendaniana (St Brendan the Voyager)*, Browne and Nolan, Dublin, 1893.

O'Donnell Lectures. Angles and Britons. (J. R. R. Tolkien, T. H. Parry-Williams, Kenneth Jackson, B. G. Charles, N. K. Chadwick and William Rees), University of Wales Press, Cardiff, 1963.

O'MEARA, JOHN J., *Eriugena*, Mercier Press, Cork, 1969.

O'RAHILLY, CECILE, *Ireland and Wales: Their Historical and Literary Relations*, Longman, Green and Co., London, 1924.

O'RAHILLY, THOMAS F., *The Two Patricks*, Dublin Institute for Advanced Studies, Dublin, 1942.

O'RAHILLY, T. F., *Early Irish History and Mythology*, Dublin Institute for Advanced Studies, Dublin, 1946.

PAGE, R. I., *Life in Anglo-Saxon England*, B. T. Batsford, London, 1970.

PARRY, THOMAS, trs. by H. Idris Bell, *A History of Welsh Literature*, The Clarendon Press, Oxford, 1955.

PEARCE, SUSAN M., *The Kingdom of Dumnonia – Studies in History and Traditions in South Western Britain AD 350–1150*, Lodenek Press, Padstow, 1978.

PEI, MARIO, *The Story of the English Language*, George Allen and Unwin, London, 1968.

PLUMMER, C., *Vitae Sanctorum Hiberniae*, 2 vols, Oxford University Press, Oxford, 1910.

PLUMMER, C., *Bethada Naem nÉrenn (Lives of Irish Saints)*, 2 vols, Oxford University Press, Oxford, 1922.

POWELL, T. G. E., *The Celts*, Thames and Hudson, London, 1958.

POWER, PATRICK, *Early Christian Ireland*, M. H. Gill, Dublin, 1925.

QUENNEL, MAJORIE and C. D. B., *Everyday Life in Anglo-Saxon, Viking and Norman Times*, B. T. Batsford, London, 1924.

RANKIN, H. D., *Celtic and the Classical World*, Croom Helm, London, 1987.

RICHARDS, JULIAN D., *Viking Age England*, B. T. Batsford, London, 1991.

SAINT-SAVEUR, E. DURTELLE DE, *Histoire de Bretagne des origines à nos jours*, University of Rennes, Bretagne, 1952–56.

SALWAY, PETER, *Roman Britain*, Clarendon Press, Oxford, 1981.

SELMER, CARL, *Navigatio Sancti Brendani*, Abbatis. No IV, Publications in Medieval Studies, University of Notre Dame Press, 1959.

SEVERIN, TIM, *The Brendan Voyage*, Hutchinson, London, 1978.

SIMPSON, W. D., *Saint Ninian and the Origin of the Christian Church in Scotland*, Oliver and Boyd, Edinburgh, 1940.

SKENE, WILLIAM. F., *Chronicle of the Picts and Scots and other early memorials of Scottish History*, Series of Chronicles and Memorials, Scottish General Register House, Edinburgh, 1867.

SKENE, WILLIAM. F., *The Four Ancient Books of Wales*, 2 vols, Edinburgh, 1868.

SKENE, W. F., *Celtic Scotland*, 3 vols, Edinburgh, 1876–80; 2nd ed., David Douglas, Edinburgh, 1886–1890.

SMALL, A., THOMAS, C. and WILSON, D. M., *St Ninian's Isle and Its Treasures*, 2 vols, Aberdeen University Studies, Oxford, 1973.

STENTON, SIR FRANK, *Danelaw Charters*, British Academy, London, 1920.

STENTON, SIR FRANK, *The Danes in England*, British Academy, London, 1927.

STENTON, SIR FRANK, *Anglo-Saxon England*, Oxford University Press, Oxford, 1943. (Revised 3rd edition, 1971.)

STENTON, SIR FRANK, *Preparatory to Anglo-Saxon England*, Clarendon Press, Oxford, 1970.

STOKES, GEORGE T., *Ireland and the Celtic Church*, Hodder and Stoughton, London, 1886.

THOMAS, CHARLES, *Britain and Ireland in Early Christian Times* AD *400–800*, Thames and Hudson, London, 1971.

THOMAS, CHARLES, *Celtic Britain*, Thames and Hudson, London, 1986.

TOMMASINI, ANSELMO M., *Irish Saints in Italy*, Sands and Co., London, 1935.

WAINWRIGHT, F. T., *The Problem of the Picts*, Edinburgh University Press, Edinburgh, 1955.

WARREN, F. E. *The Liturgy and Ritual of the Celtic Church*, Clarendon Press, Oxford, 1881.

WATSON, W. J., *History of the Celtic Place-Names of Scotland*, William Blackwood, Edinburgh, 1926.

WELCH, MARTIN, *Anglo-Saxon England*, Batsford, London, 1992.

WHITELOCK, DOROTHY, ed., *Anglo-Saxon Wills*, Cambridge University Press, Cambridge, 1930.

WHITELOCK, DOROTHY, *English Historical Documents*, Vol. 1, Eyre and Spottiswoode, London, 1955.

WILLIAMS, ANN, SMYTH, ALFRED P., and KIRBY, D. A., *Biographical Dictionary of Dark Age Britain*, Seaby, London, 1991.

WILLIAMS, GWYN ALF, *Madog: The Making of a Myth*, Eyre-Methuen, London, 1979.

WILLIAMS, HUGH, *Christianity in Early Britain*, Clarendon Press, Oxford, 1912.

WILLIAMS, IFOR, *The Poems of Llywarch Hen*. British Academy, Oxford University Press, London, 1932.

WILLIAM, JOHN AB ITHEL, *The Traditional Annals of the Cymry*, R. Mason, Tenby, Wales, 1867.

WILSON, D. M., *The Anglo-Saxons*, Pelican Books, London, 1971.

WOOLF, CHARLES, *An Introduction to the Archaeology of Cornwall*, D. Bradford Barton, Truro, 1970.

YORKE, B., *Kings and Kingdoms of Early Anglo-Saxon England*, Seaby, London, 1990.

ZIMMER. H., *The Celtic Church in Britain and Ireland* (trs. A. Meyer), David Nutt, London, 1902.

ZIMMER, H., *Gaelic Pioneers of Christianity: The Work and Influence of Irish Monks and Saints in Continental Europe* (trs. Victor Collins), M. H. Gill, Dublin, 1923.

Index